The Rise and Fall of a Prophet

By
Jan Jansen

The Rise and Fall

of a Prophet

By

Jan Jansen

ISBN 979-8-218-50451-9

It is my privilege to write the foreword for this book, "The Rise And Fall Of A Prophet", authored by Jan Jansen, senior pastor of the Fire Church, and wife of the late Jeff Jansen, author, pastor, and the co-founder of Global Fire Ministries.

I performed Jeff and Jan's wedding, during my time as senior pastor of the Vineyard Christian Fellowship Nashville, where both Jeff and Jan had powerful encounters with the Holy Spirit. We came out of the Jesus revolution days and were radically impacted by the presence of the Lord!

Later, when I would visit their church, Global Fire, in Murfreesboro, Tennessee, I was introduced as their pastor and always shown special kindness and honor, when I attended their many prophetic and healing conferences. Jeff was my friend, and I walked out many of these pages with him and Jan.

There's no question of the impact that the prophetic ministry of Jeff Jansen had on the world. That cannot be denied, and I deeply loved and appreciated his passion for Jesus, despite the things that he personally couldn't seem to overcome.

Now after Jeff's untimely passing, Jan has written a transparent, honest book about her marriage, ministry, and life with Jeff. It's her story, and I know it to be true, because she is not given to duplicity, or the need to sensationalize. I'm sure that it was a difficult book to write and yet it is so important that we learn God's lessons from their journey. Their story is not written from a place of bitterness. It's simply the way it unfolded, and I was there to witness it.

This is a book that affirms how God loves us so much, calls us individually, and trusts us with assignments to further the advancement of His kingdom.

"Your kingdom comes. Your will be done on Earth as it is in Heaven."   ~Matthew 6:10

We must realize that all of Hell resists God's callings, especially if greatly anointed, as was Jeff's. Read the book and marvel at what God did through Jeff's life. Be amazed. Find humor, even in the sadness. Just like David's story throughout the Bible, Jeff's story is a testimony of how God uses broken people who truly love him, and it doesn't matter whether we agree, or not.

Regardless of your reasons for reading this book, there is much to learn here that will enhance your journey, and cultivate maturity and effectiveness. There are also important cautions of the need to "stop, look, and listen," and acknowledge pressures and forces that will try to wrestle the steering of your ship away from you. It should remind us that no one is an island, and of the importance of discernment. We need to bless, as well as challenge each other from God's heart, along the way. Love demands this.

Even if you don't fully understand the way the Lord works good in every situation, He does and will continue to do so. Most of all, please believe that His love and amazing grace cover a multitude of mistakes we make along the way.

In the end, God's love overcomes it all.

Pastor Jerry Bryant

Nashville Worship City Ministry Alliance
(Former senior pastor for Vineyard Nashville)

Preface

You may ask me why I have written this book. Let me first tell you what was *not* my motivation. I have not written "The Rise And Fall Of A Prophet" in order to bash Jeff Jansen, or to expose my husband of twenty-eight years. Many people have drawn the conclusion that Jeff was off, or that Jeff was a false prophet.

Put his name into any search engine, and you will find both positive and negative results but sadly, the negative ones far outweigh the positive. Many have forgotten the glory years.

Countless people have contacted me to ask, "What really happened?" God directed me to keep the answer to that question to myself, until He released me. I truly believe that this attempt to tell the whole truth was led by the Lord and comes in His timing, and that the Holy Spirit guided me in the journey of writing this book.

One of the reasons I wrote it was to memorialize the Jeff Jansen that I married, the Jeff that I knew loved the Lord with all his heart, and the Jeff that had such amazing faith that He saw amazing miracles, signs, and wonders in our ministry over a period of years.

Sometimes, not finishing well can make people forget all the good a person did during their ministry or life. I don't want people to only remember the negative. You may have come to a conclusion based on what you may have heard and assumed, but there is so much more that no one has really known about Jeff, up to this point.

Although there were a lot of people who witnessed his downward spiral, and observed particular events and incidents, I was the one closest to him, and other than God, the only one who has always known the entire truth.

In this book, I am giving you the entire truth. I have tried, to the best of my ability, to explain what happened, as things unfolded and began to unravel.

If I can save one person who might succumb to the same fate that Jeff fell victim to, then this book is worth it. I want the reader and the general public to know that Jeff did not just choose to do the things he did. Many of you may have been extremely disillusioned by Jeff, and perhaps by many other recognized ministers who have fallen, for one reason or another.

Someone needs to talk about it. You need to hear the real truth and realize that as human beings, we are all vulnerable. We need to learn from the mistakes of others and minister from the wisdom we gain.

Jan Jansen

The Rise and Fall

of a Prophet

Chapter One

Humble Beginnings

Jan's Early Spiritual Life

Jeff Jansen and I did not have a glamorous beginning. Most people assume we met in church or in a glory meeting. The truth is that I was taking two-step lessons. I've always enjoyed dance, and it was a pleasant break from my otherwise quiet life as a home health nurse.

I loved my work, and the people I was able to serve as a nurse, but there was one question my patients frequently asked, and that I always struggled to answer.

"Jan, you are always so kind and caring. You must be a Christian, aren't you?"

I wanted to say yes, but in all honesty, I didn't know. It had been a long season of seeking the living, loving God I had heard about. The Lord was drawing me to Him, but I couldn't seem to find Him, no matter where I looked. I had visited many different churches of different denominations, but something was always missing or wrong.

Raised in a strict, legalistic church, I never saw evidence of a loving God until much later. As a child, going to church was not a positive experience; it was a duty. My mom taught me that attending every possible church service was my salvation. While there were good things I gained from my childhood church, like learning about faithfulness and community, I was repulsed by their elitist ways.

My mother would not allow me to visit the local Presbyterian Church with my best friend. According to her, that would put me "in danger of Hell." Our denomination believed we were the only ones that would make it to Heaven. Everyone else was in error. As a result, I rebelled from church for most of my young life.

In my early twenties, when the minister cried out from the pulpit, "All Baptists are going to Hell!" I finally had enough. I couldn't imagine a God who would cast people into Hell for choosing, or simply growing up in the "wrong" denomination.

I said to myself, "If this is God, I want nothing to do with Him." I walked out that day.

Still, the Lord is faithful to get our attention. It wasn't long before someone told me about Christ Church in Nashville, Tennessee. A large Pentecostal church, they believed in speaking in tongues and other gifts of the Spirit. By that time, my son from a former marriage was in his teens. I took him with me to visit Christ Church.

They had an amazing choir! But my soul was thirsty for more. I would sit in the balcony of the church and weep from deep longing.

Jeff and Jan Meet

Typical of his age, my son was spending a lot of time with his friends. I worked hard during the day, but often at night I would find myself feeling alone. I started going to country dance halls with friends, dancing my cares away. We would go out on a Friday or Saturday night, and sometimes Sunday afternoons for dancing lessons. We had regular dance partners, and I had become a surprisingly skilled two-stepper.

The day after Thanksgiving 1993, my friend Kathy and I were bored, and headed to one of our favorite dance halls called Rodeos. I had become weary of what I saw in these places. We went to dance, but they were still bars, and the atmosphere was wearing on me. I was determined that this Friday night at Rodeos would be my last.

That's when I saw him.

Standing there at the pool table, my eyes were drawn to him. Wiry-looking but handsome, this man seemed to have a mysterious light shining down on him. It was as if he were being spotlighted for me. Shaking it off, I turned away. Kathy and I were having a hard time finding anyone we wanted to dance with, so we agreed to leave for Southfork, another dance club a few miles away. I put the cute man who drew my gaze out of my mind, writing the whole "mysterious light" thing off as nonsense.

We arrived at Southfork and I moved toward the dance floor, scoping out the best choices for safe dance partners. Suddenly, a man appeared close to my side. I didn't want to look, but he was persistent, continuing to linger beside me. It was the man in the spotlight I saw at Rodeos!

He had two hoop earrings in one ear. It was the nineties, and this was not common at that time, except among men who were in rock bands, or the "artsy" types. Surprising myself, I blurted out exactly what I was thinking.

"You must be a musician!"

His response was friendly. "What makes you think that?" he asked, smiling.

"Well... you have two earrings in one ear." I stammered, in embarrassment. He simply laughed.

"I saw you at Rodeos. You seemed to have a light shining on you."

It was a bold thing to say. I didn't know this man, yet I felt surprisingly at ease. His response was confident.

"I would hope I have light. After all, I am a Christian."

A Christian, and there I was, standing in a dance hall bar with a beer in my hand. A surge of conviction shot through me. As much as I wanted to, I could not honestly say I was living a Christian life. In my years of searching, I still hadn't figured out how to get there.

I scrambled for something I could say that was true. Finally, I thought of something. I blurted out, "I go to church!"

Something about him felt really comfortable to me. I told him about Christ Church in Nashville. He had been attending New Song Church in Franklin. He had barely finished his sentence when one of my favorite songs came on and I dragged him onto the dance floor.

He had five left feet and no clue what he was doing. For a minute, he was a real trooper, trying to keep up. Eventually, however, clumsiness and embarrassment took over, and he left the dance floor.

Honestly, it was something of a relief. Still, the mysterious light I'd seen on him earlier intrigued me. I didn't yet know what conviction meant, but I was feeling it, and it made me want to leave. I wanted to get away from that uncomfortable feeling.

I didn't see him again until later that evening. Once again, he seemed to appear out of nowhere, asking me to join him in a slow dance.

I thought, "Why not? He's cute."

I was drawn to the way he smelled, sort of woodsy and appealing. So many of the other men I danced with smelled like cheap, dollar store cologne, which was not attractive. But he smelled good to me. I couldn't help but giggle at myself.

The music was loud, but we tried to carry on a conversation anyway. Newly divorced, he had just returned to Tennessee from his hometown in Little Chute, Wisconsin, where he had retreated to be with family and friends after his wife had an affair and divorced him.

"I have four children. They were with their mother, so I had to come back here to be with them," he said.

His words caught me off-guard. I stopped dancing and stared at him in disbelief. Was he joking?

"Four children? There is no way you have four children!"

This man looked no older than twenty-five. He had a youthful appearance and an innocence about him that was rarely seen in those places. Flipping out his wallet, he showed me pictures of all four of his kids; a girl, twin boys, and a younger son. I was positive he was joking.

"Those are your nephews and niece!"

"No, they are definitely my children."

He had been married for nine years. I told him about my fourteen-year-old son, who was staying with friends that night.

When we finished our dance, I told him that I needed to go home. I'd had enough of the bar scene. Besides, I wasn't looking for a man, and in my mind I didn't need one.

As I moved toward the exit, he caught me by the arm and handed me a scrap of paper with his phone number scribbled on it and a brief note.

"I enjoyed our dance. If you ever want to call..."

This man was different from all the other men I had encountered recently. I could feel the corners of my mouth about to break into a slight spontaneous smile. I took the paper and left the bar.

For the next several hours, I had flashbacks of meeting this man, and our dance. I wanted to continue our conversation, but I was not in the habit of pursuing or calling men.

After all, I had never had difficulty getting dates, although lately most ended up as disappointing, or even disastrous. The desire to call him lingered, but I firmly put it away.

The next morning, I greeted my son as he walked in the door after spending the night at a friend's house.

"How was your evening, son?"

In a typical teenage tone, he responded, "Fine, Mom. Why wouldn't it be? Why do you ask?"

I got started on my normal Saturday routine of cleaning my house. It wasn't long before a phone call interrupted my cleaning. Kathy, my friend who had gone to the bar with me the night before, had a situation.

"I have a date tonight who wants to go dancing, but he will only go if he has a date for his friend."

I was adamant. "Kathy, I am finished with those places!" Kathy begged relentlessly for the next fifteen minutes. "Please Jan, do it for me. Just this one last time."

"Alright, fine, just for you Kathy, but I won't go again." I was going to get my life right, whatever it took.

The man she set me up with was handsome and kind. We danced several dances, but it wasn't long before he also wanted to get out of there. We left and went somewhere to talk. He seemed to need to vent.

It turned that out he was fresh out of rehab for a cocaine addiction. He was a nice guy, but I was not interested in investing myself in a man with a recent history of serious addiction. I got home early and went to bed.

Getting To Know You

The next morning as I prepared for church, I felt a powerful urge, almost a prodding, to call the man I met on Friday night at Southfork. I couldn't help arguing with myself. It was completely out of character for me.

"I'm not going to call him! Why should I?"

I didn't know it yet, but that prodding was from God. Shaking my head at myself, I felt the words tumble out of my mouth as if I were led by some invisible force.

"Okay, I'll do it."

He answered immediately. This was long before the day of cell phones, so he must have been right next to the phone.

The conversation went on for hours. Neither of us wanted to stop talking, even though we each had plans to go to church.

Little did I know, Jeff had returned to Southfork the night after we first met, looking for me. When he saw me with another man, he thought I had a boyfriend. He left the bar and wrote me off, assuming he didn't stand a chance.

Our lives were very different. Jeff had been a worship leader at his church in Wisconsin for eight years. It seemed he had lived a life of purpose. He had been in ministry for years. I was just living life, dealing with work, my teenage son, and a new house I had just purchased a few weeks before.

Jeff revealed to me that he had been a wild teenager, experimenting with drugs and drinking. None of this was shocking to me. I was no different in my youth. Both of us grew up in the 60s and 70s and it was not uncommon. We laughed at how many of us were hippies, or thought we were.

Jeff grew up Catholic, but had become saved in a Catholic Renewal movement. Even though Jeff felt the Lord calling him, he continued to party and drink. Walking home one night from a party at a friend's house, he heard the voice of God tell him, "I love you, Jeff, no matter what you do." He did not comprehend the immensity of what God had before him.

In Jeff's words, he was "too much of a handful" for his parents. His father, being a police chief, had no tolerance for that kind of behavior. Jeff never told me specifically what led up to it, but he eventually moved in with another family in the neighborhood.

Living with his neighbors was good for Jeff. They were Christians and showed him an aspect of Christianity he had not experienced growing up in the Catholic Church. In time, Jeff and two of the brothers from this family began meeting in a small building to worship.

Although the location of the building was unusual, being on the grounds of a local cemetery, it was nearby and most of all, available. They gathered and just worshiped with no agenda. They also read the Bible and shared the Word of the Lord.

Jeff picked up a guitar and taught himself to play. He was a natural. Soon, he was leading worship on his guitar. When Jeff and the brothers invited others to join them, it wasn't long until their gatherings outgrew the little building in the graveyard.

That tiny, humble fellowship grew to eventually become a 3,000 member church. One of the brothers was the pastor and Jeff was the worship leader. During that time, Jeff met his first wife, and they served faithfully in the church for eight years.

Children came quickly. Their oldest child, a daughter, was a year old when the identical twin boys were born. When their youngest child was born, their daughter was still only two.

I marveled, "Four children aged two and under! Wow!"

"I worked hard to support them, and church was our life," he told me.

Jeff had worked at the Rawhide Boys Ranch counseling troubled teen boys. He talked little about the pastor who had taken him in during his youth and later led the enormous church alongside him, but he mentioned his unhappiness with the direction the church had taken. According to Jeff, it had become a "counseling church," and that didn't feel like a good fit for him. So, he and his wife made a bold decision, choosing to move their family to Nashville.

It was Jeff's heart to pursue a career as a Christian worship artist and hopefully get a record contract. Back then, cassette tapes and vinyl records were the standard. Jeff recorded one album. He gave me a cassette tape shortly after we met. It was a beautiful recording.

For a while, things were looking up for Jeff's music career. 4-Him, one of the most popular Contemporary Christian bands of the nineties, recorded a song he wrote with his writing partner called Wrecking Ball.

Things didn't go as Jeff had hoped, and it wasn't long before his first marriage ended. As promising as his music career had seemed, the strain of an unexpected divorce led him to lose heart in pursuing a music career. In the past, worshiping the Lord alone with his guitar had helped him heal. He just seemed tired, at this point.

I learned all of this and more in that first phone call. Finally, we agreed to meet in person for our first date.

I invited Jeff to my new house. Moments before Jeff was to arrive, the closet pole in my bedroom collapsed as I attempted to retrieve my outfit for the evening. All of my clothes completely spilled out all over the floor. Our first date was spent with Jeff gallantly repairing the damage.

"I feel like I'm not prepared. My closet pole just broke and all my clothes have just spilled out onto the floor!"

"I can fix that."

"You can?"

"Sure, no problem."

He did, and I was grateful that he was willing to.

We had no agenda for our time together. The evening ended with a walk in the cool November air. We walked around the neighborhood until we discovered a wooden bridge in front of a neighbor's house. Stepping onto the bridge, Jeff gave me a sweet and simple first kiss.

Jeff and I bonded quickly. It was as if we had known each other forever. After this night, we were practically inseparable. He would come over after work and stay with me until bedtime. Our kids quickly became acquainted, and his children grew to accept my presence in their lives.

Jeff was one of the humblest people I had ever met. His first love was Jesus, but I had rapidly become his new love. We had both experienced painful hurts from past relationships, so it took both of us a while to say "I love you". He would draw me close, look into my eyes and say, "You're moving deep inside of me." That was his way of letting me know our relationship mattered to him.

We spent a lot of time during the first six months of our courtship taking walks, or sitting on the sofa getting to know each other. Jeff often spoke about his ministry years at the church in Wisconsin.

He truly enjoyed being a worship leader, but it had been difficult to support a wife and four children at such a young age. Most of their lives revolved around church, and were spent either at church gatherings or, at times, with the families of church members.

He told me of the first time he ever encountered the Lord. When he was around sixteen or seventeen, he was simply lying on his bed, in his room. He looked up to see an ethereal hand writing on his wall. The words would touch his heart and his life in ways he could not even express. The message was simply, "I love you, Jeff." My eyes welled up with tears as I heard this.

I grew up in a broken home and was often alone. Jeff had a large and extended family. He spoke fondly of time spent with his aunts and uncles, grandparents, and especially one of his grandmothers. She died when Jeff was just a boy, and he was very fond of her. She called him "Jeffy Boy."

He also mentioned one of his grandfathers, who owned a bar where he would hang out.

When Jeff first moved to Tennessee, he had a pronounced northern intonation that he called a "Yooper" accent.

We laughed as I said, "Please, demonstrate!"

"Jan, when I first moved here, I didn't understand a word these Southerners said, but your accent is not too much. Your voice is charming."

The Tennessee weather was also much different from the weather of Jeff's Wisconsin childhood. One of Jeff's favorite winter activities was sledding. There was a special sledding hill he and his family always visited, and he could not wait to show it to me. He remembered excitedly, "When I was young, there was always snow on the ground."

Jeff was enthusiastic about how he loved the snow in Wisconsin, and how it was an important part of his memories.

The Proposal

The more time we spent together, the closer we became. We didn't talk of marriage, but we both knew that was where our relationship was heading. One of my home health clients owned a cabin in Gatlinburg, Tennessee, and invited me to use it. I thought it would be fun to take all our children there as a family, to see what that might look like someday.

Our families blended beautifully. We had a wonderful time. As we sat alone in the hot tub, Jeff surprised me.

"Jan, will you marry me?"

I was not expecting this! It was a Hallmark moment, for sure. Hearing a noise, we looked over to the cabin. All our children were peeking through the window and giggling.

I didn't hesitate in my response. "Yes, I will marry you!"

Chapter Two

EARLY SPIRITUAL FOUNDATIONS

The Vineyard

Jeff and I agreed that our first commitment as a couple was to find a church where we could take our children and worship together.

With his earlier experience co-pastoring a church, he was far more knowledgeable and mature than I was spiritually. I had been in seeking mode when I met Jeff.

I persuaded Jeff to visit Christ Church, which was the large Pentecostal church I had been attending in Nashville, but it was too big for him. He didn't feel at home in a mega-church.

As we talked about the kind of church we were looking for, I had a flash of memory. Before I met Jeff, a friendly couple, who stopped to help me with my car trouble, told me about a small new church they were going to called the Vineyard.

I had never heard of the Vineyard or its founder, John Wimber, but Jeff was very familiar, as I told him about it. He told me about the Vineyard Movement and a time when Lonnie Frisbee, a great contributor to the Vineyard movement, had called him out in a meeting and prophesied over him. Jeff was excited to find the church. I still had the phone numbers of the couple, Rhonda and Val, and called to tell them we were coming.

The Vineyard differed from any church I had ever experienced. It was very free. Not knowing its history and origins, I would have called it a "hippie" church. Being a former hippie myself, I felt safe and accepted. Nobody cared where you came from, what you wore, or called you a sinner. Nothing negative was said about both of us being divorced. I simply felt loved.

Jerry and Cindy Bryant pastored this newly birthed church, meeting in a small space on Sunday afternoons. I had never had a pastor before, only "ministers" who stood up and preached. We spent quality time with Jerry and Cindy, quickly becoming friends with them. Jeff and I felt confident calling them our pastors. We felt we could trust and rely on them.

I was learning, and pressing into this amazing new walk of faith I had found. I had not fully committed my life to the Lord at this point. I didn't consider myself to be born again, not that I even entirely understood what that meant, but the Holy Spirit was drawing me in.

Jeff had years of experience walking with the Lord. As for me, I had experienced the Holy Spirit at my Sunday visits to Christ Church, but I did not fully grasp it all. It made me feel good that Jeff didn't seem to care that I knew little, beyond what I learned in the church I grew up in, but I was hungry.

Born Again

One Sunday, the Vineyard was hosting a South African prophet. I didn't know what a prophet was.

The church I attended as a child did not adhere to the Old Testament, and rarely taught from it. I knew there were prophets in the Bible, but I didn't know there were prophets in this day and time.

This South African pastor ministered differently than anyone I had ever seen or heard. It was common in the Vineyard stream, but foreign to me. We lined up across the front of the sanctuary for him to pray over all of us, one at a time. I did not know what would happen, but reluctantly agreed.

As he approached me, he looked at me as if he were reading me. His words deeply touched my heart and soul. He told me God saw my life, my mistakes, and shortcomings, and loved me anyway.

This man saw clearly into my past, and His words were life to me. He seemed to know me on a level only Jesus could know.

That was the moment I committed myself to Jesus Christ, as my Lord and Savior. It had begun!

Jeff also got amazing words from this man that resonated deep within him.

The Vineyard Church was the first church where I truly felt the love of Jesus. Shortly after we started attending, Pastors Jerry and Cindy traveled to Toronto, Canada, after a powerful wind of the Holy Spirit came to the Vineyard church there. Many thousands were flocking to the "Toronto Blessing" to experience the presence of God.

This was all new to me. There was no question that after they returned from Toronto, the presence of God was tangible. They seemed to have come back bringing the glory with them. God was showing up in power in our church.

I was slain in the Spirit for the first time, my body shaking violently. It wasn't an uncomfortable shaking. It was wonderful. I never wanted it to stop. My body shook for hours, even after the service that Sunday. Through that experience, I was born again and filled with the Holy Spirit.

Our children were also slain in the Spirit. It was clear they were not faking it. My son was rolling on the floor, laughing hysterically as if something was tickling him. Having recently made some bad choices and been in trouble at school, he needed this touch of God. He had even been sent to an alternative school for troubled kids.

When he got up, he told me that he had seen red, glowing, terrifying eyes looking at him. He said God had taken the scary eyes away. Then God, Himself, was tickling him. Through the joy he experienced, he too was born again and filled with the Spirit of God.

My son took his newfound joy into real life and got out of trouble. He went back into a regular school the next year. He went from being a struggling student, contemplating running away from home, to an exuberant A and B student who was leading his classmates to Christ. He even started a Christian car club called Eternity. They would drive through the streets telling people of Jesus. My son has been a radical evangelist ever since.

Jeff's youngest son, who was seven, fell out in the Spirit and when he got up, he wept intensely for about ten minutes. After he stopped crying, pure joy rested on him. He needed to release some pain that was in his heart.

Home Meetings

By now it was evident that the Lord knew what He was doing when He placed me in the home I bought, shortly before meeting Jeff. It was the first house I had ever owned. I told my realtor I wanted a Western cedar, Southwestern-style home with a wrap-around porch (my taste at the time), but she replied, "Such a house doesn't exist in this region. There's nothing like that out there."

She was shocked when she discovered exactly what I was looking for. For me, it was a dream come true. God had a purpose for that house. Jeff and I were engaged, with plans to marry in a few months. It would become a place for my soon-to-be growing family. More of God's plans were about to unfold.

The Vineyard was big on home groups. The church was still small, but the revival we experienced after Jerry and Cindy returned from Toronto drew increasing numbers of people. A solid group of Vineyard members met in our home weekly. Naturally, Jeff led worship for our small group. We grew closer to one another quickly.

Jeff was truly a Davidic psalmist. When he worshiped, he did so with all his being. I always sensed the Lord smiling as Jeff worshiped. Despite all the difficulties he had as a teenager, and after going through a divorce, God was using him. He had done well. God does not look at our failures. He looks at our heart.

The Lord was manifesting Himself to us powerfully through those meetings. There was a weight of glory we had not experienced before. It was an acceleration of learning and provision for what was coming.

One night during worship, I experienced my first vision in the Spirit. I will never forget it. I could feel and see myself lying on a thick cloud. It was the most loving, comforting feeling, almost indescribable. In the vision, everyone around me was busy doing things for the kingdom, but I just lay there in a cloud of love, not wanting to get up.

In my spirit, I said, "Lord, I think I need to get up and do something." I felt guilty, just lying there.

The Lord showed me that it was His hand I was lying in. I was exactly where I was supposed to be.

Like the experience with the South African prophet, this vision impacted me tremendously. I was never the same. I did not yet understand all that it entailed, but I knew God had given me the mantle of the seer.

Jeff also received an impartation of a prophetic gift he had not yet operated in. He did not realize at the time what a high level gift this was.

Wedding Bells

Jeff and I were married June 4, 1994, after a whirlwind six-month romance. Pastors Jerry and Cindy married us at the Opryland Hotel in Nashville, in the presence of a small group of family and friends. I had become close to many of my home health patients, and a few of them even showed up to witness our wedding.

Jeff wanted to sing to me. It was a song he had written specifically for our wedding called "You Are Beautiful to Me". I felt I would overflow with joy. There were no cell phones, and there was no videographer. Sadly, it was unrecorded.

A group of onlookers gathered, and stood above us on an overhead walkway, to watch and listen.

Jeff sang another song that was accompanied by our good friend Rhonda who, along with her husband, had introduced us to the Vineyard Church.

A true shepherd and evangelist, our pastor Jerry Bryant, "preached" the entire wedding. Every observer there heard the gospel of Jesus.

At our reception in a conference room there, everyone got drunk in the Spirit instead of drunk on wine. Several fell out under the supernatural power of the Presence manifesting there. How could we expect less from Jerry, Cindy, and the living God? Then Jerry and Cindy joined us in our honeymoon suite, fellowshipping and worshiping some more. It was an incredible end to an amazing day.

The cost of paying for our own wedding, reception, and honeymoon led us to economize. Jeff's parents kept our newly blended crew of five children. We drove to Destin, Florida for a brief, three-day honeymoon.

Two weeks after we married, Jeff's twin boys came to live with us. The following year, his daughter and youngest son also moved in. Instantly, I went from being a mother of one, to a mother of five! It was quite an adjustment, but we knew it was the will of the Lord.

Although Jeff and I had no idea that we would ever have all five of our children in our home, we had faith that God was in control.

A New Business

Jeff was doing construction work, and I was still working as a home health nurse. Jeff was much more adventurous and entrepreneurial than I was. As for me, I was in great demand at work. Jeff couldn't help but notice. Gently holding my chin, he looked at me, exclaiming, "Jan, they only want you. Your home health patients love you like family, and the doctors trust you completely. You know they insist that only you take care of their patients. We can own our own home health company! These doctors want you."

I brushed his comments off immediately by saying, "It's too hard, Jeff." He refused to let it go, pursuing the idea with many more conversations in the days to come.

In early 1995, we started our own company called Compassion Care, inspired by Colossians 3:12. Jeff quit his construction job and shifted into the position of marketing director.

Success found us quickly! We signed a contract with a huge company in Nashville, but the director of our sister company warned us, "You have a good five years until all the Medicare standards change. Make the best of it, while you can."

I was already experienced in hands-on patient care, and was a natural at administrating and scheduling. Jeff had never done public relations and marketing, so he had a lot to learn to grow into his position. He picked it up quickly, using his natural gifting to stir up excitement and draw people in.

Soon we had a large team of nurses, technicians, physical therapists, occupational therapists, and social workers on our team. It was the most gratifying experience I ever had in my nursing career. Balancing a new family and a demanding business was difficult, but God gave us the grace for it. We worked together most of the time, bonding and learning more and more about each other.

Chapter Three

THE SHIFT

Leaving The Vineyard

I often thought that perhaps if Jeff and I had not met, he would have resumed his pursuit of a record contract. Jeff had become well known for his worship and songwriting ability, having recently received rave reviews for a song he had co-written for the award-winning Contemporary Christian group, 4-Him.

While we were still dating, a song he co-wrote called "Runs In The Blood" won an award for Christian Country Song of the Year in 1994. I went with him to the awards ceremony. I could tell how important music was to him.

Naturally, when the position for a new worship leader presented itself at the Vineyard, Jeff made his interest in the position known to Pastor Jerry.

There was another man who helped lead worship from time to time. He was brand new to leading worship when he arrived at the Vineyard. On the other hand, Jeff was highly skilled, with much more experience. The anointing on Jeff was palpable. It seemed obvious that he would be Pastor Jerry's choice to fill the position.

With all the changes in Jeff's life, including a new marriage and a new family, Jerry was concerned that Jeff would be too busy for the responsibilities of a worship leader. The other man was single.

After a period of consideration, Pastor Jerry decided the other man would have more availability to serve as a church leader and in his mind, he was the better choice for the worship leader position.

He explained, "Jeff, you are a married man now. You will need to spend more time focusing on your family."

Jeff took Pastor Jerry's decision hard. To him, it seemed to come out of left field.

"Jan, I was so sure he would pick me. I just didn't see this coming," he said to me with a degree of rejection I didn't totally understand.

We were both so close to Jerry and Cindy. It was hard for Jeff to not take it personally. It reminded him of the negative experience he had in Wisconsin with his friend, the pastor of the church Jeff co-founded there, and how he would frequently shut him down. When Jeff began to prophesy, he would say, "Jeff, just shut up and sing!"

Not surprisingly, their relationship fell apart. Now, Jeff was facing a similarly deep hurt with Jerry, and it was evident Jeff was struggling with offense. It was becoming more than he could handle.

"That's it. It's time for us to go, Jan." He was somber, but solid. I knew I couldn't change his mind. I did not want to leave the church. I loved Pastors Jerry and Cindy and the Vineyard felt like my home, but I knew it would be almost impossible for him to stay. It was simply too hurtful, due to Jeff's past wounds.

Leaving my church family and being a mom to five kids was quite an adjustment. I was accustomed to mothering a single child. I still didn't know how to juggle a whole brood!

Raising five children came with plenty of challenges, on top of new financial struggles. Jeff and I loved each other intensely. More than that, we were best friends. As long as we had each other, we were okay.

First Supernatural Sign

We wanted our kids to be involved in a youth group, so we found a local Assembly of God church with a decent youth ministry. The church wasn't the best fit for Jeff and me personally, but outside of church, we were continuing to learn, and growing in our faith.

It was not a prophetic church. Sharing the prophetic was frowned upon, unless it came from the leadership.

One Sunday, sitting inconspicuously near the back, I looked over at Jeff. It looked like someone had dumped a bucket of gold dust on his sweater. I was awe-struck. The gold seemed to be woven into the threads of his sweater.

"Jeff, look at your sweater!"

He looked down and gasped. We had never seen anything like this before!

At first, no one else noticed. It wasn't long before our excitement drew others' curiosity, and people saw the gold continuing to manifest. Nothing like this had happened in this church, or any other church we were familiar with, to our knowledge. What a marvel!

Jeff spontaneously began to prophesy over some other church members who were looking at the gold. This was not typical of him. It was as if an angel was in our midst. We didn't know exactly what was happening, but God had just birthed something.

Later, I talked to Jeff about the experience.

"Have you ever prophesied like that, before?" I wondered curiously.

"Well, I can remember times I would get words for people in Wisconsin. But the pastor would look at me and say, 'Jeff, just shut up and sing,' so it shut me down." He wasn't sure what had just happened.

This time, it just erupted out of him. It was a brand new experience. As the people gathered around him to witness the gold seemingly woven into his sweater, he automatically began to "read their mail," as he put it.

A Time To Be Led By God Alone

We always felt overlooked at this church. Jeff and I made jokes about being the "unknowns on the seventeenth row". But it was a sacrifice we chose to make for our children to have a nearby youth group. Maybe for this reason, he wasn't concerned that he wasn't allowed to prophesy here. After all, he didn't set out to do it. It just happened.

I don't think we ever heard anyone prophesy while we were there. It was an Assembly of God church, so we heard a lot of speaking in tongues. The prophetic was not in the atmosphere at this church. So where did this new gift come from?

This encounter spurred Jeff and me to press in to God for a deeper understanding of our spiritual destiny. There were limits to what was considered permissible to experience in the church.

After much prayer and discussion, we both sensed God saying that what He had for us was beyond those boundaries, and staying there would hold us back. Strange as it seemed, He was asking us to pull out of church for a time, and to be led by Him alone.

This was not something we took lightly. Generally, I do not believe in leaving the church. Fellowship is key to a healthy walk with God. Nonetheless, we were obedient, although we did not entirely understand.

Shortly after we left the Assembly of God, we heard rumors that numerous churches in surrounding areas were seeing revival and awakening. We flocked to these "glory meetings," hungry to soak up whatever we could of the atmosphere of Heaven. We began to see a tremendous move of the Spirit in neighboring towns. We were both experiencing many heavenly signs. We were hungry for more!

We heard revival had come to a Church of Christ in neighboring Hendersonville, so we drove to that town. Someone told us that the youth leader had been teaching the youth about the Holy Spirit. Suddenly the Spirit of God just fell on them and signs and wonders followed. This was our first experience with large amounts of gold dust falling in the church. It did not fall in sprinkles, this was more like bucketfuls! Many people in attendance were covered in "golden" glory from head to toe. We just marveled!

I slipped out to find the restroom and people were looking at me and pointing at me. I had no idea why. When I got into the restroom, I looked in the mirror and I was absolutely covered in gold dust! I just said, "Wow!" I returned to my seat and showed Jeff, and he said the same thing, "Wow!"

After that night, I acquired gold dust almost continually for many years. I could even pray for someone else to get it, and they would.

In another meeting in Murfreesboro, the gold dust fell even thicker than it had in Hendersonville. There were piles all over the floor in front of the sanctuary and people were laying in it, laughing!

Of course there were those who would question the authenticity of seeing gold dust falling out of Heaven. We didn't question it. Neither of us struggled with unbelief. We just knew it was God and that there was no logical explanation for it in the natural realm.

Through the glory meetings we went to, we discovered many well-known, highly anointed ministers we had never heard of before. Jeff was often called out by these great men and women of God, who prophesied words of ministry and travel over him. We didn't question these words, we just said, "Be it done to us according to Your word, Lord."

Seeing An Angel For The First Time

Many signs and wonders followed. Gold dust was the most obvious sign, frequently falling in the meetings we attended. The chunks of gold that were falling seemed to be getting larger and larger.

Spending time with the atmosphere of Heaven present at these glory meetings opened up a whole new level of the supernatural in our lives.

One night, while lying in bed, suddenly my spirit began to perceive what appeared to be a small person, standing in the corner of our bedroom. My eyes were closed, but I could clearly see it in my spirit. One minute it looked feminine, the next, masculine. One minute its appearance was young, like a teenager; the next minute, it appeared almost ancient. I knew I was seeing in the spirit realm, but this was brand new to me.

At the time we had two parrots, a blue and gold Macaw, and a yellow-naped Amazon, who lived in our bedroom. Boomer, our Amazon, lived in a cage near the corner of the room where this being seemed to be standing.

Larry Bird, our Macaw, lived on a tall perch next to Boomer. Boomer began flapping her wings and squawking, simultaneously. Boomer saw the angel too!

This angel had no message. I think this was just the Lord showing me that I could "see".

Jeff was growing in his prophetic gift, speaking precise, highly accurate words, over others. The more he exercised this gift, the more it intensified.

Mother Of Many

I was feeling an undeniable stirring to be a mother again, but why? Between my son and Jeff's four kids, we already had five children in the house.

When my son was two years old I miscarried, and that was it. I never had any more children.

I had seen so many happy families, and longed to experience that myself. But my dream of having a baby and raising it together, as a family, wasn't to be. I basically raised my son alone.

My parents felt children were a burden and not a blessing. They'd repeatedly say, "We hope you never have children!" Their harsh words had effectively stifled my natural desire for children.

Now, I had an overwhelming desire I could not shake. Jeff did not want more children. This led to many long conversations with the Lord.

I was praying fervently, and believing the word of the Lord that we would have a child or children. In the process, I became a prophetic word magnet. People gave me words about having children everywhere I went.

People would cry out, "Mother of many! Mother of many!"

While I was getting words about being a mother and having children, Jeff continued to get prophetic words about an international ministry and travel. The words seemed to be at odds with one another.

"Lord, I don't understand. What are You saying?"

Chapter Four

ENCOUNTERS AND VISITATIONS

Moving To Gatewood Drive

We lived comfortably in the home I purchased before meeting Jeff, for about ten years. Having never even discussed moving, it came as a surprise that one day, out of the blue, the Lord spoke to me audibly and said, "Jan, it's time to sell the house."

Because it was the first home I'd owned, and the place that held so many memories of our humble beginning, this was difficult, but by this time, we were empty nesters.

My son was married and he and his wife were soon to have their first child. Jeff's daughter was married and expecting her first child. His boys had also moved out to find what the Lord had for them. Downsizing seemed to make sense. Or, maybe we just needed a new home to match all the other newness we were experiencing?

Nonetheless, it was clear this move was God's design. He was very intentional in the direction He gave. He even alerted me the day the prospective new owners came. To my surprise, He audibly spoke again, saying, "Your buyers are coming today. Clean the house."

I was still cleaning when they showed up! I noticed a couple outside, walking around the house, looking around.

"Can I help you?" I asked.

Apparently, my realtor refused to show them the house, saying he was too busy. I was surprised, but happily responded, "Come on in. I'll show you the house. I was expecting someone to come today."

They bought the house, without a realtor. It was truly a God thing.

I developed a longing for a newly built house, one that no one else had ever lived in. It would just be ours.

After extensive searching, we chose a small house in a new subdivision where we felt the presence of the Lord. The name of the street was Gatewood Drive.

Jeff and I agreed that the name Gatewood felt significant. It seemed that there was a spiritual portal or gate over this home. Not surprisingly, God showed up powerfully in our new home on Gatewood Drive. The wind of the Holy Spirit was blowing on us, bringing us into the new and exciting things that He had in store for us.

We were beginning to see some of the prophecies that were spoken to us manifest. Jeff's prophetic gift continued to increase. My ability to see in the spirit was growing even more, and I became a prolific dreamer. We each had numerous encounters, and heavenly visitations beyond anything we could have imagined. We were in a season of encounters.

Supernatural Translation

I had vaguely heard of translations, but never experienced one before. There are numerous examples of translation in the Bible, such as encounters experienced by Ezekiel, Elisha, or John, to name a few.

I heard Joshua Mills tell a story once of being "translated" to China. He had drifted off to sleep and found himself in another land that he thought was China, based on what he was seeing. There, he was taken to an underground church where he ministered the gospel. While he was there, he met a man in an elevator. The man handed him a business card, which Joshua slipped into his pocket. Much to his surprise, when Joshua awoke, he found the same business card, from the man in China in his pocke!

One afternoon, I began to feel drowsy. Bob Jones had always told me the Lord would make you drowsy in the afternoon so He could use you and speak to you. I lay down on the sofa and swiftly drifted off to sleep.

One minute I was lying on my living room couch, and the next minute, I physically felt the soft grainy texture of sand beneath my feet as I walked, and the heat of the sun beating down on my back. All the people surrounding me were dark-skinned. Where was I? Was I in Africa?

There was an entire family sitting on a wooden wagon bed, like a trailer on wheels, but nothing was pulling it or attached to it. Several children sat with them. The mother appeared to be blind, as did one of the children. The man, who seemed to be the father, looked up at me and must have assumed I was a follower of Jesus. He crouched down and drew the fish symbol in the sand with a stick to indicate that he and his family were believers too.

Even before he did this, I sensed they were believers. I felt drawn to them, and began to pray for the blind mother. As I spoke healing over her, the earth began to shake. The Lord Himself showed up! I could feel the weighty power and the tremendous love of Jesus for this beautiful family.

As suddenly as I had left my sofa, I was "returned" back to my sofa. I shook uncontrollably for hours, as I had done when I became born again at the Vineyard. It was not a dream. It was a supernatural encounter! God had taken me to another place, for His purposes. I felt an assurance in my spirit that the blind woman I prayed for was healed.

In that same season, we were in Wisconsin doing a ministry event at Valley Harvest Church in Neenah. We were staying with Jeff's parents. I went to lay down on the bed and must have fallen asleep. I suddenly found myself sitting on a mountain top. I wasn't sure what happened, and had no idea where I was. I could feel the wind on my face, blowing my hair back with its gentle force. This was not a dream.

Looking below, I saw flowing rivers and beautiful evergreen trees. The terrain was unfamiliar to me, looking nothing like my home here in Tennessee.

I felt the presence of someone beside me. Cautiously, I looked to my right side. To my utter amazement, Jesus, Himself, was sitting beside me on the mountain top. I was speechless. Somehow, I didn't feel shocked, but surprisingly natural.

"Jesus, where are we?" I asked Him confidently.

"Calgary, Alberta, Canada. It is one of My favorite places," He responded, with total love emitting out of Him.

We sat there together in silent communion, enjoying the beauty. There was no need to speak a word.

As suddenly as it began, I was whisked back to the bed in Jeff's parents' home.

I had never been to Calgary, Alberta before. Excited about what had just happened, and curious to somehow explain it, I searched online for pictures of Calgary, Alberta, Canada. The photos I found were an exact match of what I saw sitting on the mountain heights with Jesus.

I knew somehow this encounter was more than just getting to spend time with Jesus, although that, in itself, was enough for me. But was there more?

I felt like Calgary, Alberta needed to know it was one of the Lord's favorite places on Earth. I randomly contacted several churches in Calgary that, from their websites, appeared to be Spirit-filled. They were excited at the revelation that this was one of Jesus' favorite places.

One resident there got back in touch with me months later and told me that revival had broken out because of the power of this revelation to the people there.

In 2004, I had another profound experience. There is a difference between a dream, a night vision, and an encounter. This, too, was an encounter.

Of course this is a book in itself, but let me briefly explain the difference.

—⁓⁓⁓Dreams⁓⁓⁓—

Dreams are more common to most people. Almost everyone dreams on some level. A dream is thought to occur when you are in a deep state of sleep. Bob said most dreams are soul-cleansing dreams, where information and data from your everyday life is purged while you sleep. Some people have more dreams from God than others. Many literally have the call of the dreamer, and some of dream interpretation, like Daniel. Many dreams from God contain a lot of symbolism, similar to how Jesus spoke in parables. Dreams can also come from the demonic realm.

Night Visions

A vision is a sight, something you see in your spirit. It's like you see it in your mind's eye, or somewhere deep inside of you. You can have open-eye visions when you are awake and alert, that just seem to be like a picture or a movie inside your consciousness. A night vision is a deeper level of seeing than a dream. It is not as symbolic, but more visionary. Many night visions occur when you first fall asleep when your sleep level is not in its deepest level yet.

Night Encounters

An encounter is when the Holy Spirit, or the Lord Jesus actually visits you in your sleep state. The Lord can make the Spirit realm a reality to you in these encounters, by taking you into the Spirit realm or bringing the Spirit realm to you, or He may actually speak to you on a personal level. Bob Jones said that the Lord often waits until you are asleep to encounter you, because your resistance and human defenses are down. Technically, we are just too busy while we are awake and going about our daily business, and without knowing it, we don't allow times of visitation.

In this profound encounter I had, in the middle of the night while I was sleeping, Jesus came to me driving a red convertible! He motioned for me to get in the passenger seat. Without regard for where we were going, I climbed in the car with Him. He drove down a straight road lined with evergreen trees along both sides. Reaching the end of the road, Jesus pointed up to the sky and said, "Look at the clouds."

There in the sky was a straight dividing line, with clouds on the top and a bright blue cloudless sky below. The dividing line was directly in the middle.

"This is like Heaven meeting Earth," Jesus said.

He shared at length on the principle of balance. I had no idea how important balance would become for me and others in the future. It was clearly very important to Him.

Jesus continued, "A day is coming when a plumb line will fall, and people will be forced to choose which side they are on." I could literally envision in my mind the plumb line falling, just as He spoke.

He continued, "Those who choose the right side will see a great move of My glory on the earth, like nothing they have ever seen. Those who choose the wrong side will not only miss this great move of glory, but will be caught up in deception and unbelief, and will be used by the enemy to deceive many with false religion."

His next words pierced the atmosphere, "The spirit of religion is the spirit of the antichrist."

I don't believe we can say with certainty whether these are actual physical experiences, or experiences that take place in the Spirit alone. You might say, "Well, you know Jesus did not actually come to you driving a red convertible."

As John said, *"Whether in the body I do not know, or whether out of the body I do not know. God knows such a one was caught up in the third heaven."* ~ 2 Corinthians 12:2 (Amp)

That encounter remains with me, even today. It took me to a new level, activating something deep within. I believe the plumb line Jesus spoke of has fallen in the last few years, and the division is about to take place as we see revival beginning to manifest all over our nation and our world.

Jeff also had numerous visitations and encounters during this time. One that stood out to him was seeing a large crane in the Spirit; the kind that picks up heavy items and moves them. The mechanical crane spun around from its base, and it reached over and lifted something quite large and apparently weighty. As Jeff saw the crane release and place the heavy load back on the ground it was clearly a large, numeric 11:11. He said the Lord had placed 11:11 in place.

We were not sure what this meant at first. Of course 11:11 could refer to Isaiah 11:11.

"Then it will happen on that day that the Lord will again acquire with His hand a second time the remnant of His people who will remain."

We also knew Hebrews 11:11 was significant.

"By faith even Sarah herself received the ability to conceive (a child), even (when she was long) past the normal age for it, because she considered Him who had given her the promise to be reliable and true (to His word)".

We were not sure exactly how this applied to us, but we did know the Lord had just set something in place that was weighty and pertinent for what was to come.

The Warning: Pride Will Be His Downfall

That same year, on another night as I lay in bed awake, the Lord again spoke to me, delivering a stirring word.

"Tell Jeff that his zeal will take him far, but pride will be his downfall."

It was a strong word. He didn't say might be, or could be. He said *will* be.

I took note of the warning, but I didn't realize how critical this word would be for us in the years to come. Still, I was obedient, telling Jeff what the Lord had said, word for word.

Jeff didn't seem to be concerned about it, responding simply, "I'll keep it in mind."

I have had to repent over and over for not asking the Lord more about what He spoke to me that night. At the time, it was hard to comprehend the gravity of His words because, after all, things seemed to be going great. Our lives were good, and God was moving.

It was evident to Jeff and I that we were on the verge of something great. We could feel it.

Our good friend Mary, who Jeff had known since he was sixteen, came to stay with us for a brief visit. Shortly after Mary's arrival, I had a dream of myself in an emergency room. I was wearing a hospital gown, and my back was exposed. I felt I had been in some kind of an incident, but kept saying, "I can't see, I can't see!" At the time, I was unsure what this meant.

Jeff was traveling, and that morning he contacted me with a warning.

"Jan, three dark-skinned men in black suits with scars on their faces appeared out of nowhere in my hotel room this morning. I'm not entirely sure what it means, but it felt like danger. Please, whatever you do, be careful." I took note.

Mary and I went out later to go to a hair salon. It was drizzling rain, but nothing severe. From the main road, we had to make a left turn into the parking lot of the building. Checking the traffic in both directions at least three times, I turned the steering wheel and stepped on the gas, proceeding to turn left into the parking lot.

I heard Mary call out. All she could say was, "Jan! Jan! Jan!" three times, but I had no idea why. She was too stunned to give me details about what she saw coming. I'd thoroughly checked for oncoming traffic, and the road was clear.

As I crossed the road toward the parking lot, a car came blasting down the hill out of nowhere, and crashed into the right side of my Honda Civic. The driver of the other car was speeding and distracted, talking to her child in the back seat.

It was surreal, like everything was in slow motion. The impact was hard, and Mary was obviously hurt. Just like the dream I had, we were transported to the emergency room. Thankfully, I was unhurt, but Mary's pelvis was fractured in three places.

We learned a whole new level of warfare through this experience. The Lord had clearly warned both me and Jeff that there was danger, but we did not yet know to interpret it. I believe the forewarnings showed this was a demonic attack. The enemy had apparently blinded me so I could not see the car speeding towards us, as was shown to me in my dream when I said, "I can't see!"

Between rest and recuperation, Mary's brief visit turned into a year-long stay with us at our Gatewood home. She was always a blessing and she and I became very close.

Chapter Five

THE GATE

A Supernatural Fragrance

One day I was out shopping at a fruit and vegetable stand. As I wandered around looking at the offerings, I began to smell an irresistible fragrance that drew me in.

It was a sweet, perfumed aroma that smelled better than any scent I had experienced on Earth. I couldn't help but follow it. I had to know the source.

Following the wafting bouquet, I was led to a woman with blonde hair who was also shopping. I could not see her face from where I stood. Unexpectedly, she turned around, catching me sniffing the air around her. My embarrassment quickly turned to delight.

"Lisa!"

"Jan? Is that you?"

Lisa and I had gone to school together throughout our entire childhood. I had not seen her in years. Even though we were classmates, we were never especially close. This was an extraordinary surprise.

"Lisa, it was your sweet perfume that drew me to you. It smells so good!"

"I'm not wearing perfume," she responded.

When God wants to get your attention, He can get it any way He chooses.

Lisa and I began to talk, discovering that we had both been born again and shared similar interests. We instantly bonded and exchanged phone numbers.

Over the next several weeks, Lisa and I talked on the phone frequently, sharing about our mutual hunger for more of God. What would it look like if we were to simply meet and worship?

Lisa and her husband were musicians and worshippers. I told her Jeff, too, was a songwriter and musician, but we felt more called to be facilitators than worship leaders at that time. We agreed to meet at their house, press in to the Lord, and see what happened.

Lisa and Dale had a beautiful farm in a neighboring county with a large bonus room, perfect for our plans. We first met on a Sunday morning with their two children, and our four. The ten of us joined together and engaged with the Holy Spirit in worship. We experienced a beautiful weighty presence, more than any of us had ever experienced.

Lisa and Dale were beautiful worshipers. Their voices were delightful, but it was actually their spirit of worship that changed the atmosphere. Jeff would also lead on his guitar. It was heavenly.

Eager to see what would happen next, we continued meeting, week after week. Following our worship time, we would eat and fellowship together. Each week brought fresh revelation and new levels of glory.

We would physically feel winds blow through the room. In the same way that we had previously experienced supernatural manifestations of gold dust, it fell heavily on all of us here, although we did not see it in the large bucketfuls, as we saw at the glory meetings. It just seemed to sprinkle everything in the room, and us. Many times, the heavenly dust was multi-colored and fell all over the floor and chairs, as well as something new. Supernatural oil began to flow out of our hands, remaining as evidence that God is a God of signs and wonders.

We would be so powerfully overcome that we found ourselves glued to the floor for hours. We were unable to move in the glory of His presence, laughing wildly and crying intensely, all by the Spirit of God.

We wanted to share the joy we were experiencing in our gatherings, so it was time to invite others. Our tiny, ten-person gathering grew and grew. Soon, we could no longer contain it.

We agreed to rent a space in Murfreesboro and see what happened. Searching for a small room or building in a central location, we found a space that seemed suitable. It was an upper room, so to speak, on the second story of an older, multi-use building. There was one available room that could facilitate small gatherings, so we proceeded to rent it in faith, and planned to meet on Sunday mornings.

Word got out, and we quickly filled the small room. Those who came were hungry and expecting. The presence of God that filled that space was incredible. I have never experienced anything like it since.

Every time we met, the winds of God would literally blow throughout the room as in our meetings at our friends' farm, but even more powerfully. It was a weighty glory that was almost overwhelming, ushering us into an encounter with God every time we met. I imagined how the high priests of biblical days might have felt as they entered into the Holy of Holies.

We prayed, we worshiped, we laughed, and we cried; often, all at the same time. We shook under the power of the Holy Spirit, falling to the floor in awe, overpowered by His Presence. Most of all, we glorified the living God for what He was doing in our midst!

Soon we outgrew our small "upper room". We began to look for a building that could accommodate more people. By this time, we often had twenty-five or thirty people attending our Sunday meetings.

A small storefront building on a main road would be our new home. We worked hard to remodel and decorate the space. After praying for a name, we settled on "The Gate," inspired by John 10:9.

"I am the Door (Gate); anyone who enters through Me will be saved [and will live forever], and will go in and out [freely], and find pasture (spiritual security)".   ~ John 10:9 Amp

Our attendance varied from week to week. Some came out of curiosity, because they had heard what the Lord was doing. Some had home churches elsewhere. We had a small, faithful group of regular attendees who were passionate to help us build.

The End Of The Beginning

Not long after our foundation in the new space known as "The Gate," our dreams for growth and expansion hit a wall. Lisa and Dale, our co-founders and worship leaders, had a devastating hurdle to navigate.

Unexpectedly, Lisa and Dale lost the beautiful farm where we began. It was unexpected and unfortunate. They had no choice but to move back to the childhood hometown where Lisa, her husband, and I had grown up.

Our hearts were broken for them, and for us.

Could we function as a church without Lisa and Dale? Jeff and I spoke with the other faithful members of The Gate. None of them were worship leaders, and none could devote the time that leading a church would demand. After much prayer, we believed we had no choice but to discontinue The Gate.

I didn't understand. It felt like Heaven had surrounded us, and I didn't want to see it end.

"Jeff, why would God show up in such power, only to let it fail?" I asked in tears.

He simply responded, "Jan, there was much to be learned, and hopefully, none of it was for nothing."

Jeff seemed to see other opportunities on the horizon. But my heart grieved for my friends' loss and the loss of our fellowship. I always longed to have a united church family. But now, the beautiful church family that we had been building was to be no more.

The duration may have been brief, but there was no question that the church had not been a mistake. The initial meetings at the farm and the Gate were not birthed in vain. God was giving us a prototype of how He wanted His Church, His Ecclesia, to function: Jesus as the Head, and man with no agenda of his own.

Chapter Six

MEETING PROPHET BOB JONES

Spring Blizzard

As word got out about the signs and wonders we had been encountering in our meetings, the invitations started to pour in. Jeff was asked to minister locally in surrounding towns, doing ministry in small venues where friends who had attended The Gate were leading.

Without knowing where we were going, we walked through the doors that opened before us.

Jeff looked at me one day and said, out of the blue, "I want Bob Jones!"

I wasn't familiar with Bob, so I asked him what he meant.

"I want to know Bob Jones. He was one of the Kansas City prophets back in the day," he explained.

I had never heard of the Kansas City prophets either, but I had to admit, the man sounded intriguing.

It was only a few weeks after Jeff announced his heart's desire to meet Bob that we received a call from our friends in North Carolina, Kenneth and Brenda. We had no idea, but Bob was their spiritual father. They had been going to gatherings at his home for years.

To our amazement, they invited us to join them on a trip to see Bob. Jeff and I were undone! It had been the Lord's destiny for us to know Bob and Jeff spoke that destiny forth as he felt it! That's the power of the spoken word.

The first time we drove to Bob's home in North Carolina, it was the first day of spring. Oddly, as we traveled down Interstate 40 late at night, snow began to flurry. Not a big deal, we thought.

To our dismay, the snow began to fall heavier and heavier. Eventually, we could no longer drive and had to pull over. The snow continued for hours. Thank God we had plenty of gas.

This was more than just snow. Now, all traffic on the interstate was at a complete standstill. Jeff ventured out into the blizzard to investigate. He discovered that a tractor-trailer had jackknifed in the slippery conditions, and was blocking all three lanes. Clearly, we were going to be there for a while.

Eight hours later, traffic began to move. We didn't arrive at Kenneth and Brenda's house until the wee hours of the morning. Completely exhausted, we headed to bed to grab a couple of hours of sleep before it was time to hit the road again to see Bob.

Our First Meeting With Bob

Bob's house was about two hours from Kenneth and Brenda's home. We had never met him, so we didn't know what to expect. As we entered the house, Bob's wife, Viola, greeted us. We walked into their humble home and we were invited to take a seat in the living room, along with those already gathered for the meeting.

I wasn't sure what to expect when I would finally meet Bob Jones. Would he have on a suit and tie? Would he be very professional and ministerial? No, he was extremely down-to-earth and easy to be around. He was not intimidating at all in a natural sense, but you could feel the heavy anointing on him. He had on a sweatshirt, sweatpants that were slightly too short, and white socks. He had a very "grandfatherly" demeanor.

Bob welcomed us warmly, as Kenneth and Brenda introduced us. I had never met anyone like Bob, and soaked up everything he had to say. He seemed to take a particular interest in us. Bob shared a word he received from the Lord that included the words "when the prophets would be in a snowstorm on the first day of spring".

What? He had no way of knowing we were stuck in a snowstorm on the way in, which, by the way, was also on the first day of spring!

Naturally, Bob was not shocked when we told him our story. Instead, he confidently said, "Well then, let the Lord declare you prophets!"

What a day! Bob prayed over Jeff and me, then told us he was going to "take us up" into the third heaven. We didn't know how or what that meant exactly, but we instinctively stood up and held our arms out in a receiving mode. Almost immediately, winds began blowing all around us, similar to what we had experienced in our glory meetings. This time, the winds were more like small, repeated bursts of wind directed at Jeff and me.

Referring to Jeff and me, Bob explained to the others in the group, "You feel the wind whipping up on them? This means the angels are here. Now, I'm going to take you up."

A New Spiritual Father

Many more surreal experiences would follow, but we would never forget this one. It was one of the most amazing spiritual encounters we ever had. That first visit with Bob led to many more trips to his house. Soon, he became our spiritual father. Bob took Jeff under his wing as a "young eagle," in Bob's own words. I wanted an impartation of his seer gift.

We spoke with Bob on the phone as often as we could, learning more from him in that time than I can put into words. The impartation he released to each of us was powerful. As a result, Jeff grew incredibly in the prophetic and miracle realm, and I grew in the seer realm.

I would tell Bob of things I had experienced in my own walk with God. I would usually begin saying, "Bob, I know this sounds weird, but..."

His response was always, "Honey, you're not weird. Everyone else is weird!"

Through Bob, we learned that the supernatural is natural, if we walk by the Spirit and not by the flesh. I tightly embraced the words Bob shared, particularly with me. His words were food for my soul. According to Bob, when we get a prophetic word that bears witness with us, we are to wear these words spiritually, until they manifest.

Bob always spoke with such authority, "Wear them around your neck like a necklace, honey. If they haven't come to pass, you can put them on a shelf, but put them where you can see them and not out of sight."

The Knock At The Door

During one visit, as Bob was speaking with someone else, I began looking around the room at all the beautiful paintings he had hanging on the wall. Oddly, there were screws driven through the frames or even actual paintings themselves, securing them to the wall. This was odd to me, and I was bold enough to ask him why his beautiful artwork had screws driven into them from the front.

In a no-nonsense manner, he stated, "Well, honey, the Lord would sometimes knock at my door in the middle of the night. I would get up and say, 'Okay, Lord, I'm coming as fast as I can'. I would go to the door, open it and nobody would be there. I knew it was the Lord, and He was telling me that He was taking me higher.

"This happened numerous times and He would knock so hard all my pictures fell off the wall. So I screwed them in."

That explained that. We all smiled. Subsequently, Jeff and I got the "knock on the door" numerous times. We would run to the door, and nobody was there. We simply said, "Thank you, Lord, for new levels!"

The knock on the door was an invitation.

"Behold, I stand at the door and continually knock. If anyone hears My voice and opens the door I will come in and eat with him (restore him), and he with Me." ~ Revelation 3:20 Amp

After our meetings in Bob's home, he always wanted to go eat at the Golden Corral. We had great times of fellowship dining with the seer prophet.

I was still getting many prophetic words about being a mother and having a child. Following Bob's advice, I continued to spiritually "wear those words around my neck". There was no way I was ready to shelf them.

Meanwhile, we were experiencing increasingly intense dreams, visions, and encounters. Jeff continued to spread his wings in ministry. He was traveling more, and seeing more of the miraculous power of spoken word miracles.

He was receiving high-level revelation. Jeff was even experiencing visitations from the Lord in his hotel room when he was on the road. When we were invited to minister, Jeff would speak things into the atmosphere prophetically.

It was not uncommon for Jeff's words to create a shift, causing the atmosphere to become supernaturally supercharged, and spurring the release of miraculous healing and other gifts.

At the time, we were as surprised by what came out of Jeff's mouth, and the resulting heavenly manifestations, as everyone else was. After all, we still had little experience with prophetic revelation and activation. But it seemed to come naturally to Jeff.

We were in a season of extreme expansion, seeing the "more" of God. It was during this time that Global Fire Ministries, International, was birthed. We consulted an attorney, became incorporated, and obtained a 501C3.

Word spread, and we were asked to be a part of larger events in other states. The doors for Jeff to minister began to open in Ohio. We also began hosting a few glory meetings in our own home.

Incredibly, we never had a meeting where the Spirit of God did not show up in power and we did not take this for granted. We were always careful to avoid putting God in a box, thanking Him always for His beauty and His presence.

Although the Lord had presented Himself powerfully in our Gatewood home, I couldn't forget He had told me that we would only be there for two years.

At the time, I remember Jeff saying, "No way, I will not move again!"

God had a different idea. He already knew we would need a larger house to accommodate our soon-to-be growing family. In obedience, we sold our Gatewood home, and bought another house just a few streets down, in the same neighborhood.

The Gatewood house had been marked by the Holy Spirit, with a supernatural portal over the property. It was like a direct route that brought Heaven to Earth. The divine encounters we experienced there changed us forever. In fact, one of the most remarkable things that happened while there still astonishes me.

The Visitation

Bob Jones was a key minister at a huge conference in Cincinnati, Ohio, along with several other speakers. Somehow, Jeff's name was thrown out there. I am sure Bob recommended him. Although people were beginning to hear of his signs and wonders ministry, he was basically an unknown. I remember how excited Jeff was when he was invited to be one of the main speakers. He did not hesitate to say yes.

This was one of the first large events Jeff ministered at. We were both still working full-time jobs at the time. The conference started on Thursday night, but he told the pastors he could not arrive until Friday, as we had a previous engagement.

We had already invited our good friends David and Ginny for a visit on Thursday night and we didn't want to disappoint them by canceling, or miss out on the opportunity to fellowship with them.

My friend Ginny had been in a glory meeting where supernatural bread, or manna, had fallen, and she offered to bring some. We had not yet experienced heavenly manna falling here on Earth, and were excited to see this miracle. Sitting in a circle in our small den, we took communion together with the heavenly manna.

At first it seemed like communion as usual. Then suddenly, the room seemed to shake. We felt like we were floating, and in another realm. Jeff said at one point it felt like he literally left his body, but wasn't sure where he went. It was surreal! The glory was so thick we could barely move.

Each of us encountered God in a new and profound way that night. We lingered in this heavenly atmosphere as long as we could. Eventually, Jeff announced that he had to leave early the next morning.

"Well folks, that's it for me. I need to head off to bed." Our friends excused themselves.

This time, I was unable to go with Jeff to the conference. Early Friday morning, Jeff kissed me goodbye and headed to Cincinnati for the evening session. When he arrived, a man greeted him warmly.

"Jeff, it was good to see you last night."

Assuming the man had mistaken him for someone else, Jeff corrected him.

"I wasn't here last night. I just got here."

The man looked back at Jeff with a bewildered expression on his face.

Then, another person approached and said, "Jeff, thank you for all the wisdom you imparted to me last night."

As more and more people came up to Jeff with similar statements, thanking him for what he had done or said to them on Thursday night, Jeff was confused.

Jeff called me on the phone to tell me about what was happening.

"Jan, I don't know what's going on. All these people are coming up to me, telling me they saw me here in Cincinnati last night at the conference, and thanking me for my ministry to them. It's not just one or two people. I keep getting comments from one after the other. They're all convinced it was me. Even John and Debbie."

We had spent much time with John and Debbie over the years. For a season, I worked as the booking manager for their ministry, Life Choices, founded in honor of Debbie's niece, Rachel Joy Scott, who lost her life in the Columbine High School shootings.

Their home was in Ohio, but they traveled all over the country ministering in high schools and middle schools, telling Rachel Joy's story. It was powerful and many young people gave their lives to the Lord. John, Debbie, their children, and team parked their RV in our front yard when they weren't on the road, and basically lived with us for a while. They knew us well.

They knew Jeff was a big cut-up, and rarely said anything sentimental. When it came to their sense of humor, Jeff and John were "twin brothers from different mothers," as they said. There was never a dull moment around those two.

They also shared that they saw Jeff on Thursday night, even inviting him to stay at their house, close to the church where the conference was being held. John and Debbie later explained their reaction to his response to them.

"You know, when we invited you to stay with us, you sounded a little different from 'regular' Jeff. You weren't your usual funny, bantering self. You simply and sincerely said, 'You always make room for me'. I have to admit, we kind of raised our eyebrows at each other, wondering what happened to the Jeff we knew. Not that it wasn't you. It was just a 'different' you, more serious."

A woman who had adopted a child from China spoke with Jeff about adoption, and also found his response to her out of character, more serious than his usual light style. Even my friend Georgine reported seeing Jeff at the conference Thursday night.

"Jan, I saw him too! I did! I looked up from my seat on the main floor and saw Jeff in the balcony. He was wearing a green jacket, and it seemed to be glowing."

"But Georgine, he doesn't even own a green jacket!"

This was pertinent information. It could only have been a supernatural occurrence.

One man reported that he stood near Jeff at the registration counter and watched him sign in. Jeff later asked to see the register. Sure enough, his signature was on the Thursday night registration log, and it was Jeff's handwriting. He sent me a photo of the handwriting on the log. Jeff had a very distinctive signature, and I could only verify that it was in fact his handwriting!

In total, more than forty people came forth and said they had either seen, or spoken to Jeff on Thursday night. Their testimonies are all recorded and placed on a CD set chronicling the experience called The Visitation.

Many speculated it was Jeff's "angel," as was commonly believed in biblical times (Acts 12:15-16).

Sometimes supernatural experiences are beyond our comprehension. Was it really Jeff who appeared that Thursday night at the conference in Ohio, while simultaneously, taking communion with Ginny, her husband, and me in our Tennessee home? Or was it possibly Jeff's angel?

Whether Jeff was truly bi-locating, as many suggested, or it was an angel bearing his appearance at the conference that night, we may never know on this earth. We simply felt honored to be a part of such an incredible supernatural occurrence.

The Ichabods

Another time, Jeff and I were traveling to Topeka, Kansas to speak at a church there. The pastors took us on a tour of the city, along with some of their team members. Part of the tour included a stop at the building where Charles Parham founded Bethel Bible College. The angelic presence in that building was thick. We just stood there, taking it all in.

When it was time to go, I went ahead of Jeff and the team, who were still inside talking. As I exited the building, the Lord directed my attention to the back of the building. In the Spirit, I saw an angel, chained to the railing at the back door.

He was very distinct to me. I walked up to the angel and asked him why he was there.

I clearly heard, "I have been here in chains since 1901, when the Holy Spirit was run out of Topeka."

I couldn't wait to tell Jeff what I had seen and heard. We both searched the Internet for information. We found the same dates and information, confirming the angel's report. Charles Parham founded Bethel Bible College in 1900. When he and the students went on a fast, subsequently, the Holy Spirit showed up. They all ended up speaking in tongues, causing much controversy. The community was not open to the working of the Holy Spirit. They had never experienced it before. They didn't understand it, and they weren't excited about the controversy it was bringing.

Just as the angel spoke, Charles was forced to close his school in 1901.

As we drove away, we passed the local high school. I noticed the large sign in front of the school, brandishing the name of the football team, "The Ichabods." The meaning of the name Ichabod is "the glory has departed," as mentioned in 1 Samuel 4:21-22. I knew the Lord was speaking of restoring what the enemy had once stolen in Topeka.

Supernatural Trance

Jeff and I continued to travel to Ohio frequently. During an intercessory session at a church Jeff was ministering at, I went into a supernatural trance.

As Bob Jones explained, "That's when you literally enter into a spiritual dimension and don't realize what is going on in the natural realm around you."

Basically a trance isn't much different than a vision or night vision, as far as the revelation received. The difference lies in your state of alertness at the time. A trance is like a dream, but you have no physical awareness of anything that is going on around you. It comes on suddenly. You are alert to your surroundings one minute, then you suddenly fall into a deep sleep-like state, although you are not asleep. When the encounter is over, you are again aware of your surroundings.

In Acts 10-11, Peter went into a trace-like state and "he saw an object like a great sheet descending". The Lord spoke to him and gave him revelation through the trance.

One minute I was actively praying in this intercessory meeting; the next minute, unaware of my surroundings, I immediately envisioned a big hole in the ground before me. I could clearly see what appeared to be a man in a library down in the hole. There were many, many books on the shelves. I perceived he was an angel. This angel also had chains wrapped around him.

In faith, I asked, "Who are you, and why are you here?"

The angel immediately responded, "I was left here in chains when the agenda of God was thrown out and the agenda of man took over."

"Angel, what are all the books?" I inquired.

"In them are recorded all the annals and exploits of the great men and women of God. The mighty acts of God are recorded in these books. Man covered this great library up when he chose to do things man's way, and not God's."

The angel gave me dates in the late 1800s.

When I came out of this encounter, Jeff asked me what was wrong. "Jan, you were just sitting there frozen, and seemed to be somewhere else."

"Jeff, I was somewhere else! I was having an encounter with an angel."

He was always excited when I saw things in the spirit. Jeff began researching what had happened in the region in the year the angel had given me. We found that Maria Woodworth Etter had come through the region, hosting revival meetings in that exact location, in the same year!

She was called "The Trance Evangelist," and would go into a trance-like state, similar to what I had experienced. When she came out of the trances, she would share her visions with those in attendance at her meetings.

After my encounter, Jeff was able to speak prophetically about it to those present and encourage revival over the region.

Chapter Seven

THE TORONTO BLESSING

Charles Carrin

Jeff and I highly admired Charles Carrin as a man of God. We were wowed by his ministry. Charles would humbly stand up and say, "Come, Holy Spirit!" and the power of God would fall like lightning. I've never seen anyone else operate that simply, yet powerfully. If someone had a demon, it would immediately start to manifest with no one laying hands on him, or her.

Years back, I remember seeing Charles minister in a church in my hometown of McMinnville that was a branch of the legalistic denomination I grew up in.

"Come, Holy Spirit!" he said boldly from the pulpit.

Some fell out in the Spirit. Others began screaming. The religious folk slowly retreated to the back of the room in absolute horror. They had never experienced the living presence of the Holy Spirit before. Charles followed them across the room. Many would flee and run out the back door. I had to giggle. When Charles approached me, I immediately fell under the glory. I hit the ground hard!

The awakening was still moving in Toronto at the Vineyard church. Charles Carrin was ministering there with Heidi Baker and a number of other ministers. Jeff and I had become acquainted with Charles through my first cousin, David. David had been ministering with Charles and assisting him.

Charles told us he was going to the Toronto Vineyard to minister, and invited us. We felt this was a divine invitation. We remembered what Pastors Jerry and Cindy had imparted to us after visiting there.

Toronto would be my first international trip. My mind went back to the early 2000s, recalling how I had always been terrified of flying. I would see others flying to exotic places and I wanted my fear expelled, but I was paralyzed at the thought of being enclosed on a plane.

One day, right after the tragic events of 9/11, the unmistakable voice of the Holy Spirit spoke to me.

"You need to get over your fear of flying, for you will be on a lot of planes in the future."

That very day, I booked flights for both of us to the most unexpected place of all, New York City! I was excited to tell Jeff when he got home.

"Why New York City, right after 9/11?" he asked.

I always loved diamonds and gemstones. At the time, I had a flawless, two carat diamond, set in a ring that I knew would be worth enough money to launch a ministry. As much as I loved my diamond ring, I knew ministry was far more important than earthly treasure.

"Jeff, I'm willing to sell my diamond ring and sow the money into developing our ministry so we don't have to worry about money for a little while. What do you think?"

Jeff didn't even question it. "Well then, what are we waiting for? Let's go!"

We made the trip to sell the diamond, and got to experience some of New York City. Surprisingly, it didn't bother me one bit to fly! The Lord was right. Since that time, I have flown all over the world.

The money was used to help us launch the ministry. It was a seed sown into good soil.

The Toronto Vineyard

We booked our flights and anxiously awaited for what we would experience. The day we arrived at the Toronto Vineyard, we were amazed!

Words cannot describe the glory overshadowing that place. When Jeff and I first stepped in the building, it was like stepping into a cloud. We were slain in the Spirit, fell straight to the floor, and could not get up.

This was a joyful, drunken glory that was fairly new to me. I had experienced a high level of God's glory and presence before, but this was even greater!

Jeff had not experienced much of this in his early Christian walk either, so we were both soaking it up.

Jeff had already taught me a great deal about the Holy Spirit early in our relationship. In the church he helped lead in Wisconsin, he had been hungry for more of God.

"Jan, this is what I've always longed for. All those years I was at the church back home in Wisconsin, I was waiting for this. They were all about the Holy Spirit at first, but then they became so focused on Christian Counseling, the greater glory of God did not seem to be their focus anymore. That's one of the reasons I moved to Tennessee."

Now, seeing God move in revival, signs, and wonders was a fulfillment of all Jeff had hungered for throughout his Christian walk.

The second morning of our stay there, I woke up struggling with a cold. I felt too sick to attend the morning session. I couldn't stand the thought of being stuck in a hotel room after traveling all the way there, and did not want to miss the afternoon session as well. I prayed fervently from the hotel room, petitioning Jesus to heal me so I could go. As I prayed, I was suddenly healed. That is the only time I remember being instantly healed of a cold.

By the time I walked into the sanctuary, the service was already in process. Charles Carrin had just stepped up to the platform, and in his typical manner, he simply said the words, "Come, Holy Spirit!"

Every time I saw him do this, anything not of God would manifest in people, and demons would be spontaneously and instantly cast out.

"I want that gift, Lord," I whispered.

Many people were on the floor getting unprompted deliverance, with nobody touching them. Amazing! This was our first experience witnessing mass deliverance on this level. There were many others getting prayer and assistance. I saw Jeff praying with Charles, following behind him, assisting him, and soaking up the impartation.

Scanning the room, I saw a woman lying on the floor, struggling to breathe. Instinctively, I rushed over to her and began to pray.

I thought I had seen a lot, but I was in for a surprise.

When deliverance occurs, people sometimes manifest in unexpected ways. They may cough, sneeze, have difficulty breathing, or even vomit. Some even slither like a snake, bark like a dog, or growl like a lion. Others get deliverance with no outward manifestation at all.

This poor woman, desperate to get air into her lungs, was on the floor, on her hands and knees, facing down. There was no one to assist her, and she was obviously distraught.

I bent down on the floor next to her, not exactly knowing what I was doing, put my hand on her back, and commanded the evil spirit to leave.

As I continued to pray, her head turned all the way around, 180 degrees to the back of her neck, beyond what was humanly possible, until "she" was looking directly at me.

Whatever was in her stared me in the eyes and snarled, "I hate you!"

It was a deep, scary, disembodied-sounding voice, clearly not the voice of the woman I was praying for. With that, her head swiveled back to the front, facing the floor. I had no former experience of directly encountering a demon face to face and casting it out. A righteous indignation rose up in me that wanted the woman free. The words came out of my mouth so fast I was astonished myself.

"Demon, I hate you too, and that's why you have to go!"

I knew it was the power of Christ in me that empowered me to speak with such boldness, and caused the demon to leave. Immediately, she began hacking up a wad of thick mucus, so massive that I was concerned she might choke to death. It was pretty gruesome, but thanks to my training as a nurse the mucus itself didn't phase me.

When it finally cleared, she leapt up and literally ran through the sanctuary. Her breathing was restored! The woman testified later that day that she had debilitating asthma her entire life but was now completely set free. With her former breathing difficulties, she never could have run like that. Now, she had no difficulty at all!

The Joy Of The Lord

It was a greater level of glory than we had seen before, with incredible healings and deliverances taking place. Later that evening, we ran into Charles in the hotel lobby. He laid hands on us and we all began to laugh and stumble around in joy under the tangible presence of God!

The world does not understand this supernatural drink that brings such inward and outward joy. The hotel manager thought we were literally drunk on alcohol and kicked us out of the lobby! But truly, the joy of the Lord is more than just silliness and laughter.

According to Nehemiah 8:10, *"The joy of the Lord is your strength."* Although we should be living in the joy of the Lord in our daily lives, sometimes, the Holy Spirit gives us a blast of His intense joy. As mentioned in Proverbs 31:6-7, a drink of the joy of the Lord is very refreshing, bringing strength to our weary souls and bodies.

Naturally, we did our best to honor the manager's request. But the presence of God was so powerful that we were still laughing in the elevator!

More Lord! Fill us up and let your Spirit overflow out of us!

Chapter Eight

FAMILY, ESCALATION

Reality Setting In

Although I had originally believed God would give us a biological child, that did not happen. This was very difficult for me in many ways. I did not understand all the "mother of many" words. Through two years of confirmations and amazing discoveries, God made it clear we were to adopt.

In 2006, we were blessed with a miracle; our daughter Mercy Rain. I never understood the miracle of adoption until I saw her for the first time, sitting in a walker at the Social Services office in Chongqing, China. The love I felt as I saw her for the first time was no different from the feeling a woman gets when she gives birth and sees her child for the very first time. I was instantly in love! She was just over twelve months old on our Gotcha Day.

Jeff had experienced the birth of four children, but when he saw Mercy Rain, I saw a look on his face that I had not seen. He was literally glowing! Mercy had a cold on our Gotcha Day, so she was fussy and cried a lot. Her nanny handed her to me and I tried to comfort her.

"Look! She has gold flakes on her back!" Jeff exclaimed.

I spun her around, and sure enough, she did. I knew she was marked by God.

We spent a glorious three weeks in China finalizing our adoption. We got to visit Beijing, Ghangzou, and Chongqing. We visited many historic landmarks, even The Great Wall. It was one of the most memorable events in my lifetime.

After we returned home, Jeff would often play his guitar and worship in Mercy's presence. Even within the first week she was with us, she would sit on the floor and worship with him, although she had certainly never experienced church or worship music in China.

Time seemed to fly, as month after month passed. We tried to embrace every minute with our little girl. Experiencing motherhood again and experiencing adoption was a form of Heaven on Earth to me.

We took Mercy everywhere we went, as I had been traveling quite a bit with Jeff and ministered with him. Mercy seemed to be a natural glory girl! She would dance and worship in the glory, and didn't care who saw her. I remember attending several conferences within a few weeks of her arrival.

Gemstones

When Mercy was about two, Jeff and I heard of a church in Puerto Rico, where oil had been literally pouring down the walls and out of a bible on the pulpit. We were hungry enough for God to travel there to see and experience this for ourselves.

No man could have constructed what we found. Literally, oil was pouring down all the walls like rain running down a windowpane. It seemed to dissipate as the oil got to the floor, otherwise there would have been a swimming pool of oil on the floor. The oil flowed like a river out of their huge bible which lay on the pulpit and fell into a large vat. The pastors said they emptied it regularly, and it just continued to fill back up. I don't remember what they did with the oil they emptied out.

It was here, in Puerto Rico, that we encountered a sign and wonder we had not yet experienced. The pastor there brought out a huge collection of gemstones of every size and color. They were magnificent, and you could literally feel the glory in them.

"They have been falling out of Heaven in our church for a while now," the pastor explained, "but we keep all of them that fall here."

As we stood in amazement at all we were seeing and feeling, the pastors asked if they could pray for us.

"Need you ask?" I thought to myself. We were thrilled at the opportunity!

They and their team circled around us, joined hands, and began praying for us. Mercy flitted across the room like a butterfly, seeming to just soak up the glory in the atmosphere.

After they prayed over us, Jeff prayed for them. He prayed the oil would turn into golden honey.

At that moment, beyond my expectations, I saw something fall from overhead and land on the floor.

The pastor's wife saw it too, and went over and collected it. She repeated that they kept all the gemstones that fell inside their building.

Then the look on her face changed, and she turned to look at me. It was as if the Holy Spirit had spoken to her.

"God says this one is yours." With that, she handed me the gemstone.

It was a glistening honey colored, kite-shaped cut. It was amazing and beautiful. It took my breath away. I had never seen a stone cut like this. Its color really stood out, since Jeff had just prophesied about the oil turning to honey.

As previously stated, Jeff and I had always loved natural gemstones, and I had quite a collection of natural stones and rings by now.

One of our pastimes was going to jewelry shows or jewelry stores, and just oohing and aahing over the beautiful gems God had put on this earth.

After the pastor handed me the gemstone, she blessed my daughter, Mercy, and told me she was God's gift "to you alone".

Tears ran down my face as Mercy continued to dance through the sanctuary as if nothing was going on. Little did we know, we would begin seeing a new level of "signs and wonders" in our ministry.

Sadly, after we moved to the new house on California Drive, we did not experience the level of supernatural activity that I had in the house on Gatewood. At risk of repeating myself, there just seemed to be that portal over us there, or perhaps it was just the timing of the Lord to pour out on us at that time of preparation.

I will say that along with a new ministry opportunity, a door of challenge was opened as well. It is said, "New levels, new devils." Jeff seemed to be exhausted before he had even really launched. As more doors opened and invitations began to flood in, Jeff tried to deal with the pressure in ways that he should not have.

He took sleeping pills to sleep and even became somewhat addicted to them. Knowing this was not wisdom, and fearing addiction to the pills, he found he had often been calmed down by drinking a few beers. As I think back, even in our early marriage, he would slip off and disappear for a few hours and I would find him at the local beer bar. I didn't think much of it at the time because these occasions were few and far between.

He grew up in a town with a family who didn't think having a few drinks was wrong. Even growing up Catholic, there wasn't the stigma attached to drinking as there was in the small Tennessee town I grew up in. Drinking was strictly prohibited in the church I grew up in.

As ministry began to lead him to new places and draw attention to him, I noticed he drank more, and more often. I often questioned him, and he would just say it helped him relax. I was not alarmed by it at this point.

As I pondered this, I realized he had caused me some concern early in our marriage when he sneaked off to drink. It seemed when he drank at all, his behavior was atypical of how it was when he was sober.

"Jeff, can I speak with you?" I wasn't sure how to approach this subject. "Why are you drinking more?"

"Jan, I'm just tired. No need to worry."

He would find excuses to drink. For instance, he often drank beer when he did yard work. He began a project of clearing out the woods next to our house. He was constantly out there, pulling out trees, weeds, and brush. Every time I went to check on him, he was drinking beer. He told me his dad always had beer when he did yard work, and he also just found it relaxing. Jeff actually related yard work to beer.

He had begun acting radically different when he drank, than what I considered to be his norm. Now, instead of having a couple of casual beers, he seemed to be unable to stop drinking once he started. I became more and more concerned. He was becoming more verbally abusive when he was drinking and he blew it off as nothing.

Once, he hid my entire collection of gems and rings from me when he was drunk, and couldn't remember where he'd put them. I didn't understand why he would want to hide something that meant so much to me. Eventually I would find my gems and rings, but I didn't understand his motives.

There were times that he shoved me off the bed for no apparent reason. It was as if there was a part of him that just wanted to hurt me.

I didn't try to force him into a logical explanation. Looking back, I think I was so hopeful and positive that I believed this was a brief phase due to a transition.

"Perhaps having a young child was much for him." I reasoned to myself.

Sometimes, I would catch him sneaking and drinking behind my back, and hiding alcohol from me. He would always say, "Jan, it relaxes me."

If I gave him permission to drink a beer, he would buy two cases and hide them. I even found beer hidden across the street in a ditch.

He would vehemently apologize every time he acted irrationally, and back away from alcohol for a while.

Jeff and I were raised very differently. I wanted to continue believing in him, and applied grace based on how good our earlier years had been. Previously, I had tried to rationalize his drinking as to the Italians drinking wine with their meals, or the Germans or British having beer with their meals. But I was beginning to see evidence that there could potentially be a problem. I guess, in hindsight, I thought that a man of God, filled with the Holy Spirit, who operated in such high levels of ministry, would not allow this to get out of control.

Personally, I had no conviction against having an occasional beer or glass of wine. I never thought it could get the best of him. I had never been around an alcoholic in my life, so I couldn't relate.

Having tremendous faith in God, and in my husband, I would forgive him each time and hope for better. He didn't drink daily, or even weekly, that I knew of. This seemed to occur only when he seemed to be under pressure or stress.

In Demand

Because of the giftings that had increased in Jeff so quickly, and because of the signs and wonders that followed, he became a very much in-demand minister. Invitations came from all over the world.

Mercy and I had the honor of going to many nations over a few years. Korea, Japan, England, Guatemala, Taiwan, Puerto Rico, Italy, just to name a few, as well as all over the United States. Mercy was a natural traveler.

Being with Jeff as much as we were seemed to be a comfort to him, and it also seemed to be a natural safety net to keep him in check. In fact, he never drank when we went on ministry trips together.

As I ponder this season in our lives, I recall some remarkable miracles. I went to a service where the presence was so strong, I was slain in the Spirit and felt literal raindrops fall on me inside the building.

It was as if I were laying outside in a rainstorm. I just laid and soaked it up as long as I could. I remember so many moments that are so remarkable they are hard to explain.

Jeff had a relationship with Bidal and Sherry Torrez, the pastors of Valley Harvest Church in Neenah, Wisconsin, and he had even stood as best man at their wedding when he was a young man. They often invited us to their church to minister. We had also invited other ministers to come there and minister with us as well.

Supernatural Wine

One event stands out in my mind. It was one of those "life changing" events. Mercy was still very young.

Joshua and Janet Mills and Harold and Kaye Beyer were also invited as guest ministers.

The meetings were extremely powerful. When Kaye was ministering, I was simply sitting in a chair in the front row, and I thought I saw something falling.

At first I ignored it, but then noticed something that looked like small crackers falling in my lap and on the floor. What was this? I knew Harold and Kaye often experienced supernatural manna falling in their meetings.

All the crackers were small, maybe a quarter inch sized, and shaped similarly to a hexagon. I began picking them up and piling them in my lap. These crackers looked exactly like the manna we had taken at the house with David and Ginny.

After the service, I put them in a container to show them to the pastors and other ministers and friends who were there.

Joshua and Janet had stayed back in the room to rest this first night of the conference. Joshua contacted us after the service to tell us that he had an unopened Dasani water bottle in his hotel room, and when he approached it to open and drink it, it had turned into the color of grape juice.

It was a medium purple color! He had not touched it, or prayed over it. He had simply sat it down to drink it later. He did not know about the supernatural manna until we told him it had fallen in the meeting.

We agreed to meet in our hotel lobby, as we were all staying in the same hotel.

I brought the unusual crackers, which by now we had concluded was indeed supernatural manna. Joshua brought the supernatural "wine." There was a group of about ten of us.

Joshua opened the Dasani bottle for the first time in our presence. It was obvious as the lid clicked, that it had never been opened, as if we would doubt Joshua anyway.

We took communion with the manna and the wine. It was probably the most surreal experience I have had in my entire life, even though I have already said previous experiences were surreal. That is the best word I can think of to describe something that simply cannot be explained in the natural realm we live in.

Although I had tasted supernatural manna the one time before, this manna was unlike anything else I'd ever tasted. Like Ginny's manna, it was salty-sweet, but this was very fresh, more so than the manna that Ginny had. After all, it had just fallen from Heaven.

It tasted nothing like our human food. And the "wine" was not alcoholic. It was fruity, but again, nothing like we had ever tasted in our lives on this earth.

I cannot even describe the taste. It was like a fruit we don't have or recognize. Just like the night when we took heavenly communion at our house, we seemed to be in another realm. We laughed, as the joy of Heaven fell upon us, and many of us fell on the hotel lobby sofas under the weight of glory. There is such joy in the presence of God when Heaven comes to Earth, that you cannot contain it! You have to understand that when the glory comes, you simply cannot stand.

Undoubtedly, the hotel staff didn't understand, and we were so "drunk" in the Spirit that we had no consciousness of the human realm. I can't find the right words to express the depths of what happened.

The hotel clerk accused us of being drunk, just as they did in Toronto, and asked us to go to our rooms. We respected this and tried to understand how we were not understood. We all went to our rooms, but we felt like we were walking on a cloud for days.

I also saw some of the most profound healings during these same meetings in Wisconsin.

Jeff was ministering at one of the sessions, and prayed over a woman with a thyroid disorder, and diabetes, which had caused her to be obese. As Jeff called for healing, she began shrinking before our eyes! We had never seen supernatural weight loss! This was new!

We literally watched her lose five pants sizes before our eyes. I have pictures of her transformation. She was completely healed of all her infirmities that night! When Jesus healed the infirmities that had caused her to be overweight, the weight literally just fell off.

My experiences with the powerful presence of the healing power of Jesus Christ will remain with me forever and nothing can take them away. The entire conference at Valley Harvest was completely supernatural.

We began to see many supernatural gemstones fall in our meetings, just like in Puerto Rico. There were stones of all sizes and colors. They were all exquisitely cut and polished. I had not seen anything like them of earthly origin. We gave most of them away over time, as the Lord led.

Gold dust falling in the meetings was common. Many times it was multi-colored! It would cover the people, the chairs and the floors.

Global Fire Korea

When Mercy was about three years old, we got an invitation to minister in Korea. The three of us went, as a family. The churches there are huge and people show up at six o' clock, a.m., and intercede for hours and hours. The hunger there is beyond what our American mindset can understand.

At one of the nightly meetings, the worship was so divine that Mercy spontaneously ran onto the stage and began to dance as if no one was watching. She had no idea that 6,000 people were watching!

When she looked out and saw how many people were watching her spin and twirl and dance, she began to get nervous, and ran to me. It was a moment I will never forget. She was just a natural worshiper.

I recall one of the most amazing miracles I have ever seen. Jeff was praying for healing over one particular woman. She had a finger that was partially missing.

I did not know how her finger came to be missing, and that was not even what was being prayed for, but in the presence of such a strong anointing for healing, her finger grew back out in front of our eyes!

This was remarkable in itself, but what was more amazing was that the fingernail on the finger that grew back was painted the same color as her other fingernails!

In this conference, and meetings to come, Jeff began to step into a higher level, and would continue speaking into the atmosphere in faith, believing in miracles greater than we had seen before. His faith seemed to have no limit.

Jeff founded a Global Fire Church in Korea and it thrived and grew!

At the Lord's leading, Jeff began calling for dental miracles. As he did, we witnessed teeth turned to gold, silver, and platinum. We saw gold and silver crosses form in people's teeth. Some would have numerous teeth crowned in gold, others just a tooth or two.

We witnessed metal disappearing from bodies. Metal rods or pins in hips, legs, ankles, arms, that you could visibly see, would just disappear. We could sometimes smell burning metal as it disappeared.

In the glory, legs grew out, tumors fell off. Often when Jeff released a word of knowledge about a cancer disappearing, someone who had a known tumor or growth would go into the bathroom and check and it was completely gone!

Personally, I saw amazing miracles from my prayers alone, and Jeff was seeing miracles that blew even his mind. It just got stronger and stronger.

Feathers began to manifest. Jeff was in meetings where thousands of literal feather clouds whirled in the atmosphere for what seemed like hours. There is a video on YouTube of a tent meeting with Mahesh Chavda where feathers swirled around the top of the tent during the entire meeting. Thousands and thousands of feathers! We were seeing this too, at times. Jeff received one huge white feather in a meeting that is around eight inches long and four inches wide! I have it in a glass frame.

At the time of writing this book, we have been getting feathers at the church I still pastor. I have a whole bag of fluffy white feathers that the Lord has given me. Others at my church have found feathers, too. God is up to something!

Immediately after I typed the above paragraph on feathers, I paused in my writing to go get the last load of laundry from my laundry room and finish it. Before I started writing today, I had just cleaned my bedroom thoroughly and crawled on my hands and knees to run a vacuum across my shag rug. When I went through the bedroom to get the laundry, my eyes were immediately drawn to a big, fluffy white feather laying right on my rug! I knew there was no way it was there prior. This one is the biggest I have found. God is so good! Signs and wonders will follow those who believe!

I remember a meeting in Arizona, where we saw diamonds literally grow in the glory realm.

One lady had a diamond she claims was around a quarter carat. "It was small," she said. It grew to over a carat in size, before our very eyes.

In that same meeting, diamonds appeared embedded in the face of a watch that had no diamonds before. Jeff continued to see this miracle in numerous places he ministered at.

More supernatural gemstones fell in meetings during this time. We were seeing different shapes and colors than we had seen before. The cuts and facets in these stones were beyond what human hands could perform. They were exquisite! This was particularly intriguing to me, as I loved gemstones so much. They would just appear out of nowhere and fall out of Heaven.

The glory dust was increasing as well. It often fell so thick it was as if it were dumped from a bucket, like at the Church of Christ where we first experienced it to that volume.

People would get completely covered with it. It glistened and glittered more brightly than anything I'd even seen that was made by man.

I began experiencing the fragrances of Heaven. This was more me than Jeff, but he had smelled them too. Sometimes they smelled like roses, sometimes like incense, sometimes like flowers I had never smelled on Earth, sometimes like cinnamon, frankincense and myrrh. Sometimes I would smell a fragrance that was not familiar to anything I had ever smelled or sensed.

I smelled smoke, and even popcorn, in the Spirit. I remembered Bob Jones talking about smelling popcorn in the glory, and he said that smelling popcorn is our spirits popping in the oil of the Holy Spirit.

To this day, I still encounter the heavenly fragrances in our services, even when no one else can.

I went from being a seeker when I met Jeff, to being thrust in the higher level of what I could never imagine. It would take many books to record all the amazing things Jeff and I saw, experienced, and encountered. I cannot even recall all the astonishing miracles we have personally seen, and those Jeff saw in his crusades and conferences.

Blind eyes were opened, deaf ears were opened, and the crippled walked. People threw their crutches and wheelchairs up on the stage. Cancers disappeared. Sometimes tumors would literally fall off people in our presence, before our eyes.

Crusades

Jeff did many crusades. He did three or four in Peru. There are two memorable miracles there.

One man had cancer in his eye and his eyeball had been removed. In the glory, while Jeff was ministering in the miracle realm, although the man had no eyeball, he began to see through his eye socket. No eyeball grew back in the socket, but he could see. It was almost unbelievable. This was proven and tested.

There was another man who was completely blind for years in both eyes. His wife came forward to testify to this. His sight was completely restored and he could see his wife again for the first time in years. Imagine the tears of joy that flowed from both of them!

Another testimony was that a thirteen-year-old girl named Luce had manifested a demon during the service. When asked what spirit had afflicted her, she said, "Jezebel."

When the glory came, she fell on the ground and when she got up, she appeared to be totally at peace. Her mother stepped forward to be a witness of this. This happened without anyone laying hands on anyone.

The next night of the crusades, Luce appeared and said she was completely set free and had a look of complete peace on her face, as well as a huge smile. There were many other remarkable miracles and deliverances on those crusades.

Jeff also led a crusade to Tanzania. I recall testimonies of many remarkable miracles on this trip.

A "demon tent" was set up for people who were afflicted with demonic attachments to be delivered privately. Multitudes received deliverance. Many were healed of physical afflictions. Blind eyes were healed, deaf ears opened, wheelchairs thrown on the ground and cripples able to walk or run. Many tumors fell off and cancers were healed. I am told hundreds of those in attendance received healing.

Thousands attended the crusade meetings. The stadium the meetings were held in could hold 20,000 people and it was packed every night. The crusade was held nightly for three or four nights.

Jeff admitted he saw things that he had never seen or experienced.

Darren Wilson made several movies, including Father of Lights, The God Man, Furious Love, and Finger of God. Finger of God which was partially recorded in Tanzania when he was there with Jeff. I think Jeff was in another one of the movies, too, but I cannot remember which one.

I thank God every day for the honor of encountering Him in such a personal and exciting way! I have such a desire to see signs and wonders in our midst! Once you experience something so profound and so supernatural, you can never forget.

The Power To Raise The Dead

One of the most memorable things that I can share is a testimony from Germany. This was many years into our ministry.

Jeff had written a book that was a teaching book, and one that people often studied in classes. It was called The Believers Guide to Miracles, Signs and Wonders.

A woman in Germany was leading a class using this book. During this time, her husband fell victim to an unexpected illness, and sadly, he did not survive. He was embalmed and prepared for the funeral.

On the day of his funeral, his wife had a prayer cloth that her class had prayed over. There was a chapter in that book about prayer cloths. She laid that small cloth that had been prayed over onto his chest in a private moment just before the funeral. She wanted him to be buried with it.

She walked away and began talking to visitors, but right before the service started, she walked up to just look at her husband one last time before they closed his casket for the service. She noticed his skin was pink and blotchy, different from the pale appearance you would expect from an embalmed dead body, and much different than she had seen when she placed the cloth on him.

Incredibly, there was a doctor at the service and the wife asked him to please come look at her husband. She also called over the funeral director.

The funeral director was at a loss for why an embalmed person would suddenly be pink and blotchy. The doctor did what doctors do, and took out his stethoscope and listened to the man's heart. To his absolute amazement, the man had a heartbeat! He couldn't believe it, and neither could the wife or anyone else for that matter! An ambulance was called.

He was loaded into the ambulance, still in his casket. When he got to the hospital, the man was found to be alive and breathing!

Keep in mind, this man had been embalmed and dead for four days. That simple prayer cloth of faith had raised him from the dead.

After he came back, because he was dead for so long, he needed a lot of physical therapy and rehab, but he was alive. In time, he was completely restored to health. He even fathered another child with his wife after this. We need to believe for the seemingly impossible!

Throughout his ministry, Jeff had a level of faith that astonished even me. He loved throwing the word of the Lord out and watching God fulfill His words. He didn't doubt God. He knew something would happen! He had the faith to raise the dead.

The Tornado

Another remarkable thing that stuck out in my mind was the day that a tornado unexpectedly touched down on our Tennessee community in early 2009.

My mother was with me in the car and we were going to a local grocery store. The skies suddenly got very dark. I had not heard the news or weather as we had been out all day, so I didn't know what was going on.

Jeff was at an apartment nearby where two of our staff members lived. It was just a few blocks away, so I raced there as quickly as I could.

In total desperation, I said, "Look Mom! That looks like a funnel cloud!" We headed for shelter.

I called Jeff's cell phone. "Jeff, we're two blocks away and there is a very concerning funnel cloud over us. What do we do? Please check the weather!"

"Jan, just get here as quickly as you can! Get over here immediately!" he urged. "Don't be out driving around in this."

We drove as fast as we could. I raced to the apartment and arrived in just a couple of minutes. Thank God we were so close!

I pulled up, ran inside, and grabbed Jeff. I made sure my mother was safe, and Jeff and I and our two staff members went back outside to survey what had become now a formidable funnel cloud.

Jeff didn't really think about what to do, and I honestly believe he was not trying to show out. He just did what was natural to him, and he "spoke" to the tornado.

He decreed, "Watch this! Tornado, I command you to go! You will not touch my house! Tornado, I command you to go."

One of our staff members was recording this on his phone. The tornado immediately began to lift its tail off the ground and it receded back into the sky. Jeff was not surprised. He expected it.

He concluded with, "Now that is the power of the spoken word." It was just what he believed.

Sadly, it did touch back down later, and one person was killed. It was a very destructive tornado. In hindsight, I believe we should have commanded it to dissipate completely. We are always learning.

Overall, at this time in our lives, I was feeling that although we were seeing Heaven in ways of the Spirit, it seemed that more and more frequently, Jeff began acting like there were two different people in his flesh.

On one hand, he was completely blown away at the level of miracles, signs, and wonders that he was seeing right before his very eyes.

I've said before that if I were to record all we saw and experienced, this book would be too large to read. I am just trying to highlight some of the events that stand out to me at the time of this writing.

I personally have seen healings too numerous to mention in this book. I've heard many testimonies from those who were in Jeff's meetings, leaders, pastors, and others that add to what I have personally seen. I know the power of God. I know that His ability is limitless.

Still, even with all that being said, how do people fall from grace, after all seeing such a realm of glory and the miraculous for themselves?

Chapter Nine

TRUTH

Beginning to Unravel

Even though God was so actively moving, Jeff was beginning to complain that the traveling was getting to be too demanding of him. He seemed fine when Mercy and I were with him. When we traveled with him, he seemed energized and highly motivated. Perhaps there was something going on inside of him that I was not seeing.

I remember being in Cincinnati for another conference, and Bob Jones had a concerned look on his face.

He was always cutting up with us, but this time He pulled Jeff aside, with me present, and warned him of "The Three Gs: girls, gold, and glory."

The glory of God was not the glory that Bob was warning him about. It was the glorification of oneself. It was the glory given to a man or woman of God, instead of giving all the glory to God alone. Jeff was succumbing to this, and I was seeing glimpses of it. Bob had walked this out himself, so he knew it all very well.

Bob said, "Boy, listen to your wife. If you don't slow down, you are going to fall."

Jeff would just laugh, thinking that Bob was giving him a hard time in order to be funny. No, Bob was very serious.

In retrospect, Jeff was not prepared for the attention, the travel, and the demands of a huge ministry. He was beginning to develop a rockstar syndrome. He seemed to be particularly impressed with all the attention he got. I watched his humility dwindle over time. He went from shopping at Sears and Roebuck, when I met him, to demanding the best and most expensive of everything. Sadly, I felt that I was losing the man I fell in love with.

Jeff did not realize it at the time, but there were hidden wounds in him that had not been dealt with; things neither of us knew yet, things he could not acknowledge himself.

He was building an empire that he could not manage. He was driven for recognition, magnificence, and for self-attention.

At this time, I didn't know what was actually driving him and why he was changing before my eyes. This was not an instant thing. It happened little by little, as time went by, and as the ministry grew. I couldn't fully understand it at the time.

We moved again in 2006. Jeff was filming a show called The Glory Generation and he needed an appropriate place for filming. This new house was quite large.

Our bedroom was the size of a small apartment. We had a bed for baby Mercy in our room at first, as she was still adjusting but eventually, Jeff demanded a larger office. We moved our bedroom and Mercy upstairs so that she could have her own room. He set up his office and studio in the huge master bedroom. It turned out to be to his detriment, because he could easily lock himself away in there, alone and unsupervised.

In January of 2007, Jeff received a DUI. This happened when Mercy was not quite two and we had no other children at home.

He said he had gone into Nashville to look at property. Of course, he downplayed the incident to me, but when I read the police report it said he had been at a popular country bar in downtown Nashville called The Wildhorse Saloon. I was shocked! Why would a happily married Christian man and father want to go to a country bar? Or any bar, for that matter?

Keep in mind, I was seeing some bizarre personality twists in him, but couldn't put my finger on it, or explain it. I always dismissed it because I didn't understand, and I wanted to believe the best.

When I confronted him about the police report from the DUI, he confidently said the police officer had made it up!

As I tried to ponder how this happened, my thoughts drifted to earlier that evening.

We had gone to Red Lobster for a romantic dinner alone and he asked if he could have a glass of wine. I agreed to one glass, but surprisingly, the server brought him an entire bottle. I wondered if perhaps he had asked for the bottle, while I was in the ladies' room?

Because we were deep in conversation, I didn't even notice that he had continued drinking it until the entire bottle was gone. He apparently drank an entire bottle of wine before our meal even arrived. As I said previously, I had begun to see that if he started to drink, it was very difficult for him to quit.

When we got home, he started acting angry. There wasn't an argument, prior cross words, or even a point of conflict. He just began flailing his arms above his head, yelling at me for no apparent reason.

Anger and a violent disposition seemed to go with the alcohol, more and more. He pushed me off the bed again, as he had done a few times before, and I landed flat on my back, on the floor. Struggling to get off the floor, I whispered to myself, "What just happened?"

While I continued to ponder the situation, I clearly recalled several other occasions when he became very aggressive after drinking.

I recollected him doing things he claimed he hadn't done, including hiding my jewelry twice. Once, he took my jewelry box and could not remember taking it or what he had done with it. A year later I found it stuffed down in a bush in the front landscaping. When asked why he would do such a thing, he simply responded, "I didn't do that."

When we try to believe for the best we don't always see the warning signs that are so obvious. We blow things off much easier when we are still in the honeymoon phase. Jeff was the love of my life, and it was very difficult for me to grasp that there were serious issues that needed to be dealt with.

I wouldn't find out until the next day that he had driven into Nashville after our "romantic" dinner, and continued drinking, even after the entire bottle of wine. It made no sense to me at all. The thought of him actually driving in a big, busy city in that condition was frightening! The danger was not only for him, but for others.

Back then, we still had land-line phones. That night, after he pushed me off the bed and mysteriously stormed off in anger, it had become very late and he had still not returned home. I knew when our land-line rang that something was wrong.

"Hello," I said, afraid of what I was about to hear.

Nobody said anything. I repeated, "Hello? Hello?" No one spoke, and I hung up.

Then my cell phone rang, and again, when I answered, nobody said anything.

I came to learn that a policeman pulled Jeff over in Nashville because a brake light on our van was out. The policeman smelled alcohol and pulled him out of our van and initiated a sobriety test. Jeff failed the sobriety test, but the officer agreed to let him come home if someone could come get him, or at least that is what Jeff later told me.

So Jeff had given him our land-line number and my cell phone number, not knowing who else to call I guess, and the officer told him nobody answered. This was Jeff's explanation and it always seemed sketchy to me.

I did ask him why an officer of the law would lie, and say that I hadn't answered? Or did Jeff make all that up?

Jeff was hauled off to jail at this point, and the next morning, he was allowed a phone call. He called me, not knowing what else to do.

"Jan, I'm in jail. I'll explain when you get here," he said with a tone of regret, rightfully so.

I had to go bail him out.

He was so apologetic, as he always was after his binges, and promised me he would never do it again. He played the innocent role, blaming the officer. He didn't admit to actually going to that bar until a few years later.

"Why Jeff? If you loved me, why would you go to a country bar in Nashville? What motivated you to do that?"

He could not come up with an answer. After much pleading for me to forgive him, of course I did. Again.

As time passed, he began distancing himself from me emotionally. I tried to talk with him about it many times, but he was always too busy and didn't seem to appreciate the distraction of my asking for his attention.

My frequent comment to him was, "You continually just hit a reset button and life just goes on."

As a consequence of the DUI, he was ordered by the courts to go to a drug and alcohol counselor. The man was not a Christian, and the dominant Jeff would spend his time with the counselor "ministering" to him, instead of getting help for himself. The counselor would often pull me into the sessions to have me express my feelings and how the uncertainty of Jeff's behavior made me feel.

I think Jeff did try to abstain from alcohol, but usually after a few months, he would become so agitated, so exhausted by travel, that he had to drink just to quiet his mind and calm himself. Hence, another binge, while he continued to minister and travel as if he were a perfect man.

The struggle was becoming more and more apparent to me, and I didn't even realize how many others were seeing a change in him, even this early on.

I had been his booking agent since the ministry started in 2003 and didn't continue to practice nursing after Mercy came along. I booked all of his flights and travel and coordinated with churches and ministries he was to visit. Many times, I warned him he was taking on too much. He just shrugged me off.

In the wee hours of the morning, on occasion, he would whisper in my ear, "Can we just quit ministry and get a farm somewhere?" He said people pulled on him, demanded and expected too much from him, and he was weary from all the traveling.

"Jan, I am absolutely exhausted!" he would complain to me. Although he could admit he needed to slow down for a season, and possibly even quit for a while, he had too much pride to actually do it.

He didn't want to go back to a menial job. He even felt pressure because of the vision of a filled stadium he had when he was newly saved. He felt the Lord was telling him he would see this in his lifetime. He felt a great deal of pressure to accomplish this, or he would fail God, so he continued pushing himself beyond his human capacity, despite many warnings.

Although Jeff verbalized in vulnerable moments how he was really struggling, life went on. One minute he was frail and weak, and the next minute he was on top of the world. Again, it was almost as if he were two people. This had become more pronounced as time went on.

God was speaking to me about another child. Just because Jeff had his issues, that wouldn't stop the Lord from fulfilling His plans for me. I spent years petitioning the Lord for children, and had many, many prophetic words spoken into that desire.

I had many dreams about another baby girl, and even saw her and knew what she would look like. My vision didn't seem to match the realities of what I was experiencing in my world, but it was obviously God to me. I knew when the Lord was speaking.

I found time when Jeff was relaxed and happy and asked to speak with him. I shared a dream I had, showing me our next child. I explained that part of my destiny was to be a mother. I shared all that the Lord was speaking to me and had shown me.

He believed my dreams and visions were from God, and although having more children was my heart's desire, not necessarily his, he adored Mercy. If he had second thoughts at this point, he didn't express them to me.

I still believed and prayed things would level out and be fine. When he wasn't drinking, we found a way to live a pretty normal life. We went out to eat. We took Mercy to the pool and the park. We saw movies. We went to church and church activities. We had friends. We both believed that God would ultimately be in control of our lives and continue to bless us.

We both felt led to do a domestic adoption this time. The child I had seen in my dreams was of mixed race. After much searching, we found an adoption attorney in Sacramento, California.

Six months later, we were matched with a birth mother who was seven months pregnant and couldn't keep the baby.

In answer to my prayers, Jeff had taken a turn for the better and had done well for many months. He tried really hard and didn't seem tempted to drink. I prayed this was the end of a cycle, and the beginning of life the way we knew it earlier in our marriage. I was excited about our growing family.

Greater Glory Gatherings

We also began hosting meetings we called Greater Glory Gatherings on Tuesday nights. It was so named after a word the Lord gave me about hosting gatherings.

The Lord had said to me, "Gather the people. Call these 'Gatherings'. The people will come."

We used the building of another church in our town. We chose Tuesday nights, so that people who went to Wednesday night church could still come.

The presence of the Lord was there, and we continued to see amazing evidence that God was moving. As the Lord had said, people came. We had around one hundred people every Tuesday night and on some level, we were seeing revival.

Jeff was operating in a stronger and stronger prophetic gift, and I could see the intensity of it increasing consistently over a period of time.

It wasn't that I wasn't gifted or experiencing spiritual maturity, but I was simply caught up in the administrative duties of running a ministry and in the tremendous joy of being a mother, and of a growing family.

Global Fire Ministries hosted our first conference in this building in September, 2009. Our new baby girl was due any day. I was afraid we would have to leave the conference to go get her. She held on until after the conference was over, but just barely.

We flew into California just in time to be present for the birth of our daughter Truth, on September 24, 2009. She was a hefty eleven pounds, six ounces! Her birth mother was diabetic and had other health issues, which was why Truth was so large. She looked like she was three months old at birth!

As I looked at her beautiful face, my mind was flooded with memories of all the prophetic words that I had received of being the "mother of many." She looked exactly like she did in the prophetic dreams I had about her.

God announced each child before his or her arrival. All of my adopted children are four years apart in age. God carefully planned it this way.

When I began my adoption journey, I only asked for one child. I had no idea I would have three more beautiful babies in addition to my grown son!

God didn't start that journey until I was later in years. I was forty-four when Mercy came along. I have been able to counsel or assist many families that led to them adopting as well. Many thought they were too old to adopt. I have the honor of being the spiritual mother of many children, who have found their forever homes!

Chapter Ten

BUILD ME A HOUSE

Global Fire Church

Shortly before Truth was born, people began telling us that we should start a church. They wanted a church home and a place to settle in, that embraced the supernatural and the glory of God.

We prayed about it. In no way was it my desire to start a church, but it seemed like the natural thing to do, considering we were packing out our Tuesday night gatherings. It just seemed like the next step.

The Lord spoke only one thing to us. "Build Me a place where My glory can dwell." It hit us both hard, and we knew that it was God.

In faith, we began searching for a building. This was an exhausting process, since Jeff was still traveling and ministering fairly often.

After much searching, we found an empty insulation warehouse, leased it, and soon began turning it into a proper place for a church. Much work was needed! We had very skilled and confident people partnering with us to fulfill the vision. There was excitement!

We named the church Global Fire Church. Jeff also wanted to host other events and conferences there, so he made the official name Global Fire Ministries and World Miracle Center. For him, it was a center for the ministry, but for me, it was a church.

We began meeting on Sunday mornings in mid-November of 2009. Truth was not even two months old.

In what seemed like no time at all, we also launched a full-time school called the Kingdom Life Institute. People of all ages relocated from all over the country to be students at our school.

Jeff was definitely being pulled in every direction. He had found success and recognition in every way, but as his wife, I was concerned he couldn't handle it all.

I would frequently ask him if he needed some time off. He simply responded, "I can't."

Although we had a long season of him seeming to be in a good place and not drinking, I could see that he was tired. I prayed his fatigue would not get the best of him.

We were seeing much fruit in the school and the Lord brought us competent leaders to steward it, in Jeff's absence. He would minister when he was in town, otherwise our leaders and anointed guest ministers would carry it.

Kingdom Life Ministries had three years of classes. Many great men and women of God received wisdom, knowledge and impartation to graduate into leadership positions and to lead powerful ministries.

The Child Will Be Given

When Truth was about two, I was sitting on the bed one day and heard God say to me, "The name of your next child will be Given, for the child will be given to you."

Another child, Lord? The Lord saw my future. All those prophetic words about my being the mother of many were literal, as well as spiritual.

Despite new warnings about pushing too hard, and his appearing to be so tired, Jeff continued to travel. Now, it seemed that he was gone more than he was at home.

At the time, I didn't consider myself a preacher, so we had a team of ministers who would speak at the church if Jeff was gone. At times it was overwhelming to have two young children on my own a lot of the time, and soon three, but I was filled with joy at the opportunity to be a mother. I knew this was the blessing of the Lord.

Our adoption attorney offered us another baby girl, due in a few months. Jeff was adamant about our only adopting girls. He felt I could manage them, but a boy would demand too much from him, i.e., playing sports, etc. We agreed to take this baby girl, and I spent the next few months preparing for her.

I can't explain why I agreed to bring more children into my home at a time when I saw Jeff again being so challenged by the pressure he was under. All I can say is that I heard the voice of the Lord and yielded to it, despite my natural circumstances.

We felt confident about the certainty of the birth mother to relinquish the child, and she had good reasons to. We had developed a relationship with her. We had provided thousands of dollars in support to her.

To our dismay, at the last minute, she backed out and decided to keep the baby. I was devastated, when it became clear to us that she had taken our money with no intention of giving us the baby.

I'm the one who needed a reset button, this time. Without even thinking beyond my emotions, I booked a last-minute trip to the Dominican Republic. I just needed an escape. As I began to pack for the trip, the phone rang.

When we made plans to go get the baby girl in Sacramento, California, we contacted a pastor friend of ours who lived in nearby Yuba City, and told him we would be coming into their area. He and his wife were excited to get to spend time with us while we were there.

When we learned that we wouldn't be going, we immediately called him and told him the sad news. He told us that he understood.

We packed for the trip and hoped we would receive some kind of refreshment by getting away. As we were preparing to go, this pastor called us out of the blue. He seemed to be very surprised, himself, at what he presented to us.

God is so amazing and nothing is an accident. You cannot imagine the shock I felt when this pastor, who was going to assist us in the adoption of the baby girl, told us that he had gone to get a haircut, as he did every six weeks, or so. He was going to his regular hair stylist.

She told him she had taken custody of the newborn son of her niece, who was homeless and could not keep the baby boy. She and her boyfriend lived down by the river in Yuba City, California, by choice.

His hair stylist asked this pastor if he knew anyone who might want the baby. He knew we had just experienced a tremendous loss, and he couldn't wait to call us.

Jeff immediately and adamantly dismissed the idea.

"Jan, boys just shouldn't be adopted. They should be biological sons," he reasoned.

He thought that since I was at home alone with the kids while he was traveling, I needed girls, not boys. The pastor said he had also offered the baby to another international minister whose daughter desired to adopt.

Since Jeff was refusing this boy, and I felt confident the baby would be offered to the other minister's daughter, we went on to the Dominican Republic, as planned. In my mind, I had just moved on.

While there, I cried over the loss of our baby girl. We were going to name her Given Favor, as the Lord had said our next child would be called Given. Her name, Given Favor, was still hanging on her bedroom wall. I had left everything as it was when we left for our trip. Now and then, I would think of this baby boy, but not holding out hope. I just needed my heart to stop hurting.

We returned a week later, hearing nothing further from this pastor. Jeff continued to refuse the baby boy, at least to me. I didn't press the issue. Otherwise we had a nice trip and this time, he didn't drink.

On our returning flight, when we arrived back in the United States, Jeff checked the messages on his phone as we prepared to land.

There was a message from the Yuba City pastor.

He said, "It turns out that the aunt doesn't want the other pastor's daughter to have the child, because she lives in Mexico. She wants you to have him."

Wow, this was a lot to process! Jeff was still adamant about not adopting a boy. I was simply confused. I had to just pray and leave it in God's hands.

A couple of days after we returned, Jeff was ministering in the pulpit on a Sunday morning.

As he shared his message, he stopped mid-sentence and tears began streaming down his face. This was not normal.

"What?" I asked. He continued to preach. Nobody knew what was going on. I looked at him, completely bewildered.

After the service, he sat down next to me.

"Why did you stop, and why were you crying?" I asked.

He looked at me with perhaps the most intense look I had ever seen on his face, as if he had seen an angel.

He said that the audible voice of God Himself, had spoken to him while he was preaching, and said "Jeff, will you take My son?"

We both realized this baby boy was meant to be ours, or at least I was certain. I was still not sure about Jeff.

God's will is sovereign and sure. Our son, who we named, Given Justice, was born October 17, 2013. He was three weeks old when we flew to California and received him into our family. Our adoption story is supernatural and amazing.

All three of my children are gifts of love from God Himself, and proof that He hears our prayers and wants to bless us more than we want to be blessed.

Life

It was becoming more apparent to me by now that Jeff was not dealing very well, combining three small children with constant travel fatigue and jet lag. We had a crying baby, and two young girls. Just tending to the children was consuming. I was in Heaven, but Jeff was obviously feeling more stress than he could deal with.

I took care of the children, and he did what he did. I was still booking his flights and managing his travel arrangements.

He had gone to new levels and had stepped into an anointing of great signs and wonders and new levels of the power of the spoken Word. Often he would prophesy strange weather happenings in different towns and nations he went to, and it would happen immediately.

I recall one time he prophesied powerful straight line winds. People shook their heads in unbelief but sure enough, it happened within twenty-four hours.

It was so bizarre and unexpected, that it made the front page of the local paper where he was.

I wanted to believe we had a pretty normal life at home when he wasn't drinking. Like any dad, he got annoyed at the kids. He enjoyed playing with them, and sometimes I could see a real father's heart in him for them.

I overheard him on the phone with his mother one day. He didn't know I was listening. He was telling her how I had demanded that we adopt children, and how it stressed him. Again, it was as if I was living with two completely different people. He went on to say, "Mom, it makes my ministry look good to have adopted kids."

I am not convinced that Jeff's motives for adopting were the same as mine. I wanted to build a family, the family I didn't have growing up. He seemed to want to impress people. This is difficult to explain. I'm not saying he didn't want the children at all. I think his intentions were good, it was just not his particular heart's desire, as it was mine. Deep down, Jeff loved me greatly and just wanted me happy and fulfilled. As much as he had changed, I knew he loved me.

I tried to calm and comfort him as much as I could. I missed the best friend I had married. He wasn't the same person I had grown to love, most of the time.

His ministry had changed from what I saw in the beginning. He was so humble then. His ministry and worship were also very pure and humble. In my eyes, he had lost much of that simplicity.

I saw brief glimpses of that man sometimes, but that was usually when we first woke up in the mornings, before he encountered the demands of the day.

He would look at me with love and in tears, and tell me that he felt he would have a breakdown and could no longer live the lifestyle he was living. I continued to warn him that he was traveling too much and should slow down. I could still hear Bob's voice of caution.

He agreed and wanted to quit, buy a farm, and live the simple life. I told him I would do whatever we needed to do, but that we did have a church, and couldn't just abandon it. He did not want to go back to driving a truck. I felt that he thought he was trapped in a world he couldn't keep up with. He seemed desperate at times.

He was completely torn between having the quiet life he envisioned as peaceful and non-threatening, and the life of high level ministry and fast-paced travel that he believed the Lord had called him to, and he couldn't find balance between the two.

Chapter Eleven

DISCOVERY

Dealing With Monsters

One morning, his words shocked me. I woke up to find him staring at me, as if he were waiting on me to open my eyes.

"Jan, the Lord spoke to me and told me that if I pervert His anointing, He will take my life."

He spoke these words to me with fear in his eyes. I wasn't sure if he had just heard this from the Lord, or if he had been holding it inside for a while.

"What do you mean, pervert God's anointing?" I asked.

"I'm not sure," was his response.

I think he knew more than he was telling me. Jeff was obviously scared, but didn't know what to do. I don't think he wanted to admit that he was spiraling out of control.

After he told me this, he immediately began to hide himself in his man cave of an office. I thought perhaps the alone time he would have with the Lord would be good, but apparently his drinking had escalated and I wasn't aware of what he was doing in there, especially late at night.

His personality was very unpredictable, but I couldn't put my finger on it. I continued to press him to take a sabbatical, but he pressed back even harder, and traveled even more. He seemed to be driven by a force that was unknown to even him. I was quite sure it was not from God. He was moving further and further away from the closeness we once had.

I would have thought that the sobering words the Lord had spoken to him about not perverting the anointing would have gotten his attention, but instead, it seemed to have the opposite effect.

He begged me to book vacations for the family. I would usually give in, just to get away as a family and break him away from the demands of a church and international ministry. Everyone who knew Jeff knew he was tired, and overextended.

We loved the beach, but along with that came challenges. Most of the resorts we stayed at, were "all-inclusive" which was a great way to experience the cuisine of the region without additional cost, but drinks were also included, as well as alcohol.

As I recall our beach vacations, dating back to 2006, we had gone to the Bahamas when Mercy first came home with us. He drank too much one day, became angry towards me, and ruined a couple of days of our vacation.

In faith, I agreed to go again to a different island in the Bahamas in 2010 when Truth was a baby.

I refused to book all-inclusive. I thought this would relieve him of the temptation to over-drink. He promised me he would not drink at all. He gave me his word.

For several days we had a wonderful time. We took a boat to an outlying small island, but there was a restaurant with a bar there. I was busy tending to the girls, and without my realizing it, he was sneaking off to the bar and becoming terribly drunk.

I didn't realize this until we returned to our hotel room. I was concerned for the girls to be around him, so I put the girls in their stroller and walked around for hours, on an island where there were only strangers, until he sobered up.

The same thing happened in St. Thomas, U.S. Virgin Islands in 2011. He won some kind of contest at the pool and the prize was a bottle of liquor. I looked at him and said, "Don't even think about it." He agreed.

As I was preoccupied with children, he began drinking the liquor. This time, he became irate for no reason and was cursing at me and other people he didn't even know at the pool. I was humiliated! Again, I had to take the girls in a stroller and walk around until he sobered up. It was hours, but it seemed like days.

I can only remember one or two trips that he did not ruin from drinking. We loved the beach, so that was typically where we wanted to go. Although the girls and I still traveled with Jeff for ministry when we got the opportunity, we rarely got to go to a beach on a ministry trip. We did get invited to Hawaii once for ministry and had a glorious time. Since he was surrounded with other ministers the entire time, he didn't drink.

He was always focused on ministry, pastors, and his assignment when we went to conferences, so he longed for vacations where nothing was demanded of him.

Because we did have a few good vacations, I would reluctantly agree to try it again.

We had a nice time in La Romana, Dominican Republic. That was the trip we took when we found out we were not getting the baby girl. He didn't drink on that trip.

He did over-drink only one day when we went to Jamaica during the Christmas season of 2013. He admitted to sneaking over to the swim-up bar. It was a one-time incident and the rest of the vacation was very enjoyable.

Overall, in regards to vacations, I felt like I had to treat him as if he were my child and not my husband, constantly looking out for him, helping keep him from making bad choices and giving in to temptation.

I felt like I was spanking him on the hand. "Don't sneak off and drink, okay?"

Even though he believed a few drinks now and then in moderation wasn't sinful, it was apparent that he wasn't able to drink in moderation. His alcohol counselor said that only 20% of the population can have a few drinks and know when to stop. The other 80% don't have the ability to stop, once they start drinking. These are the people you see who black out when drinking and can't even remember what they did. Jeff refused to believe he was an alcoholic.

It was nice to travel to conferences with him and the kids and I have some wonderful memories from these trips, but you could hardly have family time at a conference. Sometimes we had the opportunity for down time on ministry trips to just see the sights and breathe, but then we were never alone. We were always accompanied by our hosts.

He stayed so stressed, so exhausted, and unwilling to slow down most of the time. It was as if during our vacations, when nobody knew who he was, he just let his hair down, but the exposure to such easy access to alcohol was too much of a temptation for him. Vacation was a huge trigger to tempt him to drink because most of the people we encountered on these trips were drinking.

Somewhere around May, 2014, we took all of the kids to Punta Cana, Dominican Republic for a much needed getaway. It was against my better judgment, as this resort was all-inclusive.

"Jeff, I don't want to go on vacation with you again. You have ruined almost every vacation we have been on, because of your need for alcohol."

"But Jan, I promise I will not drink any alcohol on this trip," he insisted.

"Well, you and I both know you've said that before. The temptation is just too great."

I felt like I was lecturing him, but there had been too many times that he had simply been unable to keep his word, no matter how hard he tried.

He said, "Jan, I just really need to get away and not think about work, or ministry." At least, he was admitting it! "I need to take a deep breath."

After much discussion, I very reluctantly agreed. Our kids really needed it, and the truth is, I gave in to the kids. At the time, they were eight years, four years, and six months old. They were excited!

Jeff did well for a few days into the trip, but about four days in, after he had been constantly surrounded by alcohol, he admitted it was difficult. I watched him like a hawk and we tried to stay busy. We talked about it often.

It seemed sometimes as if something just took him over, leading him to drink. He could be doing really well and out of the blue he would be compelled to have a drink.

On the fifth day of our vacation, we took the kids to the pool. It was early in the day, so I didn't really worry about him drinking. He would usually drink later in the day or evening.

The pool was circular. He claimed to be taking the kids all the way around the pool and back, and just like in Jamaica, he kept swimming away from me with one or the other of the children. I eventually followed him and found that there was a swim-up bar in the middle of the large circular pool.

He was sneaking up to that bar each trip around and getting drinks. I guess the temptation was just too great for him. The kids didn't know to tell me, and didn't understand about drinking alcohol. He was getting them non-alcoholic pina coladas, and they didn't know the difference between alcoholic drinks and non-alcoholic drinks.

When I discovered he was drinking, he admitted it, but downplayed it. I insisted we go back to the room, having no idea that something catastrophic had already been set in motion. I somehow thought that removing him from the alcohol would solve the problem.

He said he wanted to rest, and Truth had gone down for a nap, so he agreed to stay there and rest with her. Mercy and I went for a walk with baby Given in his stroller.

We were gone for about an hour, giving Truth time to finish her nap, then we had planned to go to dinner as a family. When we returned to the room, Jeff was not even Jeff any more. I had never seen him as I saw him now. I had seen him drunk, but never like this!

As I opened the door, he began cursing at me and raising his voice loudly. I knew all the neighbors were hearing him. I tried to hush him, but he just got worse. His face was red and his words were threatening and just mean. Mercy just looked up at me, eyes wide open.

"Jeff, obviously, you've had too much to drink. Please give Truth to me and we will leave you alone."

His response was typical of drunk Jeff, firing off a spew of vulgarities. He refused to release Truth. At this point, he was in a actual state of rage, not only verbally aggressive, but threatening physical abuse as well. It was the worst I'd ever seen him. Truth was now crying, begging him to let her come to me.

All of our children were horrified. I tried to break through his restraints that were preventing me from entering the room, not considering the danger I could be in, but being concerned for Truth being stuck in there with him as she screamed in total horror at what she was hearing and seeing.

"Jeff, let me have Truth! Can't you hear her crying?"

It was difficult for me to conceive that Jeff would actually follow through with some of the threats he would make when he was drinking. I had seen what a kind man Jeff really was. When you are in such a position, you always want to believe for the best, which can leave you rather naive.

It was obvious that he was incoherent, at this point. Desperate for him to realize what he was doing, I told Mercy to push Given away in his stroller. I was afraid Jeff would reach out and grab Mercy and Given and pull them into the room as well.

Jeff shoved me away from the door with one hand, and put the chain lock on the door so I could not get in. Mercy took off running and crying, and I ran after her. I was very torn about leaving Truth with Jeff, but we needed to get help urgently.

We found a security guard.

"Sir, can you help us? My four-year-old daughter is being held in a room by her drunk father, and we are afraid for my daughter's safety, and ours."

The guard followed us to our room. He was able to get the lock off the door and go in. By this time, Jeff had gotten in the bathtub and apparently passed out. The guard was able to get Truth out without disturbing Jeff.

Management got us another room so we would be safe.

The officer wanted to arrest him, but I was afraid I wouldn't know how to get him out of a Dominican jail, so I told them to please just leave him in the room, because he would eventually sober up.

I felt it was safe to return by mid-day the next day. At this point, he typically did not drink the day after he pulled a bad binge. I walked in the room to find a very much hung-over Jeff, along with what seemed to be a hundred empty glasses that had the residue of alcohol in them, and even an empty wine bottle and an empty liquor bottle in the landscaping outside.

He remembered nothing of the evening before, denying it happened, until Mercy recanted what we had experienced.

"Daddy, don't you remember?" she said with a pitiful longing for her dad to be normal. The look on his face was one of a sorry child who realized what a mess he had made.

This was the beginning of the end so to speak, now that I look back. Little did either of us realize at this point, that he was dealing with a much bigger monster than we had realized.

The Breakdown

This was, or should have been, a huge eye-opener for Jeff!

When we walked around and he saw all the liquor bottles, wine bottles, and empty alcohol glasses, he said to me, "Jan, I remember nothing. What did I do?" He cried and apologized over and over, and said, "I need help."

We tried to salvage the remainder of our vacation. I found it difficult to act normal around him, and he could sense the sadness I was carrying. We just tried to get through it.

When we returned home, he simply hit another reset button and went right back into work mode. Perpetually, he would adjust over and over again, and he never pursued help. He acted as if the Dominican fiasco never happened.

He was still filming his show, The Glory Generation, and other opportunities were becoming available. We were beginning to realize that he was a natural behind a camera. I kept one eye wide open for what could happen next, but had to tend to children and the church. The church was doing very well, and he had hidden his secret life very well.

I can't describe my emotions. I think I was still in denial in some ways. It's hard to admit your husband is spiraling out of control, and this could destroy your home, your ministry, and your church. We were the senior pastors of the church and many people looked up to us.

Often Jeff would awaken in the morning, desperately crying out to me for help, but refusing everything I did to get him help. As soon as he got up, he became this driven man, who thrived in the fast lane.

Since I still did all his event booking, I became very upset that he wanted me to book flights to three different countries, back to back, within just a few weeks time. This was sometime in early 2014.

"Jeff, there is no human way you can pull this off. You just admitted you needed help during that disastrous vacation." I begged him to simply say no to these invitations.

Australia and Dubai were two of the places he wanted to travel to. I can't remember the third, but I knew they were far away with too much travel and too many time zones in such a short period of time.

"Jeff, use wisdom! That is not an easy itinerary for anyone, and you are already exhausted!" I exclaimed.

He heard me but said, "Just book it, Jan, and I'll slow down after this."

He couldn't even tell me why it was so important for him to push so hard. There was usually no arguing with him, or convincing him. He was driven to do what he thought was God, but I never believed that God would push him to the point of breakdown. That was not the God I knew.

Jeff had been warned, but would not heed the warning. There was no way to convince him when he was *this* Jeff. This was the pride Bob and the Lord had warned him about. It was literally driving him to collapse.

I worried about him the whole time he was gone on this trip. Typically, he contacted me frequently when he traveled. This time, I had not heard from him at all.

The day he returned from this demanding itinerary, he arranged for someone besides me to pick him up at the airport.

I was upstairs in our bedroom when I heard the back door open and close. I heard footsteps coming up the steps, then a big THUMP! The floor even shook. It was as if an elephant had just fallen over.

I ran down to see what had made the loud noise. Jeff was lying face-down on the floor, motionless. I shook him and called his name repeatedly.

"Jeff! Jeff! Are you okay?" Nothing happened.

I felt his pulse to see if he was alive. His heart was pounding hard. I checked to see if he was breathing. He was, but I was unable to rouse him. He was out cold, so I called one of his sons to come over and get him off the floor and into bed. His son said he wasn't available so somehow, with superhuman strength, I eventually got him up off the floor and into bed.

He literally slept for three days. When he finally got up, he was not the same man I married. He was not even the man I had lived with for the past few years. He was a completely different person. It was as if something had happened. His greatest fears of literally "snapping" under the pressure had come to pass.

It was sadly obvious that he'd had a complete physical and mental breakdown.

Chapter Twelve

COMING TO GRIPS

Struggles

You might ask me how could I act normal in front of people at church, and be around other ministers as if nothing was going on? Why didn't I tell them of his struggles? Our struggles?

"Struggles" is just the best word I can find to define it.

This was probably one of the most difficult things I ever had to deal with.

Jeff was very convincing when he was in repentance mode. He would cry and beg and make a million promises, stating it would never happen again. It was in my nature to believe in the man I thought was the one the Lord had given me as my life partner and trust that somehow, God would help him to overcome.

I never suspected there were underlying issues that had yet to be discovered. I thought it all stemmed from his drinking to help him deal with the pressures of a life he had created. To this day, I believe the real Jeff was sincere and truly wanted to be clean and pure. But there were many cracks in his armor that had not yet been totally revealed.

I began to take note of how short he was with everyone. We had a wonderful church staff. We had an amazing church family. We had been building the church for six or seven years now, and since Jeff traveled so much, I basically administered the functions of the church.

I still didn't particularly desire speaking and preaching, and preferred serving behind the scenes. I did several teachings on things that were important to me, such as dreams, angels, numbers, and supernatural encounters.

We had associate and assistant pastors who took the pulpit in Jeff's absence. The real Jeff loved and appreciated our staff and our church but on the other hand, he had begun making negative remarks to them, and about them.

He frequently said, "They'll do what they are told to do." I would just look at him in disbelief.

He began to say that the church was a burden to him, and he wanted to shut it down. This was during our church's peak years and more and more people were coming. He would minister from the pulpit, but it appeared to me that he was putting on a show, instead of ministering. Again, rockstar syndrome had overtaken this once humble man.

The process of this transition in him was a slow one. I think I just didn't want it to be true. You don't want to believe that your fairytale is a figment of your own hopes and dreams. I'd been seeing fatigue in him for so long, now. I saw frustration. This had taken the ultimate toll on him. He was now behaving like a totally different person, not just some of the time, but most of the time.

He insisted on calling our church Global Fire Center all of the time, and refused to call it a church, eliminating even a hint that it was, in fact, a church.

"Well, it's not a church. It's a center for my ministry," he announced to me.

He said he didn't want a church. He wanted a place that would bring glory to himself. He hinted at this in the beginning, but he was adamant about it now. I never failed to express my complete disdain at all of this. This church was birthed to house God's glory, not to showcase Jeff Jansen.

The next thing that happened was a total shock and came completely out of the blue.

We had closed our school by now. Our main director had gotten married and wanted to pursue other interests. We were thankful for the three years of success and blessings we had seen in the school, and many students had remained with the church. Some were even eventually on our leadership team. Jeff had imparted great things to so many!

My staff and I were in a meeting one Tuesday morning, as usual. We always met with leaders and staff on Tuesday morning to pray and strategize. I believe this was in 2015, and we were discussing closing out our Kingdom Life Institute Facebook page, as the school had closed by this time.

Jeff was on yet another trip, gone more than he was home. I had come to accept this, even though I asked for him to slow down. In the meantime, I just carried on.

He claimed he was fulfilling the call of the Lord. I almost felt that I couldn't argue with this, if he was so sure.

No one knew how to get into the Kingdom Life Institute Facebook page, and nobody seemed to have admin rights. I suggested that perhaps we could log in to Jeff's page, because I knew Jeff's log in credentials for Facebook.

I logged into Jeff's account, hoping to be able to access the Kingdom Life Institute page. My staff and I had more important issues to discuss, so we decided to come back to this later. Just as I was closing my computer, still on Jeff's page, my eyes were drawn to his Facebook Messenger. I saw many familiar names of ministers we both knew, acquaintances I was aware that he spoke with on occasion.

I hadn't created a personal Facebook page, because I felt Jeff was often addicted to looking at it. I had no desire to join Facebook, at this time.

Suddenly, my eyes were drawn to a female name I was not familiar with. I will call her Emma, which is not her real name, to protect her identity.

I clicked on his chats with her on his messenger, out of curiosity. What wife wouldn't do that if she found her husband communicating with another female?

He often conversed with females. Many were pastors and leaders, or the wives of leaders he knew, so I typically didn't think much of it. But this day, it was different. I was being led to this person. God was showing me something.

What I found would change our marriage forever.

As I opened his messages with Emma, my eyes seemed to bulge out of my head and my mouth hung open. I couldn't believe what I was reading.

In a state of panic, I hurried into a private office and continued reading there, fearing that my emotional state would be obvious to the others.

One of our ministers followed me and asked, "What's wrong?" I couldn't speak. I could barely breathe. Tears were streaming down my face.

Jeff and this Emma were having a very wrong, very intimate conversation.

He said things like "Ooh la la!" and he sent gifs with hearts and love symbols. He told her he was sending her his ring, a ring he had designed, containing a supernatural fifty carat red stone that an angel had brought him in Coeur d'Alene, Idaho.

It was one of thirteen identically sized stones of many colors that were dropped by an angel. He valued this stone highly and had designed a mounting to hold the stone. It put any Super Bowl ring to shame. I always felt the gaudy ring was just another sign of his arrogance and actually hated it, but the stone itself was heavenly and breathtaking.

The mounting Jeff put the stone in was a symbol of the Jeff I didn't know. He called it his "fifty carat ruby". He would often loan it out so others could "get the impartation from it".

Jeff told Emma that the pastor of her church in Australia, who was a personal friend of his, would receive the package and give it to her. He also told her that hidden in the box would be a gift of diamond earrings he was giving to her. The pastor had no idea what was in the package, by the way.

My mind raced back to a month or so back, when Jeff had asked me if I had any extra diamond earrings he could have. I asked him why he wanted them. He said, "I want to start wearing earrings in my pierced ear again."

He had two piercings in one ear but hadn't worn earrings in years. I wasn't really suspicious when he asked for the earrings and gave him a pair, as I had several.

I recalled that I never saw him wear them. In reality, he had packed them up in a gift box and sent them to that woman!

It was more than apparent that he had been speaking to this woman often and it was not for the sake of ministry. Their conversation was very intimate.

This is an exact quote of Emma's closing words to him. "I just want to leave a message for you when you wake up. You are amazing and every time I speak to you, you bring peace and understanding to my mind. I've never experienced anything like it before! Absolutely amazing. Ahhh, you are really and truly so awesome. Loooooove you!"

Still sitting in the church office, I called Jeff on the phone and told him I was in shock and could not believe he would do this to me, to us, and to his children! As one can imagine, he denied anything inappropriate and said he was "mentoring" her.

I never wanted to see him again. I knew I would have to take a deep breath and deal with him when he returned. My heart was broken. My mind raced. I am not sure if he felt worse about what he had done, or about getting caught.

He swore he would just stay away from her and acted like it was nothing for me to be upset about. I felt like my heart had been ripped out of my chest. I needed to talk about it, but he just dismissed it and acted like I was a silly, jealous wife. That was my first experience with gaslighting.

I started remembering details that seemed maybe small to me at the time, but that I could now see were obvious signs that something was really wrong.

He had a way of turning things back on me and making me think I was the one who was off. I came to discover more about gaslighting. I was clueless then, but I was about to enter into a period of discovery.

After he returned home from his trip, he continued to dismiss my discovery. He downplayed it and said I was at fault for even suspecting he would do anything inappropriate.

At this point, Jeff locked himself in his home office for hours and wouldn't surface, claiming to watch what he said were "documentaries" on TV or his computer. He always locked the door and we had to knock to get in. Rarely did he watch TV outside of his office.

One evening, after I had gone to bed early, I was awakened a couple of hours later. Oddly, Jeff was in our bonus room, right outside our bedroom. I awoke because of the sound of the television being on.

I walked towards the bonus room, and he was sitting on the sofa staring intently at some show. As I looked at the TV, there were several women walking around topless. This was a key moment when something so shocking was revealed to me, that I almost could not believe it! He had always claimed to keep such a high level of integrity.

He said he fell asleep. His eyes were definitely not closed when I walked in. His response to this was, "Things like that don't affect me. I can let it just roll right off."

He finally admitted he had been watching this show regularly. This was a series called Game of Thrones, and he said he liked the storyline. He claimed nudity was not normally on this show and it just happened to pop up this once. It was one of those moments where again, there was something very different about him. Early in our courtship and marriage, he was always very careful not to even look at another woman. He only had eyes for me. What changed? Was he no longer attracted to me?

We all know you cannot let perversion come into your eye and ear gates. It does not just roll right off, as he had said to me. You become what you embrace. I found other movies on his Amazon account that were rated R and questionable. Keep in mind, purity and humility were two things that drew me to Jeff in the first place. He would have never entertained such things early in our marriage.

Of course, I confronted him again and again. He promised it wasn't a problem, and that he would never do it again, but these were signs that he was embracing sin. He was beginning to compromise. He believed his own deception. That is the danger of even opening a door of compromise.

I eventually began turning off and cancelling movie channels, because his habit of watching bad movies was becoming too frequent.

He watched movies with violence, cursing, murder, and even nudity. You can imagine what I was thinking by now. Who had come and hijacked my wonderful husband? I was beginning to lose trust in him for many reasons.

He had also gone from drinking beer and occasional wine, to drinking vodka. This happened almost overnight, after he had collapsed on the floor. I found vodka bottles in his office and confronted him on this as well.

He was never a liquor drinker to my knowledge, other than maybe on vacation. When confronted, he always just blew it off and said I was the one who was wrong. I wanted to believe him. I tried to believe him. He acted like it was my imagination.

He was blaming me for everything I confronted him with. He tried to make me think I was losing my mind. Again, at this time I did not know much about gaslighting, or about blaming someone else for what you are doing.

I was on the verge of a huge wake-up call; in fact, the wake-up call had already slapped me in the face. I just didn't want to believe it.

One night, I literally pushed the door to his office open while he was shut up in there, and he was obviously seriously drunk on vodka, watching a weird movie, and holding a knife.

I called out, "What in the heck are you doing?"

He became angry that I had just walked in without knocking, and he began yelling at me for invading his privacy. I can't even describe how I felt when I began catching him doing things that I would have never expected or imagined. It was disappointment, pain, sadness, shock, and anger, all packed into the same moment.

I ran into the kitchen, not sure what to do. He followed me, still holding the knife.

Mercy came running downstairs when she heard him yelling, and she immediately saw the knife. She looked at me with great concern. He was not threatening me with it, but the thought of him holding a knife at all at this point, and realizing that he was drunk, scared both of us.

Mercy grabbed hold of me and silently pleaded for help, yet without saying a word. I became terribly frightened, and decided to call 911.

As the police arrived, Jeff had gone back into his office like nothing was going on, while I grabbed the other children and waited outside. The police found him to be almost in a state of unconsciousness, but they were able to rouse him. He confessed he had a knife in his hand, but denied coming at me with it. My children and I fled to a hotel.

This would be the first of several times I had to call the police, and the first of many, many trips to sleep at hotels. The police wouldn't arrest him because they said he had a legal right to drink in his own home.

The next morning, he remembered nothing and denied it all. I don't think the Jeff I married was capable of the harsh reality of realizing who he had become. Jeff could never realize how bad it was, because he never remembered what he did when he drank. The suspicion that I was living with more than one person in that body, had become a cruel reality.

This was not a sudden revelation in a single moment. This was a slow realization that something was very, very wrong. It was revealed over time and got worse, as we went along. I took note along the way, but because we had such a great beginning, I had tremendous hope in him, even at this point.

Although I have many very good memories of this man, the love we shared, and the good he did, and although I have always tried to focus on the good, there are just some memories of the bad Jeff that particularly hurt and stand out. These are the moments that proved to me that I could no longer pretend everything was okay. I prayed. I prayed a lot. I cried out to God.

"Lord, I thought You put Jeff and me together, and I thought it was You who was growing our family, our church and our ministry. Please help me to understand what is going on!" This became my heart's cry.

Jeff called me into his huge office one day. He was sitting at his desk and had been working on something. He was good at pretending everything was perfectly normal with him, and that I was the delusional one.

He looked at me rather matter-of-factly, and calmly said, "Jan, you are just not the wife you used to be. You are cold and unloving. I am moving to Australia to be with Emma and her daughter. I will make sure you are financially cared for, as well as the children, but I'm sure that we will all be better off with my moving there."

This came completely out of the blue. Although I was trying to keep up a good front to everyone around us, my world was beginning to crumble because of Jeff's bizarre behavior.

As often as he had denied having anything more to do with Emma than ministry and mentoring, he was now telling me he was leaving me, my children, the church, and this country, to be with her? I just shook my head and said "What?"

He repeated himself. He was absolute and had apparently made his mind up and was making plans.

"But what about the church?" I asked, expecting him to respond as if he cared.

"I don't care anything about the church," he replied. "It's just a thorn in my side."

Shocked would be an understatement of how I felt at that moment. My heart sank. I felt sick.

When Jeff was Jeff, which was becoming more and more infrequent, we got along fine. I would not have said we had a bad marriage in any way, were it not for his drinking and personality changes. To say that I was cold was outrageous!

I had spent a huge portion of my time and my emotions trying to help him deal with the drama he himself had created. I never withheld my passion from him. I spent so much time dealing with him, and the needs of my children and church, that my own needs went seriously unmet at times.

"Cold? Really Jeff?" I struggled to say these words, feeling completely broken. It was a effort to remain calm, but I simply added, "Okay, well, if that's what you want."

I walked out and went into another room and just cried to God and prayed.

Several hours later he walked out of his office, and I asked him when he would be leaving to move to Australia.

He looked at me as if I were nuts! "What are you talking about? Are you losing your mind, Jan?"

In silence, I waited for his next comment.

"I have no idea what you are talking about. Moving to Australia? Ha! That's ridiculous! You're delusional!"

I could tell he sincerely had no memory of saying any of this to me, and he truly thought something was wrong with me.

He added, "I told you Emma and I are simply ministry acquaintances, nothing more. I was only mentoring her. I haven't spoken to her in a while."

This was truly a Dr. Jekyll and Mr. Hyde moment and I felt like I'd been kicked in the gut.

Chapter Thirteen

DISSOCIATIVE IDENTITY DISORDER

Is It Like Sybil?

I had never heard of dissociative identity disorder, or D.I.D. Like many, the movie Sybil, starring Sally Field, was my first exposure to even be aware of things of that nature, although I actually never watched the entire movie.

It came out in 1976 and I was quite busy with school and friends and rarely watched movies. I also found the content to be too intense, at my young age.

I had heard that Sybil had sixteen different personalities, that it was very rare, and can only occur when there is severe mental illness.

Sybil, the lead character, suffered with what was then called multiple personality disorder, caused by horrific, ongoing abuse throughout her young life at the hands of her mother.

As more understanding was gained, the term multiple personality disorder was formally changed to dissociative identity disorder in 1994, in the DSM IV (The Diagnostic and Statistical Manual of Mental Disorders), the professional publication released by the American Psychiatric Association.

Webster's 1828 dictionary describes dissociation as the act of disuniting, a state of separation or disunion. It's not unlike the shattering of a mirror.

There are varying beliefs about the prevalence of D.I.D. In the past, most insisted it was extremely rare.

However, with a growing understanding of trauma and the increasing numbers of those who have experienced traumatic abuse, many now believe that D.I.D. is much more common than previously thought.

My friend Wendy Hibbard, one of our graduates from Kingdom Life Institute, regularly ministers to survivors of traumatic and ritual abuse. As she explains, dissociation occurs on a spectrum. Most of us engage in dissociation to some degree. We might temporarily zone out, or daydream on an everyday drive to work, while at school, in meetings, or so forth. This is considered normal.

Others dissociate as a coping mechanism for dealing with trauma, disengaging from what's happening around them. At a more serious level, some people experience blackouts, missing time, and amnesia.

We often use the term "parts" or "fragmented parts" (of consciousness) in ministry to those with less severe dissociation. With more severe dissociation (blackouts, amnesia), we typically use the term "alters," short for "alternate identity".

Alters are alternate personalities. The way God designed us, He knew there were times when the trauma we experienced would be more than our fragile humanity could endure, and He gave us help that would come from within ourselves.

Over the years, the ministry team at my church has done hundreds of sessions and never found one person who did not have "parts" on some level.

Have you ever had times when you felt like you were not yourself? You may just cry for no reason, laugh for no reason, but afterwards feel much better. There is a chance that was a part expressing. I believe that God designed parts for our protection. Something may rise up in us that gives us strength that we didn't know we had. We may be hurt or threatened by another person, and suddenly we step up and defend ourselves and think, "Gosh, that came out of nowhere."

Quotes From Survivors

Here are some quotes from people I have known that have dissociative identity disorder (D.I.D):

"It's like watching a movie in my head. Like you're watching a movie and you get all absorbed in the movie. And you forget who you are, where you are, what time it is, and what is really going on in your life".

"You know that you're doing something, but you feel that somebody else is doing it. You have no control over what they do. You feel you are watching yourself from a distance."

"Sometimes I just feel like a little girl and want to curl up in a fetal position. And sometimes I feel angry and like I just want to hurt someone. "

Alters or parts sometimes choose to take over when they believe the core person is incapable of dealing with the pressures that are upon them, and could be in danger of a breakdown. Other times, they may be triggered to take over, or "switch".

This may result in literally knocking the consciousness of the lead personality out of the way, or it's possible that they may be "co-conscious," meaning that they are aware of alternate personalities presenting at the same time, either in the front of their consciousness, or rumbling around elsewhere.

This is often noticeably expressed through uncharacteristic mood and behavioral changes, or simply distraction or agitation. It's common for a person to experience a sudden onset of fear, dread, panic, anxiety, paranoia, and rage, as some of the most commonly displayed behaviors. In addition, they may engage in negative self-medicating behaviors, such as an array of addictions, violent outbursts, even cutting themselves.

In some cases, alters or parts may have their own agenda. This is particularly true when the individual has occultic roots in their family history, or has been subjected to SRA (satanic ritual abuse), and a part will frequently have a "demonic" attachment. Typically, this would corrupt their will, and interfere with their ability to make a positive, free will choice.

SRA stands for satanic ritual abuse. It wasn't until we had to deal with it head on, that I learned what it meant. A victim of satanic ritual abuse can be someone who was born into a cult or targeted by a cult, and was innocent of what happened to them. Some are recruited. Others knowingly delve into satanic worship, although they often misunderstand the realities of it, at first. SRA victims may be abused mentally, emotionally, physically, and spiritually. The abuse ranges from mild to severe.

When we had the Kingdom Life Institute, a few of our students were survivors of satanic ritual abuse. The school was wonderful, because of our dedicated, spirit-filled leaders, and a collection of passionate students from across the United States, eager to grow in the Lord. Each meeting began with a time of worship and soaking, led by a beautifully anointed worship leader. It was not uncommon for students to be overcome by the power of the Holy Spirit pouring out, falling to the floor with no one touching them, receiving supernatural healing as they lay there, basking in the glory of God.

Yet, the glory of God is highly confrontational to demonic strongholds. As some were touched by God and experienced spontaneous healing, there were others who, on occasion, would experience an internal battle being stirred. For some of them, it was overwhelming at times.

One of the hardest things in supporting survivors of satanic ritual abuse is the potential danger involved to themselves, others, or both. The enemy considers them his property, and is not about to let them go without a fight. Firewalls are put in place in an attempt to prevent meaningful deliverance. When these firewalls are disrupted, it often triggers extremely self-destructive behaviors within the individual, ranging from avoidance and isolation to even attempted suicide.

Sadly, this is not an isolated experience. Survivors of SRA tend to be very gifted, and drawn to ministry. Often, part of the reason they were victimized has to do with their natural gifting, and the enemy's desire to crush or pervert that gifting before they are able to use it for the kingdom of God.

We have had reports from numerous others who have attended supernatural ministry schools all over the United States, and experienced severe spiritual backlash or worse as they pressed in for more of the glorious presence of God. It is heartbreaking to hear how poorly many of them were treated by leaders that had little to no understanding of the realities of SRA.

Thankfully, God led us as we learned more and more how to support those in need, through the challenges that arose. It wasn't easy, but the good news is that God is able. We saw them receive freedom and healing in amazing ways. God allows us to experience things we don't understand so that He can educate us and so we can help others.

Freedom Encounters

Between the survivors of SRA that came to Kingdom Life Institute, or came into my life in other ways during that time, I knew I wanted to be able to help and deliver these folks.

I searched for someone to train a deliverance team at the church. A ministry associate mentioned Freedom Encounters, with Ken and Sylvia Thornberg.

I spoke with them at length. They explained how people's souls can fracture, allowing the demonic to attack and attach to them. After extensive conversations, and with much prayer with my church leaders, I scheduled a time for an in-service training.

I felt they were trained and knowledgeable on how to bring freedom to the captives. Jeff was adamantly against it.

"It's all a hoax, Jan," he said.

Nonetheless, our entire leadership team was for it, so we literally outvoted Jeff.

Ironically, I was always drawn to the deliverance ministry. When we were at Charles Carrin meetings, I would comment to Jeff, "I want this!"

I felt that the Lord was bringing this new knowledge of deliverance to our church but I also felt personally compelled to know more, in a way that I didn't yet understand.

With a team of about fifty people in training at the church, Ken and Sylvia spent several days with us, teaching us things about "alters" or "parts". Because this was relatively new to me, I was almost leery, myself.

Jeff struggled to believe Ken and Sylvia, and arrogantly dismissed himself.

We required that all of our staff, including our leaders, go through this process, which included deliverance, inner healing, and integration as needed, while Ken and Sylvia were with us.

I felt we couldn't rightly ask our staff to go through a session if Jeff and I did not submit ourselves. Jeff completely refused at first, and even I said, "I do not have parts. I don't know if I believe in any of this!"

Over time, I learned that everyone has parts. No one is exempt. God revealed this to me in a very personal way.

The night before my deliverance session, I had a dream. In my dream, Sylvia was driving a car. I was in the passenger seat. She insisted we stop the car and get out.

Out of the back seat came at least fifteen "people". They stood in two lines, one in front of the other. Some were beautiful women, some children, some thin, some obese. Some were elegant, some were awkward. I didn't understand.

I looked at Sylvia and asked her, "Who are these people?" She answered me as if I were dumb to not know.

"Well, these are parts of your personality."

Dreams can be symbolic, but the message in the dream was to reveal to me that we could all have "parts" or fractures in our souls, and this was not something limited to people who were mentally ill or had come out of darkness.

In fact, parts are more accurately described as mental injury than mental illness. Simply put, they are the result of trauma-induced fragmentation.

I found some great articles online and purchased several books. Below are excerpts of one article I found:

Dissociative Identity Disorder and Its Impact on the Brain

In this day and age, humans are well-equipped to detect their own consciousness rather than jump to conclusions. For example, a demon is possessing them. Lucky for us, modern science helps us better understand the idea that we are in control of our own minds. However, the human brain is still quite complex, which means there are a lot of opportunities for it to malfunction, especially in the form of disorders. One disorder that many are starting to raise awareness of is dissociative identity disorder, known as D.I.D.

D.I.D has been mistaken for other disorders in the past, but with modern research and technology, we know that D.I.D has real biological impacts on the brain.

So, what exactly is D.I.D? It is a disorder in which a person generates two or more separate personalities to cope with a distressing situation. For example, physical or sexual trauma. A person dealing with the psychological consequences of a traumatic event may view it from an outside perspective. Each persona has different traits or backgrounds, and it controls the person's behavior when shifting into that personality. The other personas are more of a fragment of their original identity rather than an entirely different entity.

Famous actress AnnaLynne McCord, who has opened up about her struggles with dissociative identity disorder, described this experience as a fragmented identity, stating, "You are not multiple personalities when you experience D.I.D. You are fragmented versions of yourself. The reason that the brain splits in this regard, it's always a protective mechanism." (Mental Health: Multiple Personality Disorder, 2020)

Symptoms of D.I.D include anxiety, delusions, depression, disorientation, memory loss, and suicidal tendencies. Different personalities may generate different symptoms than others, resulting in a further lack of consistency of thought. D.I.D could be mistaken for schizophrenia or bipolar disorder due to shared symptoms, but brain scans show this is not the case.

(Dissociative Identity Disorder: What Is It, Symptoms & Treatment, 2021)   *~End of article excerpts.*

I took this to the Lord continually. I have been asked, "If D.I.D. is real, may I have scripture to back this up?"

Is dissociative identity disorder mentioned in the Bible? Not by that name. Of course, neither is diabetes, high blood pressure, or any other modern name for infirmities.

Certain afflictions were mentioned in the Word by name: drunkenness, atrophy, paralysis, fever, hemorrhage, leprosy, blindness, deafness, dumbness, boils, dysentery, epilepsy, even obesity, indigestion and baldness. Cancer wasn't mentioned by name, but there are two scripture references to "wasting diseases". (Leviticus 26:16 and Deuteronomy 28:22)

Deuteronomy 28 speaks of the blessings of the Lord for obeying His commandments but also the consequences of disobedience. Tumors are also mentioned in Deuteronomy 28:27. So were scabs and "itching that you cannot heal".

Mental illness was referenced in several ways, in the Bible. Deuteronomy 28:28 refers to, "madness and with blindness and with bewilderment of heart and mind."

The word "lunatic" is also mentioned in Matthew 4:24 in the King James Version. This word derives from the Latin word "Luna," which means "referring to the moon". It was believed that mental illness was dictated by the phases of the moon.

In fact, most medical conditions in the Bible are simply referred to as sickness or infirmity.

"Now may the God of peace Himself sanctify you through and through (that is separate you from profane and vulgar things, make you pure and whole and undamaged- consecrated to Him- set apart for His purpose); and may your spirit and soul and body be kept complete and (be found) blameless at the coming of our Lord Jesus Christ." 1 Thessalonians 5:23.

Would this prayer ask that a person be made whole and complete if there could be no brokenness or division?

Different versions of the Bible use different wording, but all would indicate that perhaps there could be a possibility that your spirit, soul, and body may not all be whole, and that one or the another could be independently afflicted.

Double-mindedness is mentioned twice in the book of James. In both cases, the root word used for double-minded is di-psychos, which means "two spirited, two souled", or literally, a person split in half.

"Being a double-minded man, unstable and restless in all his ways (in everything he thinks, feels, or decides)." ~ James 1:8 (Amp)

"Come close to God (with a contrite heart) and He will come close to you. Wash your hands you sinners; and purify your (unfaithful) hearts, you double-minded (people)." ~ James 4:8 (Amp)

Actually, James 4:8 points to one of the most common barriers in helping people dealing with dissociation to find healing. Often, at the time when fragmentation took place, there was no visible sign of Jesus coming to their rescue. This leads many to believe that maybe God isn't good, or doesn't care, or in some cases, that He was behind the punishment.

The key is to reach the fragmented parts is to lead them into an encounter with the true Lord Jesus Christ of Nazareth, Who came in the flesh. Then their hearts may be delivered of all doubt and defiling, their hands cleansed of every stain.

Access Points

"My people are destroyed for lack of knowledge..."
~ Hosea 4:6 AMP

People can unknowingly open demonic doors and open themselves up to demonic attack. I've known people who loved watching horror movies or playing video games, thinking it was innocent, and they unwittingly opened a door to spiritual attacks upon themselves.

Others mistakenly believed that there is such a thing as "good" witchcraft, and became entangled in darkness. Many are drawn to witchcraft for the desire to belong, not feeling accepted by the church, and not realizing the true dangers.

"So, come out from among (unbelievers), and separate (sever) yourselves from them, says the Lord, and touch not (any) unclean thing; then I will receive you kindly and treat you with favor".
~ 2 Corinthians 6:17 (AMP)

Gloria's Story

Let's look at Gloria. Gloria had a tumultuous childhood. Her parents divorced at an early age. She often felt alone, but was able to press through.

When she was seventeen, she was in a terrible car accident when a tractor trailer hit her vehicle. She remembers that during the actual trauma, she felt surreal. She felt as if the *real* Gloria was not present, and that someone else was there to protect her. She always thought it was a guardian angel. She had memory loss for a few days after that, and felt like she was not even herself anymore. Eventually she felt normal again, although she could still feel the residual effects of what she had been through and of almost losing her life.

Sam's Story

Sam was only five when his father started sexually abusing him. It started as something playful. Sam's mother was the sole breadwinner of the house and was gone a lot, so he welcomed the attention from his father.

Gradually, the playful interactions began to escalate to something uncomfortable and inappropriate. Sam's father made him feel that this kind of physical attention was normal.

Sam's five-year-old self could not handle the tremendous damage this did to him. Even though he was conditioned to believe what was happening was normal, his spirit person knew it was not. God allowed a part of him to separate that would house the difficult memories (as an amnesiac barrier), to help him cope. This fragmented part of Sam's consciousness kept the knowledge of this severe trauma from disturbing him by hiding them away.

As Sam grew up, he was unable to remember what had happened to him until his father was dying of cancer, and all those repressed memories resurfaced. He had a breakdown, traumatized by the realization that his father had sexually abused him for years, and his mother had done nothing to stop it.

Although Sam's mother had no idea what was going on, the child within Sam blamed her for abandoning him and not being there for him. He was able to remember the trauma and confess this to his mother.

It was shocking to her. Sam's mother was initially unable to cope with the devastating news, and had a breakdown as well. After Sam's father died, his mother and a skillful counselor were able to help him find ways to cope with what had happened to him, and move toward healing.

Mary's Story

I've known those who were in an intimate relationship with someone in the occult and suffered the consequences, even though they were innocent.

I had a good friend named Mary M (not the best friend Mary, I spoke of previously). She loved the Lord dearly and served him faithfully her entire life. She was a powerful minister, healer, and prophetess. I witnessed mighty miracles occur during her meetings.

Mary had been going to a local prison for over twenty years, ministering to the inmates there. Although this seemed odd to me, she had met one of the inmates and had entered into a relationship with him.

He was serving a twenty-year sentence, and had given his life to the Lord through her ministry there. During their time together, they fell in love and eventually married, even though he would not be released from prison for a long, long time.

I remember so clearly when her husband was released from prison. He felt like a new man, for a while. But much had changed in the twenty years he had been incarcerated.

Often, when people are released from a long prison sentence, they feel lost and out of place. They don't know how to survive in the outside world.

As with another friend of mine who was imprisoned for fifteen years on drug charges, he told me when he got out, he almost wanted to go back to prison, because it was more predictable than being in the world. He was even homeless for a while because he didn't know where he belonged.

Mary had to step back from ministry to help her husband adjust. This was to be expected, but it took a bad turn. His family had always been heavily into witchcraft, and they still were before he met Mary.

Mary knew this when she married him, but she thought he had overcome that influence. Not long after he became a free man, it was as if he were automatically drawn back to it.

His challenge in getting back to a normal life and suddenly cohabitating with a new wife that he yet didn't really know, was overwhelming to him. As a dog returns to its vomit, Mary's husband returned to what was familiar to him, witchcraft.

He began doing rituals in their basement. Soon, Mary found herself being attacked by demons in the middle of the night. She was healed many years back of a serious heart condition in a Kim Clement meeting. When these demonic attacks began, subsequent to his rituals, her symptoms of heart disease began to manifest again.

In desperation, she called me.

"Jan, I don't know what to do. He's become horrifically abusive, verbally, spiritually, and physically. At times, he even locks me in the bedroom!"

After Mary finally had enough, she was able to escape while he was asleep one night, and call the police. He had apparently been involved in other crimes behind her back, so he was arrested and went back to prison.

Being in the same house with a practicing warlock had opened many demonic doors, and demons continued to attack her during the night.

Mary told me this story with a broken heart, and I could tell she was truly afraid. She was not at all the once powerful woman of God that I had known.

"Jan, I live in constant fear that the demons will kill me, especially during the night."

I went to her house to minister to her and took a team with me. We could feel the evil presence that remained there. We prayed over her, and her home.

After that, I called Mary frequently to check on her. She told me that she felt freedom, at least for a while, but my discernment told me there was still a connection that allowed her to be tormented.

"Mary, can you think of any soul ties that may remain between you and your husband?" I inquired of her.

"Well Jan, I do still receive support checks from him. Do you think that could be it?" She had not thought of soul ties remaining.

"I do, Mary. I really do. I strongly advise you to cut all ties with him, including his money, and move out of the house."

She admitted that when she was sleeping somewhere else, even in the hospital, or at her son's house, she was not attacked by these demonic spirits. It only happened in the home she'd shared with her husband, where he had performed satanic rituals in the basement.

Sadly, the thought of leaving the home, and rejecting the support she'd come to depend on, was too hard for Mary.

Shortly after, I realized I had not heard from her. I tried calling, but she never answered her phone. Eventually, her son reached out. He had found Mary dead in her bed.

It was a devastating loss. This woman who demonstrated the love and power of Jesus so well to many had unintentionally allowed a door to the dark side to be opened, a door she had been unable to close.

Chapter Fourteen

SEEKING HELP

In Denial

Eventually, I began to realize there was more than one "person" living in Jeff, calling the shots. There was the good Godly man I fell in love with and married, my best friend and soulmate. Then, there were the others. I didn't completely understand what we were dealing with, but I was determined to learn as much as possible.

Because this was so personal to me, I continued to research based on what I had observed in Jeff. It was a lot to learn, and I needed more understanding.

Not only had Jeff refused to submit himself to Ken and Sylvia's authority, he also chose to deny that anything they taught was reality. He went through the motions, but his unbelief rendered it ineffective. Even Ken and Sylvia said his inner healing sessions were pointless, as he did not respond.

By this time, I had gone to several prominent ministers and asked them if they would be willing to help hold Jeff accountable. I was afraid his behavior and drinking habits were out of control. These were good men of God that Jeff had walked with and ministered alongside. He respected them, so I was hopeful he would submit to them, in an attempt to remain clean and sober.

I was very candid and honest and did not hold anything back. I prayed for wisdom and asked what I should do. They all felt that Jeff must get a grip. I think it was difficult for these ministers to believe Jeff could do some of the things I told them he had done. They agreed to check on him regularly by phone. Sadly this was not enough.

Always after a drinking binge, he would submit to the authority of these great ministers briefly, but ultimately he just lied to them and told them everything was wonderful, and that he was completely healed. His pride would never allow him to humble himself and truly seek help, even though he knew, deep down inside, he was falling apart.

When the real Jeff surfaced, which was becoming less and less frequent as we moved forward, he verbalized his deep concern about himself. He realized that he was even having brief memory loss.

Admitting how deep his shortcomings were to men he considered his peers, was just too difficult for him. In moments of vulnerability, he could confess to me, but pride kept him from opening himself up to others.

Without revealing the truth to anyone else, I continued to schedule inner healing meetings for Jeff. Reluctantly, he went. It seemed he did have some degree of breakthrough.

I remember after one session, he got in the car, looked at me like a scolded child and said, "Jan, I was abused."

I let him vent, and in tears, he told me things he had never revealed before.

I thought we were making progress, but eventually he said these inner healing sessions were a waste of time and he rebelliously refused to go back. I didn't understand. Jeff wanted help, but whatever had surfaced in him, did not. It was as if he was on the edge of something huge, but he didn't want to know what it was.

We talked about an alcohol treatment center. I suggested that he check into a rehab facility. His response was "I have to keep working. The machine has to keep running." He still downplayed the fact that alcohol had a grip on him and that he was using it to cope.

I told him that the machine was about to break down, short of a miracle. The Jeff I was now living with most of the time was completely driven, and refused to acknowledge he had a problem serious enough to require intense treatment.

The Lord spoke to me one day while I was in prayer and said, "You know, Jan, if you continue to hide Jeff's behavior, you are just as guilty as he is."

I will never forget how I felt at that moment. I was afraid. I was afraid the church would be destroyed. I was afraid many people would be disillusioned and hurt. I did not want to hurt innocent people. I loved our church. I loved people. How could I tell them that their much admired and respected leader was living a completely double life in many ways?

I had to ponder this word of the Lord for a while. I knew I had to obey. I knew His voice. I did not want to be held in contempt because I continued to cover for Jeff.

In fearful obedience, I called a meeting with a few of our church leaders. Humbly, I told them what had been going on, all of it. I told them I had believed that somehow a miracle would occur and save Jeff, but this had not happened, and that Jeff was unwilling to seek help on his own, at this point.

They were loving and supportive. They admitted that they had also witnessed the change that had occurred in Jeff. Often, even in staff meetings, his personality would flip on a dime, leaving everyone shrugging their shoulders.

We called a meeting and Jeff was confronted, calmly and matter-of-factly, by our leaders. I stepped back and let my trusted pastors lead the confrontation. I was too close to the issue and didn't want Jeff to think this was a "wife" thing.

"It's not that bad guys," he said. I remained silent.

He felt comfortable with two of our pastors who had risen up to lead our deliverance ministry. They had proven to have a great track record. Many people had been integrated, delivered, and set free.

In private, in a rare moment where Jeff was humble and remorseful, I asked him to please go through this process of deliverance, as his behavior had become very different from the man I married. After all, he was drinking heavily, lying, accepting immorality as normal, and had even been inappropriately involved with at least one woman that I knew of.

He agreed to the session, but not because he thought he needed it. It was more that he was intent on proving that he did not have alters, and that there was nothing wrong with him.

Our deliverance ministers had several sessions with him. Although he was somewhat resistant and not completely submitted to the process, it wasn't hard to get his alters to talk.

There was, of course, the real Jeff. This was the humble man I married who, at this point, was only occasionally able to break through to express his desperation to me. This was the man who spoke his heart to me early in the mornings.

Another called himself "Jeffrey". He seemed very dominant and mean to the deliverance ministers and used foul language towards them. Jeffrey was very arrogant. He said that he didn't care for me very much, or for Mercy.

There was another part who acted like a little kid and called himself "Jeffy Boy". I remembered Jeff telling me early in our relationship that this was what his favorite grandmother called him, when he was a child.

Although his alters presented and identified themselves, Jeff was still hesitant to be totally transparent to these ministers who had walked with him daily for quite some time. They were too close to the situation. When we confronted him on our discovery, Jeff resisted further sessions or rather, it was Jeffrey who resisted.

In light of Jeff's reluctance, I insisted that he visit several HeartSync ministers. This is also a ministry that deals with the integration of alters or parts. Again, it was always me taking him, not his seeking help. He was able to recall and admit some details from his childhood through these sessions.

It was becoming more apparent that Jeff had suffered abuse. I wondered why he had not confided in me. He just said he "went through some painful things" when he was young.

When Jeff confessed to me that he was abused, I knew that this was real to him, even though he had never expressed anything like this to me before.

The only thing he said to me was that he was a rather wild teenager and that was why he moved in with friends. When I asked him to expound on this abuse he was talking about, he changed the subject.

Jeff was too prideful to simply humble himself completely and admit how seriously he was traumatized as a child. After all, he had achieved great things for the Kingdom of God. How could a man of his stature and recognition be flawed?

There was something even deeper, even more damaging, that was still repressed in his memory.

Ultimately, despite all my efforts to help him and get to the bottom of his real problem, he just laughed it all off.

"I don't think he is taking this seriously," his HeartSync counselor had told me in private.

My reply was, "I don't think he is willing to believe he could succumb to this."

Again, this was proof that the word I had received from the Lord in a night vision about pride was genuine.

There wasn't much more I could do, but at times I would get flashes of what was to come, and it gave me cold chills. One can guide a thirsty horse to the water's edge, yet be unable to compel it to drink.

The breaking point now was that things had become so bad, I had to get travel partners to go with him on all of his ministry trips, so he could manage himself. I was becoming more and more a caregiver to Jeff, rather than a wife. I was trying to save something that was spinning out of my control, from what I could observe.

Jeff had been invited to minister in India and despite expressing my concerns to him, he still went, alone.

He apparently got through the services, but as he went to the desk to check out of the hotel, apparently he was completely drunk, as it was later reported to me.

The desk clerk had called the pastor there because Jeff had put large amounts of alcohol on his room bill. That pastor was very upset and called me. He had my number because I had communicated with him to book Jeff's travel arrangements.

The Indian pastor was irate. It was clear that his guest minister had been drinking heavily the entire time he was there.

I felt angry and embarrassed.

"Sir, I don't know what to say."

I asked for a copy of the bill with the room charges. That was all I knew to do. Sure enough, there was over $400 in alcohol charged to Jeff's room. I had to pay this bill as the pastor refused, as well he should have. A bridge was burned there that was never restored.

Jeff was too drunk to even check out and get on a plane. To this day, I'm not sure how he even got to the airport, or how he managed to get home.

This happened several other times, whether he had a travel partner or not. He would order large quantities of alcohol to be delivered to his room, then leave the charges for the pastors. I could not even reason why he would do something so blatant, or what he was even thinking.

I had numerous men who could travel with him. Their main job was to make sure he traveled safely and behaved. Some didn't see him do anything wrong. Some would tell me later what they observed.

It was obvious that he was not doing well, not traveling well, and was leaning heavily on alcohol to cope. He was even now sometimes drinking before ministering, I was later told.

Nobody wanted to tell me what they were observing at the time. This all came out in the end. Why didn't they tell me? I think they were just as afraid to expose the man, as I was. We all wanted to believe the best. They loved Jeff and considered him a friend, and somehow they felt they could not challenge him.

Typically, when Jeff was not on an alcohol binge, he tried to be a normal person, a normal dad, and a normal pastor. A part of me still felt very deeply for him and I hurt because I knew he hurt. Still, I felt betrayed and helpless, and at times, I felt like a hypocrite, because most people around us were clueless and put him on this religious pedestal.

Jeff was outgoing, funny, and charismatic by nature and people were drawn to him. He was the life of the party, so to speak.

He was obviously very knowledgeable of scripture and spiritual matters. He was a powerful minister. Signs, wonders and healings continued to follow him wherever he went, as much as I did not understand this.

The gifts and callings of the Lord are without repentance, or irrevocable, as some versions of the Bible say. (Romans 11:29) God doesn't just take our spiritual gifting away if we struggle, or even fall into sin. This is something that is difficult for most of us to understand. God is patient and longsuffering, but scripture is full of evidence that when God says enough, it is enough.

I intentionally watched, looked, and listened to try and figure Jeff out. Privately I cried out to God to deliver me from this nonsense. The kids and I were completely victimized and we were fleeing to sleep in hotels more and more. The level of intensity and abuse when he was drinking had escalated. I begged the Lord for a solution. I begged for a way out, so that no one would be hurt.

To clarify intensity and abuse, Jeff never just slugged me with his fist or hit me across the face. There was much yelling, cursing, and threatening. He had hit me on the arms, shoved me, pushed me, and knocked me down. I always managed to get out of the house before any further harm could be done. He never remembered any of it the next morning when he sobered up. It is never okay to tolerate abuse on any level.

Reflection

Throughout our marriage, Jeff spoke very fondly of his childhood. He spoke about being an altar boy in the Catholic Church, going on camping trips with the extended family, swimming in the river, and also being a troubled teen growing up in the 70s. If he had other memories, he didn't seem to talk about them much.

He experimented with drugs, grew his hair long, and in his words, was a hippie. Being from a broken family, I could relate, because I was the same way. It wasn't an anomaly back then.

We would laugh, because if you weren't cool back then, you were treated as a reject. We would thank God we overcame, because some of our school friends did not, and some of them even lost their lives.

Apparently, his father, being a police chief, was pretty hard on Jeff and was upset that his own son was going against the grain. Jeffrey possibly surfaced then and felt he had to be meaner than his dad, to protect Jeff from his dad.

Jeff (or Jeffrey) may have made it almost impossible for his parents to manage him. It was Jeff's perception that he was treated unfairly, or that it was an abusive situation. Since I had known him, he had only spoken very highly of his parents and his family. Only when Jeffrey began to surface, did he mention any type of mistreatment.

Alters don't always have reasoning ability. They just jump in when needed and if the threat feels real enough, they will take over, at least for a while, until they feel that they are no longer needed to intervene.

It was becoming impossible for those who were close to us, particularly our church staff, to fail to notice that there was something abnormal about Jeff.

For instance, we would be with others at the church and Jeff would be perfectly calm and normal one minute, until he would become agitated and irritated over something or nothing, and we would experience an immediate flip into the impatient, intolerant, and cruel Jeffrey.

Fatigue would also frequently be a factor. He would often storm out of a room and tell us how we were wasting his time. He would call us all idiots. When he and I would get in the car to leave, he would make very cruel remarks about our staff.

I felt helpless and afraid. If our staff was recognizing and dealing with him as he was, what next? Who else had noticed?

I even confided in a man he trusted at the church, who was a men's leader at the time, and asked him to please speak with Jeff and help him be accountable. He said he understood, but I'm not sure if he ever even brought it up to Jeff.

I also contacted other men of God, Jerry Bryant being one of them, and asked for advice and counsel. The sad fact was that there was no easy solution.

It was difficult for even me to believe how Jeff was now, so I know it was almost impossible for others to witness how the powerful man of God was battling something, and believe he was not as he appeared.

My children were even making comments that Dad was very unpredictable, and they were beginning to feel unsafe. Having to flee to hotels all the time was creating fear and trauma in them. My older daughter became adamant about not wanting to be around him at all.

You might ask, "Was he acting strangely all the time, or were there just random episodes?"

I will say that most of the time, he was not the man I married. There were occasional, fleeting moments when he would look at me with those eyes and ask me if I loved him, and he would say that he loved me. He occasionally even asked me urgently to please forgive him, to help him, for he never meant to hurt me. I knew that the Jeff I married was still there.

When we were in public, he acted normal to most people, but I knew this over-the-top, more than charismatic man, was not the real Jeff. This man was always after the last word, always after attention, and was the opposite of the humble man I fell in love with. I don't mean to say that Jeff was never charismatic, but I knew him and his nature, and now, as a whole, he was just different. He was totally different.

When the real Jeff managed to come to the front, as I explained it, even he realized there was something really wrong, and he panicked. He would cry, as he recalled God telling him that if he didn't get a grip, his life would be taken, as the anointing could not be perverted.

He applied this directly to his abusing alcohol. If he was conscious of multiple personalities at this point, he had not yet verbalized it to me. I would reassure Jeff and tell him I was always willing to help him, but I also began to take a stand and tell him his behavior could no longer be tolerated.

He was a mean drunk. He had become an obnoxious mean man in my world, and that of my children.

"Jeff, you live a double life, and it's just plain wrong. Nobody really knows what the kids and I live through," I would insist, as I tried to reach some sort of a consciousness deep within him.

He continued to travel, against my advice, but I was seeing him doing more and more online meetings and events as well.

We were soon coming into the pandemic years. Zooms and online events had become more popular. I was amazed that I had not just bailed at this point. The part of me who had suffered and yet endured, wanted to escape. I simply wanted to take my children and go somewhere where we could find peace.

By now, we had moved twice and as previously mentioned, his office was upstairs. He could easily just lock himself in. He had only approved houses where he had a room to escape to. This had been the case in our last two houses.

I was very concerned that the children's bedrooms were also upstairs. He spent more time in his office upstairs than not, and in many ways he and I were like strangers.

I can't tell you how many binges my children and I endured and how many nights we continued to have to escape to hotels. We even slept at the church. I was embarrassed for the hotel clerks to see that I lived in the same town, and I was having to explain why I needed a room in a hotel.

They would often ask, "Have you had some kind of damage to your house?"

I could honestly respond, "Yes, there is much damage in my house." There was.

Once I actually pulled receipts and counted over twenty times that we had to flee to hotels in a two-year period. We were afraid of drunk Jeff, and even sober Jeffrey was not nice. In fact, he was a nightmare!

We were scared of who he had become and of the unknown. We all kept an overnight bag packed in the car, in case we had to flee.

We knew we could step into the house at any time of day, to find him drunk, yelling, threatening, ranting and cursing. We had become accustomed to the reality of literally turning around, and hopping right back in the car.

If I was brave enough to unlock his office door to check on him, sometimes he was studying or watching videos, but it became more frequent that I found him completely wasted. His every two month binges had turned into more of a weekly or even daily habit. I had stopped confronting him in that state. I would just gather the children and leave.

He had also developed a fascination with guns and knives. He had quite a collection, and sometimes when I would sneak up on him to see what he was doing in his office, he would be throwing knives into the carpet or playing with his guns. He had watched so many violent movies, this had possibly triggered some of his obsession with weapons. I began to tell the children to lock their bedroom doors at night. I had my young son sleeping in my room with the doors locked.

I knew the real Jeff was nothing like Jeffrey, who seemed to be dominant. I can't tell you how many times I sat down to talk to him to ask him what was going on. I can't tell you how much research I did. I often went online to figure out what was wrong with my husband, the love of my life. I truly felt like someone had taken my husband and replaced him with someone else. I compared it to an alien abduction.

It is common that someone with dominant parts or alters will actually turn on those who are trying to help them. The parts feel the person is being controlling and making the core person feel uncomfortable, since they may be unable to meet up to expectations. We just wanted our loved one back.

The alters feel we are trying to get rid of them, and they are threatened and can't understand why we can't understand that they are trying to help, too.

You can't imagine what it's like to see someone you deeply love and respect just seem to turn into someone else you cannot stand, and who literally could be a danger, not only to himself but to his family.

Jeff was kind, loving, thoughtful, humble, and loved the Lord and His people with all his heart. This Jeffrey, who had taken him over, acted like a perverse, disrespectful teenager who pushed the limits of everything.

I searched and searched online for his symptoms and was constantly led to borderline personality disorder and dissociative personality disorder, as well as narcissism.

I had heard the word narcissism before, but didn't even know what it meant. I will talk more about that later, but I do know it is a demonic spirit whose head is the Jezebel, Leviathan, and Python spirit.

I continued to act like nothing was going on when I was at the church, although it was one of the hardest things I had ever had to do. My pastors would ask how Jeff was doing. I could not answer. He was still traveling a lot and gone most of the time.

I went to some of them privately a few times and told them I was at the end of my patience with him. They never encouraged me to leave, or stay. They just agreed that we needed to be safe, and that the situation had to change. We all wanted to believe the best.

He wasn't preaching false doctrines, but the style in which he ministered was very different. I dreaded him ministering, because it was no longer pure. It was unclean in some way.

Although he was still getting high levels of words of knowledge, it was obvious that the words he got were like "data" that even any demon could know: name, address, how many kids you have, phone number, etc. The general public was amazed at how accurate he was, but he no longer got prophetic words that called out people's hearts, their history, or their future. It was nothing but data.

I asked him not to minister for a while. Of course, he didn't understand or agree. Our church leaders had already asked him several times to step down. He would always just promise he would be okay, and that he would do better. We all wanted to simply believe him, and none of us knew what to do.

We continued to host big conferences at the church. I knew this was a mandate the Lord had given Global Fire

Ministries. Thousands of people throughout the years had come to our conferences and received high levels of impartation that they could now take back to their homes, churches, regions and to the nations.

My leadership team and I prayed a lot, and we trusted the Lord, since He is ultimately in charge. I know that this seems impossible, given the circumstances, but, the glory of God would always be present in our church and conferences.

We had powerful ministry time, despite Jeff. The ministers who came to minister at our events were those in relationship with Jeff and myself. He had many ministry friends and acquaintances that he had met over the years. He knew them well and they thought they knew him.

A few times a minister would ask me if Jeff was okay and state he was different. More and more people commented that they just sensed something not the same about Jeff. Jeffrey was very blatant and was not good at hiding his intentions.

Jeff was increasingly realizing he was not himself. The moments when he would wake up in the morning and look at me with the eyes I once grew to love, and beg me for help were becoming few and far between.

Wake-up Call

I remember one morning he aggressively grabbed my arms and pleaded, "Jan, something has taken me over. I can't even remember what I am doing half the time. I want to quit. I don't want to minister any more. Please, please help me! I don't know what's happening to me! It's like I can't control anything about me anymore. I'm afraid I'm going to die."

He would cry, and beg me over and over to move to a farm somewhere. I am not sure what there was about a farm that enticed him, but then, as he would continue, he would admit stepping down from ministry was complicated.

As soon as he got up from bed after pleading with me, like clockwork, he quickly shifted, as he jumped into the activity of the day. Honestly, any stress, particularly with demanding phone calls, confrontations, or just simple decisions, seemed to trigger this shift. If we just went about our day, went out to lunch, and tried to have fun with the family, he was more able to relax and stay normal.

I was still believing that either a miracle would occur, or the Lord would release me from this marriage and somehow save my church. At times I was hopeful. At times I had given up.

I tried to talk to Jeff about a plan. I tried to reason with him when he was the real Jeff. What could we do? We could send him to rehab. Where could he get help? An alcohol rehab center would not know how to deal with parts or alters.

We had tried numerous things and he admitted nothing had really helped on a deep level. Going to HeartSync had done little. I believe they are a very effective ministry, but he simply would not submit. He also refused to completely trust our church deliverance team. He was guarded. Jeffrey would not allow total submission, as he feared being eliminated.

Jeff had now begun to acknowledge Jeffrey by name. He said that he, Jeff, could not stop Jeffrey from manifesting. He talked about Jeffrey like he was a completely different person, not part of his own personality, as if he was perhaps a cousin or a brother. He told me Jeffrey had taken control.

I wasn't even sure what this meant. He was obviously clueless as to what had caused this. In processing this himself, he finally told me he thought Jeffrey first appeared when he was a teenager feeling that he was being abused. He referred to his father's strict discipline. He added that Jeffrey had to be meaner than his father was.

Although this was a remarkable revelation, I did not have a solution. I told Jeff over and over that he would have to come forward and confess his condition, and step back from all forms of ministry. But if he was too proud to submit to other leaders to get healing, how could he admit to the world that he was failing and needed help?

The real Jeff was open to this, but anxious about it. Jeffrey wouldn't hear of it. He was on a mission. He had something to prove. The more Jeff wanted to quit, Jeffrey pushed Jeff that much harder. I recalled conversations throughout our marriage where Jeff would tell me he often felt like a failure when he was younger, especially in his teen years. He even mentioned someone telling him that he would never amount to anything. Perhaps this is why Jeffrey felt he had something to prove.

Almost as soon as I would suggest to him that he had to publicly choose to step down, Jeffrey would immediately come to the surface.

I could tell when Jeff switched to Jeffrey. His eyes would twitch, and his personality would immediately change. Jeffrey would tell me he had no idea what I was talking about and stepping down was out of the question. This could be five minutes after Jeff begged me for help, or hours later.

He repeatedly mentioned memory lapses to me and that he was not remembering things. I was starting to notice this was becoming more and more frequent.

One example was when we noticed a leak in our kitchen ceiling, and had to get a man to come repair it. Jeff was there the whole time, watching and completely involved with the process.

A couple of months later, the sheetrock began to peel again in that same spot, and I asked him what I should do. He had no memory whatsoever of it ever leaking or being patched. He acted as if I was crazy and losing my mind.

I was getting used to this astonished look he would get when he realized something was deeply wrong. I often said that I felt that I was living inside an insane asylum. In addition to his bizarre symptoms, he continuously blamed me, trying to make me feel like I was the problem. Gaslighting, at its finest.

I would spend countless hours praying, crying out to God, begging Him to release me from this prison! Oftentimes, feeling complete defeat, I would accept that there may be no hope, and I would beg for the Lord to say, "You are released. Take the children. I will save your church and its people."

Nothing about any of this was simple. The death of a marriage, the death of a church, and even Jeff fearing the literal outcome of what God had warned him of, regarding his own death was just overwhelming!

I wanted all of this to be a nightmare. I wanted to wake up! I wanted to go back to the happily-ever-after beginning.

Of course, I prayed for Jeff to recover. I continued to press him to get help. Jeff was very willing, even desperate, until Jeffrey found more important things for him to do.

Up to this time, I had not heard from the Lord about what was to come. In fact, sometimes I felt like I heard very little, in relation to the time I spent pleading with Him, literally crying so hard I felt my insides would explode.

A few times I even collapsed on the floor in front of my children, weeping uncontrollably. They knew why I was crying, yet they didn't know. It was a little of both. How much could children really understand? I had tried to protect them, but I couldn't protect them from what Jeff was exposing them to. He was robbing them of a feeling of safety and stability that all children should be guaranteed, by parents who love them.

A few days after we talked about the sheetrock, I heard a loud shout from the kitchen and ran in to see what was wrong.

"Jan! Come quick!"

Jeff was standing by the microwave. He looked frozen, as if he couldn't speak. All he said was, "Jan, you have to get me help! Take me somewhere. Please help me!"

Apparently, he had put his phone in the microwave and cooked it. He pulled it out of the microwave, still smoking. I couldn't keep from laughing and told him that could happen to any of us, if we got too distracted. He had stuck his phone in the microwave, instead of his coffee.

"No, Jan, this is serious." He looked very worried. It was apparent he had been processing the changes in himself more than he spoke of it. This was a wake-up call of sorts to him.

I wasn't sure what else to say or do. Jeff wanted help when he was Jeff, but Jeff never stayed in place for long, and we never knew when the switch would take place.

As much as I tried to create fun, memorable family time to keep him relaxed, and as much as I overcompensated to take on managing our home life and church, eventually anything he perceived as pressure, exhaustion, and stress would always cause a flip. Sometimes it would just happen out of nowhere, for no apparent reason. Normal, mild, daily stress that all of us face, would seem to push him over the edge, and it was getting worse.

A perfect example of this was going to a church family's house for a meal one afternoon. This was the men's leader he was so fond of. They were buddies and they just loved to laugh and hang out together.

Jeff and Mercy got into a minor squabble in the van, which was really no big deal, and happens in every family. I warned them both that they needed to let it go, as arguing wasn't solving anything. Jeff became more and more agitated. I knew what was coming. Mercy was particularly resistant to her dad and had been for a while now.

I looked at him and saw his eyeballs twitching.

"Calm down Jeff. It's not worth it," I urged. I often tried to prevent the shift.

It was too late. Suddenly, he became very aggressive. Out of nowhere, he began verbally attacking me and my daughter, Mercy, for no real reason. He told her that she should have stayed in China, as that was where she belonged, "with all the other rejects".

My heart ached for my daughter as she began to cry. I continued to try to calm him down, but you couldn't calm or quiet Jeffrey. He loved hurting and humiliating us.

As we reached our destination, I advised him to stay in the car until he calmed down. Instead, he jumped out of our car, began ranting and raving loudly in front of all the church people who were gathered there.

His language was atrocious, and he began yelling out accusations against me and my daughter that were completely false and embarrassing. He yelled out to a number of our church family who were standing in the yard that I was a drunk.

"Jan is a drunk!" he shouted.

I was undone! Why did he even say this?

I was so humiliated, I just left him there, took my kids, and drove off in disbelief that he had behaved this way in front of church members.

My daughter was heartbroken, and was crying hysterically. "Mom, I can't take this any more," she said through her tears.

Rejection is often harder for an adopted child. For him to say she should have stayed in China with all the other rejects was an arrow in her heart.

"Me either, honey. Me either. God is going to have to rescue us." I didn't know what else to say. I feared the kids were beginning to blame me for not just leaving.

I had to do damage control with Mercy all afternoon. I had tried to protect our family and our church family, but he was beginning to expose himself, and I couldn't cover for him.

I messaged the people who had invited us to their home, and told them I was sorry. They just blew it off as if it was nothing, but I knew they were very puzzled at his behavior. I believed they thought we had just had a minor disagreement, but they had no idea of the magnitude of our reality.

I began seriously wondering how much of a toll Jeff's unpredictable behavior was really taking on the emotional and mental health of my children, the church, and me. Most of the time my children tried to act like it all was okay. I did my best to make sure that they were safe and had as much of a normal childhood as possible.

I was also deeply concerned about what dark spirits were being brought into my home with the media he watched and the choices he made. Again, I cried out to God daily. There was no apparent answer. I knew the Lord loved me, loved all of us, even Jeff but at times I felt that He had forgotten me. I wondered how He could seem to continue to favor Jeff, when he lived in total sin much of the time.

I had removed Netflix, Amazon Prime and every other movie channel that came into our home. But he would just order them again and at one point we had four Netflix accounts.

I would sit him down like I was his mother and ask him why on Earth he wanted to watch filth. I felt like I was truly dealing with a teenage boy, and I was, since an alter frequently acts the age that the core person was, when it was created.

I found different movies on his computer that were beyond anything I thought he would ever watch in a million years. There was a lot of cursing and violent content. Some had illicit sexual content. When I confronted him, he denied it all and said it was my imagination, even though I showed him proof of what I had found.

He would then say that he was just scrolling over the Internet, and something would pop up and he watched it until he realized it was bad, then he turned it off.

I was confused and humiliated. I felt completely betrayed. What wife wants to acknowledge that her husband is watching other women in seductive situations, even if it is on a screen?

"Jan, I swear, that was not me! It was not me! I would never do that," he would say. He could be very convincing, and in a sense, it wasn't Jeff who was doing this. Much of what he did, he couldn't recall later on. It was Jeffrey.

At this point, he seemed to realize that there was another part of him who obviously would do these things. He even began to acknowledge more and more that Jeffrey was taking him over. He called himself Jeffrey a lot, now. He knew. I think this realization grew steadily. As the real Jeff became weaker and less able to manage stress, Jeffrey felt he had to save Jeff, and finally just took over.

To the best I could assume, based on my own research and observation, Jeffy Boy had been a part or alternate personality that was created to protect young Jeff from some sort of early childhood trauma. I asked him what happened in his early childhood. He had no idea. He only recalled happy adventures with his parents and siblings.

Jeffrey was the alter who was created when he was a teenager, mean enough to protect him from his father. Now that Jeff was acknowledging Jeffrey as reality, the horror story had begun to intensify.

As previously stated, trauma and abuse are subjective and in the eyes of the beholder, and to the one experiencing it. What is abuse to one, would not affect another. Just because Jeff perceived his father to be abusive doesn't mean he was.

Jeffrey was a fracture of Jeff's soul that helped him cope with what he perceived as abuse. Jeffrey was exactly what Jeff had to become to survive, and it was Jeffrey's responsibility to protect Jeff.

Jeffrey wasn't able to conceive that he was doing anything wrong. When he was in control, there was nothing to talk about. I couldn't reason with Jeffrey.

Jeffrey had a particular disdain for me and my daughter Mercy, but was always playful and acted like a child around my two younger children. Perhaps this was Jeffy Boy being playful and childlike. Jeff never acknowledged to me that he knew that Jeffy Boy was there.

In other words, he called his alter ego Jeffrey, but never called himself Jeffy Boy. He just knew Jeffy Boy was identified in some of his healing sessions.

Jeffrey seemed to hate everything pure and holy. He could pretend well, but his pretending was just that, with no sincerity. He seemed intent on destroying the Jeff I knew. This just didn't make sense to me at the time.

I began to fear that I could not leave my children alone with him. One day, I walked in and Jeff was literally lying on top of Given, and it was obvious that Given could barely breathe. Jeff was laughing and acting as if he were a five-year-old, playing with a friend. He didn't realize this was not normal dad behavior.

"Mom, please make Dad get off me! He is hurting me!" Given said in tears.

Jeff would laugh and tell Given to "man up".

I told him, "It's okay to play with your little boy, but you don't seem to know when to stop. You're frightening your son."

I knew he truly was just trying to play with his son, but he had no balance.

He really didn't get it. These episodes also became more frequent, indicating that his personality fracturing had many facets. All this madness was taking a toll on me.

I sought wise counsel myself with Christian therapists and I even saw a couple of HeartSync ministers, as well. The conclusion was always that I could not control another person's behavior or struggles, and the main priority was to keep my children and myself safe. Most of those from whom I sought counsel would tell me to leave him. Simple as that.

It was not that simple. It was not simple at all.

He had those who believed in him and trusted him, all over the world. We had church members who trusted both of us. I couldn't simply just file for divorce and leave.

I knew if I did that, I would ultimately be blamed by Jeffrey, and he would just continue doing what he was doing, behind closed doors.

The bigger factor was that although I had begged God to release me, He simply had not, at this point.

I had seen other pastors literally live in sin and when it all fell apart and their wives could take no more, the man would blame the wife who left, saying, "She abandoned me, for no reason." I knew Jeffrey would do this if I just left. The real truth may not ever surface.

Desperate for some explanation, I finally scheduled an appointment with a psychiatrist, just to ask questions.

"Doctor, I am not here for myself, I am actually here to try and identify what is wrong with my husband."

"Go on," she said, not knowing where I was going.

"He is more than one person. He even admits this, and calls himself different names. The best I can tell, this is called dissociative identity disorder," I explained.

The Psychiatrist told me this was very rare in the medical world, and she seriously doubted this was what was wrong with Jeff. She described paranoid schizophrenia and said this was much more common than D.I.D.

In having a deliverance ministry, we found that although most everyone has parts, or fractures, of the soul on a minor level, they typically do not manifest in a harmful way.

We didn't label people with a diagnosis, we saw it more as a spiritual affliction than a physical or medical one. This may explain why the medical community isn't aware of how common it is. Medical science frequently dismisses and ignores spiritual realities.

Knowing and treating people who were SRA (satanic ritualistic abuse) survivors, and a few with severe dissociative identity disorder over the years, helped me to arrive at my conclusions.

There was a woman who used to contact me for ministry who did not hesitate to tell me about her seven or more personalities, their names and their characteristics.

Many of the people who have parts actually love their parts, and come to know them as their brother, sister, or friend. In fact, they would rather keep their parts just as they are, even knowing some of their parts are even evil, because that is the only security they know.

Another woman who was obviously D.I.D. came for prayer and freedom and told me that she didn't want her demons to leave because they were her "best friends". She even named them. She called one Pan.

Perhaps Jeff didn't really want Jeffrey to integrate. Jeffrey was seemingly the strong one who would carry Jeff in his weakness. Jeffrey knew much was expected of Jeff in the life and calling he was walking in, and Jeffrey stepped up to fulfill what Jeff could not.

Jeff seemed to need someone to carry him because he could no longer cope and represent himself well. His pride, or just fear, was preventing him from stepping away from the ministry and doing whatever it took to be whole.

This was all totally consuming to me. Normalcy was a distant dream. I had to continue to be a home school mom, a pastor, a daughter, and a friend. I often just had to leave the house and go for long drives to cry out to God to give me the strength to endure!

"Show me what to do, God!" I would plead from the depths of my soul, and cry out so loudly I feared someone from outside the car would hear me.

I even wondered if the neighbors wondered who this lady was, who was crying and driving up and down the streets again and again.

Chapter Fifteen

MORE REVELATION

Under The Influence

We both began feeling we were to move again. I hated moving, but I could discern God's hand in it. I suspected the Lord might be moving me to prepare me for life without Jeff.

Jeff always wanted to live in a house that had woods behind it, or at least a view of land. This seemed to bring him peace in some way. I was hoping he wouldn't be as isolated in this next house. I wanted to downsize, realizing I could end up on my own soon.

We found a house we both liked, that was surrounded by woods and trees. He seemed rejuvenated at having the opportunity to just go for walks with nature. I saw another brief glimpse of hope. Working in the woods was good therapy for him in the past. Maybe he could find healing and at least not desire to drink all the time.

This house also did not have a separate office he could isolate in. I talked to him often about this. He felt it would help him, overall. I agreed.

We were both devastated when the house deal fell through literally at the closing table, through no fault of our own. It seemed that the mortgage company had made some serious mistakes with numbers.

With nowhere to go, we were forced to find temporary housing until the situation could be worked out. We tried to look at things on the bright side. Maybe God didn't want us to have that house and another would come.

We had three children, two large parrots, and cats, so a hotel or an apartment wasn't an option.

Jeff's friend, the men's leader, said that his grown daughter had a house she was trying to sell, and we could possibly stay there until we found another suitable house to purchase. We called that house the "creepy" house because something just didn't feel right about it. I was praying it would be very temporary, but we were thankful to have somewhere to stay. Perhaps it was just the season we were in. Our lives felt rather "creepy" at times. We were thankful, no matter what.

We put three blow-up air mattresses on the floor of the master suite, and the kids and I all slept in there, as they were all afraid to sleep in the other bedrooms.

Jeff continued to book ministry dates, even internationally, and all I could do was send someone with him. In his absence, he didn't seem a bit concerned that we were there alone and that we felt unprotected.

To add to existing tension during this time, he got a second offense DUI on his record. Since it had been ten years since his first, the courts lowered it to a first offense, and he served twenty-one days in a half-way house.

He had come home from a late-night flight and rented a car to get home. When he never came home, I feared the worst. Apparently, he had gone straight from the airport to meet one of his sons at a Buffalo Wild Wings to watch a football game.

I don't know what happened after he left, but he was seen slumped over behind the wheel of his rental car in a convenience store parking lot. The officer tried to wake him, and he became belligerent and violent with the officer. He failed his sobriety test and had a pretty high blood alcohol level so of course, he was arrested for DUI.

He didn't call me until the next day, and I was very upset that I knew he had flown in the night before and not come home. I was worried something horrible had happened to him. He told me he was in jail on a DUI and please come get him. I was tempted to leave him there, but that wasn't an option. My grace for his bad decisions had worn very thin.

When I picked him up and got him released this time, he still reeked of alcohol, was unshaven and disheveled.

He was not apologetic at all this time. He was angry, swearing, and totally Jeffrey. I took him to a hotel where he could dry out for a few days.

I felt like I didn't care if he ever came home. But here we were, no real home, having to stay in a temporary place, and not knowing what to expect from one minute to another.

After he dried out in a hotel for a couple of days, he begged to come home. As usual, he promised the moon and stars and swore that this time, the DUI had been another serious wake-up call for him.

This temporary place we had landed in was in the same small town Jeff and I had lived in for the first ten happy years of our marriage. We tried to find good times with the kids. Jeff seemed to need some fond, peaceful memories. We took the kids to some of the places we had gone early in our marriage. We shared our humble beginning with the kids, which seemed to bring security to them, following such uncertainty.

I didn't even ask Jeff not to travel any more. I had resigned myself to the fact that he would ultimately do whatever he wanted, anyway. He informed me he planned yet another trip to Australia, and I didn't even care this time.

I invited my best friend Mary to come and visit and I looked forward to catching up with her. My children loved her, and she was their godmother. We welcomed a few days of joy and laughter. While she was with us, we got a babysitter for Truth and Given, and Mary, Mercy and I went to a theater performance in Nashville. This was a first for all of us and so refreshing just to enjoy ourselves without worry. We had a great time with Mary while she was with us.

After Mary went back home, the kids and I just tried to make the best of it. We found fun things to do and stayed busy. It was nice not being in a house where not everything reminded me of something bad Jeff had done. There was even a total eclipse of the sun during this time.

God had always been faithful to speak to me. He had been, since I was born again. He had spoken to me often, and in many ways, as He does to His children.

He spoke to me in dreams, visions, and signs. But the audible voice of God came as well.

While Jeff was in Australia, I was sitting on my blow-up mattress in the rental house, and from nowhere, I clearly heard the voice of God in my spirit say, "Pick up Jeff's iPad". Jeff had left a computer tablet behind.

I questioned if I'd really heard it, and immediately, the voice again repeated, "Pick up Jeff's iPad."

Obediently, I did as I was asked, and reluctantly turned it on, not sure what I would find. I reasonably feared another "Oh, no!" moment.

The voice of God distinctly said, "Go into his Facebook messenger." It was as if the Lord Himself was standing beside me, directing me.

I was still not registered on Facebook myself, at the time, but was able to log into Jeff's Facebook account and found his messenger and clicked it open.

The Lord said, "Click on the name Everett". Who was Everett? I didn't know any Everett. Jeff had never mentioned anyone named Everett. Surprisingly, I actually found the name "Everett", clicked on it, and held my breath.

It was a conversation Jeff had with Emma, from Australia, the woman he swore he would never speak to again. He had changed the name so I could not track it.

The conversation went something like this:

Jeff: "I am coming back to Australia and need to see you. I have missed you so much and just need some closure. I know you may not want to see me, but would you please meet with me? I really need to look into your eyes again."

Emma: "I had to go to my new pastor about you after I was asked to leave my old church. I've been in counseling. I don't ever want to see you again."

Jeff: "Well, f*** you then. I'm not asking for anything but a meeting and just to talk."

Emma: "Jeff, are you drunk again? Why can't you just move on?"

You get the picture. After much dialog, she finally agreed to meet with him.

I was determined to file for divorce and to pray that Lord would just cover the whole thing in a miraculous way.

I called my former Pastor, Jerry, for prayer and advice. He was the only true pastor I ever had. I often reached out to him. He said I was justified in leaving. He connected me with another man who ministers to pastors.

I met with this man a few days later, and this minister told me the same thing. Nobody should tolerate abuse and infidelity.

My response was always that I didn't want to hurt my church family. I loved them and they would be extremely disappointed. I almost felt like a martyr for the cause.

We prayed and asked the Lord to please intervene supernaturally. I felt hopeless and powerless. Nobody seemed to understand why it was so hard for me to leave. Deep in my spirit, I didn't feel the release to leave.

Of course, when we feel this way, we must realize God is not oblivious to anything. He has a plan even though we can't always see it. I could hear His voice so clearly, but honestly, I didn't know what to do next.

The next time Jeff called me from Australia, I told him the Lord had shown me his messages with Emma. He denied everything, saying he just needed closure with her. Closure? Why would you need closure with someone you deny ever being intimate with, in the first place?

I had a lot to process between then and when he was to return home. When he got back to town, I wouldn't let him come back to the house we were staying in. This time it was Jeff who was in the hotel. At least it wasn't me and the kids.

He begged to speak to me, as he had so often done before. He asked me to please come to his hotel room.

After several days and repeated begging from him, I went, but I was absolute in my decision to end it. At least, I felt that way at the moment.

He submitted to go into rehab, or do anything he needed to do. He promised me there was nothing with Emma.

I didn't believe him and part of me was getting to the place where I was just numb.

Interestingly, he had still never initiated any form of help, counsel, or intervention on his own to this point. It was always me who sought out help and took him to it. I think he could see I was just done, and despite all he had wrestled with, I didn't think he wanted our ministry, marriage and church to end.

At his urging, I began researching alcohol rehabilitation centers. I presented the choices to him. He wasn't convinced an alcohol rehab center was the answer, and neither was I.

I told him I saw no other options, as he had not been able to pull it together. I reminded him of all the times he had admitted to his condition. The real Jeff always realized the truth and the need to change. Jeffrey laughed in the face of the risks he posed to his family, his church and the ministry.

I wanted him to go into rehab immediately. He was willing when talking to me in his hotel room. At least if we eliminated the alcohol factor, perhaps it might solve much of the problem, then perhaps we could get to the root of it all.

I was content with him continuing to stay in a hotel until we got him into rehab. He said he missed me and the kids. After a couple of weeks, I let him come back to the house we were staying in, based only on his willingness to get treatment. Of course after he got back home with us, he hit another reset button and just kept booking travel and making excuses not to go to a rehab facility.

He was not drinking in front of us now, so perhaps he really was awakened by the second offense DUI.

Contrary to that, what transpired next was proof to me that Jeff had no control at this point.

Jeff had traveled somewhere for a conference. He was booked to fly home early on a Sunday morning, so that he could attend our church. He booked a ride-share from the airport and came straight to church.

He reeked of alcohol, and everyone knew it. He was unshaven and looked awful. His behavior indicated he was still a little inebriated. I feared people would smell the alcohol and that others might notice.

Nobody said anything at that time, but later many admitted they knew he had been drinking. Of course I had to once again act like the perfect pastor and pretend nothing was wrong. I can assure you, we had a serious talk when we got home. He admitted to drinking the night before. He took no responsibility for what just happened at the church.

"Jeff, it's bad enough that you live a double life a lot of the time, but to even consider showing up at our church and mingling with people who look up to us, reeking of alcohol and looking like you just walked out of a bar, is shocking to me!" I had raised my voice. I didn't remember ever being this angry.

He didn't want to admit any wrong-doing and just went to his office and shut the door. I had come to realize confrontation got me nowhere, except even more frustrated.

Only a few days after that incident, my children and I came home from being out all day, walked in the back door and found him drinking and demonstrating an abusive nature. I could expect this at night, but this was early afternoon.

Furious and exhausted by it all, and unwilling to be forced to leave and drag my children somewhere, I asked him to leave. In fact, I demanded that he leave.

"These children and I have had enough!"

He knew that I meant it.

During our confrontation, little Given walked up to his father, feeling helpless, I guess.

Jeff lost his temper.

Why? Because my son was just being a normal little boy? Jeff obviously thought he was too loud, and he smacked little Given on his bare belly and left a bright red handprint.

Given wailed, and both of my girls ran into the room to see what had just happened. They lashed out at their dad this time, for being so harsh with Given. Given clung to me, unsure why his dad was even angry with him. We were all just done.

Feeling no remorse at all, he called his oldest daughter to come and get him and I told him as he walked out, "You know we have a worship night at church tonight and in no way will you be there!"

Nothing surprised me any more, but knowing he was drunk earlier in the day, I couldn't believe he actually showed up at our worship night. I didn't go, because I was just too rattled with what had transpired earlier in the day.

I was told the next day what happened.

He showed up smelling like alcohol and walked into our green room. His daughter and her boyfriend were with him, when he came to church.

One of the worship team members asked him if he was drinking. He actually showed them a small liquor bottle and said, "Watch this."

He proceeded to arrogantly march into the sanctuary and hug and greet several people, then came back into the green room. There were only a few people in there, thank God.

To this day I cannot even imagine what the people who witnessed this thought. Someone asked him, "How can you drink and be around people and they don't smell the alcohol?"

"I simply turn my head the other way and use lots of mouthwash." He cocked his head and seemed proud of his response. Jeffrey had no conscience or remorse.

A revelation came to me. In the recent years of ministry, when my kids and I weren't traveling with Jeff, I would often pick him up at the airport. He always smelled strongly of peppermint, which I rarely smelled on him at home. Apparently, he would drink on the plane, then cover it up with peppermint oil and lots of mouthwash.

In some of his humble moments, he admitted that all the times that he told me that his flights were missed due to airline errors, it was because he was drunk and passed out in the Admiral's Club and missed his flight. He even admitted he had been kicked off several flights because he was drunk and was rude to airline staff members.

There was another occasion in which he had been at our church all day one Wednesday, dealing with some pretty stressful issues involving another minister he had a disagreement with.

I did some work and when I was finished, I told Jeff that it was time to go.

He was still unable to drive, so I became taxi driver on top of everything else. He refused to leave, saying he had things to take care of, and said he would just stay there until church. I took the kids and went back home, intending to return later.

It seems that he and this other minister, not a church or staff member, were having words with each other on the phone that day. When I showed up for church that evening, Jeffrey was in full form. He smelled like he had been drinking and had put on a lot of other scents to cover it up.

When I confronted him, he told me to stay out of his business, then literally stormed out of the room and stepped up on the stage to "minister". He put on quite a show. Although everyone in attendance knew something was really not right, no one would have imagined the truth. I literally could not believe he had the audacity to step into the pulpit drinking.

How was he able to drink while at church? I thought this would always be a safe place for him. Later I did find beer cans in his office. He must have taken them to church with him and hidden them in his bag.

I immediately called all of my church leaders into a serious meeting the next day.

"This has gone to a new level. I don't think he is coping at all anymore and he is drinking more and more. He has even shown up at the church drinking three times, that I know of. A few people from other churches have contacted me to say he has ministered at their churches appearing drunk and his behavior was not normal.

"We have to do something. I am at my wits' end." I hung my head in shame.

I had also recently gone privately to two of our pastors, who were also close personal friends of ours, and told them how serious this had become. I told them that I was afraid, and was even afraid to go to sleep at night, fearing what he could potentially be capable of.

"Michael and Trina, will you please come and get all of his guns and knives?" I petitioned our associate pastors.

Michael came to the house when Jeff was gone and took possession of his gun and knife collection and kept them with him when Jeff was traveling. Of course Jeff was livid, but I told him I no longer felt that the kids and I were safe. Jeffrey had actually threatened to kill me before in a drunken rage. I knew it wasn't Jeff, but due to his severe behavior when he was drinking, I felt frightened.

Since the first offense DUI, Jeff had randomly continued seeing the drug and alcohol counselor. These sessions had no effect on Jeff at all. He just seemed to think he was above the law, so to speak.

REALITY SETS IN

Watching It Unravel

Somehow, we worked through the events that occurred at the temporary house, the discovery of his continued relationship with the woman in Australia, and his second offense DUI. He apologized profusely and made many, many promises.

I can't explain why I continued to forgive him time after time. Sometimes I asked myself what someone else would have done if they had to walk in my shoes. I just wanted my best friend back. I wanted to go back to our early marriage when we were inseparable and there was deep love and total trust.

We stayed in the temporary home we so affectionately called the "creepy" house for about two months in the summer of 2017. The kids and I were thankful to have a place to stay, any port in a storm so to speak, but there was so much negativity during those two summer months.

After looking, and looking, I found a great house while driving through a neighborhood called the Reserve. It was a new build. It looked like a nice neighborhood for a family. There was even a community pool. Jeff's office would still be upstairs, which I was not happy about. I compromised, because I just wanted to be in my own home.

I was surprised I was even willing to buy another house with him. I was such a believer in miracles, I just felt like somehow, breakthrough had to be coming. God couldn't have forgotten all the prayers I had prayed.

I was hoping for a new start with a new house, but things continued to get progressively worse. So many times, I think I agreed to move to a new house, just hoping a change in environment would bring a change in Jeff. Sadly, nothing changed for the better.

I continued to have travel partners go with Jeff when he traveled. He had come to accept it. The man who had been traveling with him sat beside me one day in my driveway and cried his eyes out.

"I just can't do anything to help him. I love Jeff, but he is out of control".

"Why haven't you told me this before now?" I asked him.

He admitted, "I thought I could help, but it's obvious that I can't. And I didn't want him mad at me for telling you."

I told him I had pretty much demanded Jeff to come off the road and the church had asked the same. We were using our associate pastors to preach most of the time, for fear of what Jeff would say or do. I would also preach, from time to time.

If I didn't agree to book his flights and travel, he would do it behind my back and just walk out of the door with his suitcase. I refused to pick him up at the airport anymore because he was almost always drinking, and I couldn't handle the tension, so he got a ride or called Uber or Lyft. I would cry for days before he was to come home, dreading what we may encounter. I lived in constant anxiety.

I had found alcohol treatment centers who would take him, but he never really followed through with going. They all told me that he was the one who had to initiate treatment, not a family member. He did agree to interview with a couple of them, but this had not yet happened. One minute, he would agree to go to rehab. This was always after a bad binge. Other times, he seemed to literally give in to things the way they were and had no intention of changing. At the risk of sounding cliché, he had a devil-may-care attitude.

He was refusing any spiritual care or counseling at this time. He basically just did whatever he wanted, and the kids and I did whatever it took to stay safe. Progressively, I was seeing the toll this was taking on my children and me. Why wouldn't God just speak to me and tell me what to do?

The intensity of his behavior had become slowly but increasingly worse since his initial breakdown in the floor, years ago. This had been a period of about four years.

Mercy was literally terrified of him and wouldn't let him anywhere near her. I understood her being afraid of an abusive drunk, but this seemed to be even more than that. I reasoned that Jeffrey did target her, as well as me. He was particularly cruel to her, although she was so angelic. There was no natural reason for his aggression towards her. Most people would have considered her a perfect child.

She was now almost a teenager and struggling with the normal challenges that brings, which is enough in itself, without all the excessive challenges we were subjected to.

Jeff adored Mercy, but I had not yet figured out why Jeffrey had such disdain for such a precious child. I often wondered if he was jealous of her.

Truth seemed to be able to pretend nothing was wrong. She was quite close to Jeff, which greatly concerned me at times. Given was showing obvious signs of inner turmoil, such as unrealistic fear of the dark and other exaggerated fears. He absolutely refused to sleep in his room.

My biggest fear, even greater than not wanting to hurt people who believed in him and the ministry, was that if I filed for divorce, he would get visitation rights to the children and have them alone, without me there. I couldn't stand the thought of that and would cry out and beg God to help me.

I saw what Jeff did with me around. What would he do if I wasn't around? I stayed, because it seemed I at least had some control of the situation. Even if I couldn't control him, at least I could protect my children by being there when he was around. If we needed to flee, we would flee.

What would happen if he was the sole guardian of the children, even for a weekend? I had decided a while back that the children were not safe alone with him. Now I was horrified!

Not every day was bad. It never had been. There were periods he seemed to be under more pressure than usual, or exhausted from travel, and he would drink more frequently.

He hid it from us. Sometimes it was obvious, other times not as much. We had days of normalcy when we would just live life. I tried desperately to find a thread to hang onto.

Although there were times when I would breathe and feel like he was doing well, almost like clockwork, every two months, he would drink too much for no reason apparent to us, and we would have to go to a hotel, or force him into one, or even just sleep at the church. I think when we slept at the church, we felt close to God, if that makes any sense at all.

To match what he had done in the Dominican Republic, Mercy and I had gone out grocery shopping one day and left Truth and Given alone with him. We thought since it was early in the day, and most of his drinking was in the afternoon or evening, perhaps he could stay straight.

He was sober when we left, and he promised me all would be well, so we prayed it would be okay. When Jeff promised, he did it with passion, and would say, "Jan, I want this as bad as you do. Please trust me!" He could be very convincing. He was the love of my life and I so wanted to believe him.

When we arrived home from shopping, he met us at the door and was probably in the worst shape that I had seen him since the Dominican vacation. He acted like a literal demon had taken possession of him.

I couldn't reason with him at all, and he wouldn't let me in to even see my two youngest children, let alone get them to safety. When I tried to get in the door, he would threaten to hurt me, and slam the door.

I called the police, and they came quickly. I was so embarrassed at what my neighbors might think, but I was terrified! Mercy and I sat in the van and the two police officers went to the front door. Mercy and I prayed, and waited. I cried, and I was concerned for the safety of Truth and Given.

When the police came back to our car, one officer said that Jeff told them I was the one who had been drinking. Of course, they knew that was not the truth, and so did Mercy.

The exact words of one of the officers was, "He is the meanest S.O.B. I have ever run across. We can't force ourselves into your home, since he has a right to be drunk in his own house. He is obviously very drunk, and not safe to be around."

I became frantic and reiterated that he had my younger children held captive in my own home. The officer said that Jeff showed them a video of the children, and they were asleep. They suggested I take Mercy and get a hotel as there was nothing else they, or I, could do.

Words cannot express the apprehension that I felt as I had to drive away and leave my innocent and vulnerable children, a nine-year-old and a five-year-old, in the hands of a drunken and aggressive madman.

I got no sleep that night in the hotel but reassured Mercy that all would be well, although I wasn't convinced it would be. I had to put my total faith in Almighty God. I prayed all night, and, weary the next morning, I called Jeff.

"Well, you did it again Jeff. Does it ever end?"

He remembered nothing and asked where Mercy and I were. He had no memory of anything that had happened. He was actually quite worried that he didn't know where we were.

Thank God, Truth and Given were fine and had no idea what had transpired.

"This madness has to end, Jeff!" I cried out to him.

I gave Jeff an ultimatum. He cried, and told me he knew things were spiraling out of control, but he didn't have the power to change what was happening.

For a brief moment, although he didn't seem capable of realizing how frustrated as I truly was, he could see the toll this had taken on the family, and on me. I told him I was ready to walk away from it all so the kids and I would have a chance of having a happy life.

I required several more meetings with church leaders about his declining condition. He always asked that we all give him one more chance. I am not even sure why we granted it. He promised he would not minister at all anymore and would focus on himself and getting healing.

We, as children of God, always want to believe for the best. I did still love the man I had fallen in love with and married, even though I rarely, if ever, saw that man.

Although he kept his word about stepping out of our church pulpit, he continued to travel. As I said, I no longer booked his airfare, so he would book it himself, and just go anyway.

It was really hard to understand how the core man just wanted to quit, but there was this driving force that didn't care what damage was caused to Jeff, his family, his church and our international ministry. Jeffrey almost seemed willing to destroy everyone and everything. I couldn't understand how someone's alters could think they were helping the person, but were destroying them, in order to do so.

More and more people he came in contact with were contacting me about his irrational behavior.

The Lord spoke to me again and said, "Sell the house." We had only been there for two years. It seemed much longer than two years. We had moved several times since we married. Jeff said he was not moving again.

I told him, "Well, perhaps it is time for us to talk about what it would look like to get a divorce. I know it is complicated, but I am at my wits' end."

He would always end up in tears, begging me to give him another chance. He was completely torn inside. On one hand, he did not want to lose everything, but on the other hand, he seemed to have lost interest in his home and family much of the time, anyway.

God had orchestrated all of our moves and He must have a good reason to move us again. I felt more confident that it was to secure my future and that of my kids, possibly without Jeff. I insisted to him that we must listen to the word of the Lord and put the house on the market. I wouldn't take no for an answer.

Jeff finally agreed. He knew if he didn't, I was ready to move on without him and just accept whatever consequences came from that decision.

This time it took only six days to get a contract on our house. The Lord told me the exact day the buyers were coming and again told me to clean the house that day. The people who viewed the house that day were the buyers. God is faithful.

I still wanted to downsize because in my heart of hearts I just knew Jeff would not be around long after we moved. I wanted a much smaller, and much more affordable house. Jeffrey had always demanded the best of the best. Jeff's humble beginnings were consumed by Jeffrey's arrogance.

In searching, I found a house online that was my dream house. It was not exactly affordable, but was everything I ever wanted. I was more curious than anything, and didn't want to pursue buying this house, but just enjoyed seeing it. Oddly, it brought me peace somehow. I couldn't explain it.

One day when he seemed to be normal Jeff, I told him I just wanted to see the house out of curiosity. He insisted on going with me. We had always loved looking at model homes and open houses.

I said, "Jeff, I don't want to buy a big house, we need to downsize, but I just want you to see what we could have, if only you would try. Maybe we could still have the fairy tale." I had hoped somehow that if he saw this beautiful house, it would inspire something in him, I guess.

Jeff looked at me while viewing this house and whispered, "Jan, I believe the Lord wants you to have this house, and you will continue to raise the kids here. This house is for you."

I knew that was my Jeff, but I just didn't see the whole picture at that time.

As we toured my dream house, it literally felt like my house. My flesh said no, but my spirit was hopeful.

Although I felt that I needed a much smaller and more manageable house, I felt that I had some sort of an unspoken agreement in the Spirit over this new house. God had never once led me astray.

All of our moves had been to our advantage financially. I even felt a time or two, that God had moved us just because He knew we would have good equity in our investment. This was the case with the house we were presently moving out of.

Of course every time we had moved, Jeff was conveniently traveling somewhere, leaving me to do all the packing and unpacking. I prayed this would be the last move for a while.

I was exhausted from it and every time we moved, although I tried different moving companies, they destroyed much of our furniture and keepsakes. Dishes were broken, as were family heirlooms. I was exhausted from moving every two years. We had moved six times since we married.

The couple who originally put a contract on this home wanted a great deal of upgrades, such as upgraded appliances, and an inside and outside security system. The builder had agreed to their requests, and had added a lot of extras to please the original purchasers.

An issue transpired between the builder and the potential buyers, and the builder could not add the cost of the upgrades to the house, as it would be over market value. We were basically offered the house without paying for all the extras.

In faith, I agreed, even though buying this house did not make sense to me in a rational way.

I believed that somehow, either things would work out and Jeff would be healed, or that God would just remove him, and he wouldn't be with us. Either way, I trusted God no matter what. I can't explain feeling peace during such uncertainty. I think the Lord was preparing me somehow. I knew it could easily go either way. We purchased this new home in December of 2019.

My kids and I managed to endure and survive. We home schooled, and my kids were active at their home school tutorial that they attended every Friday. They had many friends there and at church, and so did I. My church was my family. I did everything that I could to make my children's lives happy and as normal as possible.

Jeff did well in the first months we moved into our new house. He pressured me to agree for him buy a truck and resume driving, but he had proven that he would just head straight to alcohol. I had to drive him to church and everywhere else we went. I knew this was embarrassing to him, but also humbling.

We continued to go to staff meetings, attend church, go to movies, out to eat, meet with church members and friends, and try to find the good along the way. I felt like I always had one eye open to what might happen next. I never felt entirely comfortable with anything.

His office was again upstairs, as were the kids' rooms, which I was completely uncomfortable with. My son Given was still afraid to sleep in his room, so he slept in our room on a daybed. Jeff was pulling all-nighters in his office and when I questioned him, he said he was studying. I would just let it go. Arguing didn't solve anything.

He spent more and more time upstairs in his office and sometimes I found him sleeping on the bonus room sectional. At times, I felt we had become nothing more than roommates, and not husband and wife.

Once again, we walked into our house one day after school, to find him apparently drunk. This launched a quick downhill spiral. We continued to have to leave our secure home to go to hotels, even more often than ever. I tried to make these overnights fun for the kids and sometimes we would stay somewhere that had an indoor pool so they could swim.

Mercy was starting to show signs of severe PTSD. She was just having a really hard time. At her age, she longed for a normal life, like her friends all seemed to have. She begged me for a dog and just seemed to need something to love, that would unconditionally love her.

I agreed for her to buy her own dog, then that led to a second dog for the younger children, then I had a weak moment in the pet store. So now, we had three dogs and it was more difficult to stay in a hotel. We found we could just sleep at the church and be able to manage the dogs and care for them more easily. Nobody in the church had a clue. I slept on the couch in our green room. The kids slept on pillows in the nursery. This wasn't nightly or even weekly, but any night having to flee for safety and security was too frequent.

You may wonder how the church and ministry were doing through all our personal challenges. The church seemed fine on the surface. We had our faithfuls. Other people came and went, but that is not uncommon in our stream.

We had what Jeff called tumbleweeds, that would blow in and blow out. Our numbers were around a hundred and twenty on a good Sunday. We had powerful assistant and associate pastors who were strong speakers, so nobody seemed disturbed that Jeff was no longer ministering in the pulpit. Jeff and I were still senior pastors, although with Jeff, it was in name only. He had completely lost interest in the church and just went through the motions, if even that.

Global Fire Ministries followers basically had no idea, as Jeff was still traveling, still recording livestreams and videos that kept them engaged. The presidency and politics were the main topic and he drew a larger and larger audience.

On one hand, Jeff had influenced many people. He had raised up numerous spiritual sons, several from our school, Kingdom Life Institute.

He had met a lot of people and had developed friendships and relationships with countless ministers all over the world, a number of them considered spiritual generals.

He had gained the admiration and respect of any number of people. He had become an accomplished author. I applaud him for this. He had a special gift and anointing that could not be denied. I don't want to downplay any of that by telling the darker side of his story.

This being said, I didn't know at this time how many had actually experienced some kind of incident relating to Jeff's instability. More and more pastors at churches he was traveling to were noticing that he was beginning to behave differently, and some suspected he was drinking. More and more church members were whispering that Jeff was off, and not himself. Concerned people were starting to come to me.

I wouldn't realize the gravity until it was all over. The wheels kept spinning and the machine kept running, but I feared that at any time it would all disintegrate.

Some events just stand out. One Friday, we returned home from home school tutorial. The kids went in the house first, while I unloaded things from the van.

"Mom! Dad is drunk again!" They had come running outside to report to me.

I quickly went inside to find him drunk, in the middle of the day, and one of the kids said, "Well, back in the van."

I was just done. I guess I snapped. Years of intensity had taken a toll on me emotionally.

"I will no longer take my children and have to run off to a hotel or the church just to feel safe when I find you drunk! You will leave and I don't care if you ever come back!" I shouted. I was absolute in my decision and stood on it.

Without even arguing, he got up, packed a bag, called Uber for a ride and checked himself into a hotel. I took the opportunity of him being gone to inspect his office, and as always, I found alcohol containers hidden in every corner, behind the curtains, and in the attic.

"He must be drinking almost constantly now," I whispered to myself. "I thought he was doing better."

While in the hotel, he would call me and swear in tears that he would enter rehab. In the past, I would let him come home, only to repeat the cycle, over and over. I was always the one who pursued getting him treatment, but he never went. Instead, he would call me after he sobered up, completely apologetic, and begging to come home.

This time, he even admitted he was feeling suicidal and unable to control himself. He reiterated that the Lord had again told him that He would take his life if he didn't straighten up.

Jeff was afraid. I was seeing a frail helpless man I had not seen before. As the real Jeff began to even more realize how fractured he was, he told me in tears that Jeffrey told him what to do almost all of the time.

I had deep compassion for him, but yet I was just done with the constant anxiety of what might be next, and whether it would be far worse than anything we had experienced so far.

Something in me wanted to save him. Ask anyone who lives with someone who has mental illness, a sickness, and an addiction. You know that you know, that you know that the real person is still in there. The real person is crying out for help. I was holding onto that real person and praying. A lot.

He repeated to me over and over, "Jan, I'm afraid God will kill me. He keeps telling me He will take my life if I don't straighten up."

I could feel the intensity of his distress. I could see that he was remorseful for his actions and was trying, but he didn't have the mental strength to press through.

Eventually I let him come back home. I am not sure how he could still travel at all, but he continued to book ministry dates. He was unwilling to lay it down.

We had been through several travel partners by now, and were running out of options. Having someone with him didn't seem to keep him from drinking, but now I had a man traveling with him that he highly respected and at least he would not drink in front of him and he could make sure Jeff got to wherever he was supposed to go.

Kat Kerr was a good ministry friend of ours and had invited us to go on a ministry cruise with her in February of 2020. My birthday would occur while we were on the ship.

Despite my concerns, I prayed that Jeff wouldn't drink while he was around Kat, and I agreed to take the family. We were long overdue for a vacation and I had refused to go to an all-inclusive resort ever again.

The cruise was at the beginning of the Pandemic, and Covid checks had begun as we boarded the ship.

We had a great time and Jeff didn't touch a drop of alcohol while on the ship. We were free during the day and at night there were ministry sessions, much like a conference.

We had several friends there and Steve Swanson was doing worship. It was a glorious time! We visited the Bahamas and Labadee, Haiti.

There was free-flowing alcohol everywhere and I knew he was probably tempted, but he didn't touch a drop. I told him I was proud of him.

"Jeff, this is a sign that you can overcome this thing. It's not too late. Please try. For me, for the kids, for the church, for the ministry, and for you!"

He agreed! I allowed myself to have a mustard seed size hope, for the first time in a long time. It's hard to explain how I vacillated between hope and hopelessness.

A few days after we returned home feeling refreshed, believing for, and praying for the best, Jeff became very ill. His temperature quickly elevated to over 103°F. He complained he couldn't breathe and he was scared.

I rushed him to the emergency room. On the way there, Jeff began talking out of his head. He was apparently talking to dead people.

He said, "Jan, I see your father and he said to tell you he loves you. He is wearing a plaid shirt and is sitting on a green Naugahyde chair."

This was uncanny, as my dad did frequently wear plaid shirts and the chair he sat in when I was growing up was green Naugahyde, common in the 60s and 70s. Jeff didn't know this.

He was also saying hello to other people who had passed on. He was giving me a report of who he saw.

I grabbed his hand and in a loud voice said "Jeff! Don't leave this earth! It is not your time!" I wasn't sure if it was the fever making him talk out of his head, or if he really did have a glimpse into Heaven.

I wasn't allowed in the ER with him, as Covid-19 was rampant. I was told that I could wait in the car until I got a call updating me of his status.

He tested positive for the flu. I was allowed to take him home, but they also tested him for Covid-19. The results would come in a few weeks. There were no instant tests at this time.

I brought him home, and in order to protect my children and myself from sickness, I isolated him in the bonus room upstairs on the sofa. He willingly stayed there, and I brought him food, fluids and his medication. I was reminded of how much I felt like his mother and not his wife, over the past few years.

We thought he was over the hump with the flu, but five days after his diagnosis, he became more acutely ill and could not catch his breath. Again, I rushed him to the ER, and he was diagnosed with double pneumonia.

He would have a difficult recovery. I prayed they would keep him in the hospital, but hospital rooms were full of more seriously ill Covid patients. He was not considered high risk.

An extremely threatening and stressful situation is almost more than the victim can bear, when he is already struggling with D.I.D. It was like adding insult to injury and any progress he might have made was reversed. The real Jeff was incapable of handling this illness. Jeffrey would now step up in an even bigger way. Jeffrey knew Jeff needed rescuing.

He did recover from his illness in time, but what surfaced was even worse than Jeffrey.

An Unexpected Turn

After he recovered, he stayed locked in his office continuously, even more than before. He only came out for food or coffee. He had become obsessed with promoting Donald Trump's campaign and spent almost all of his time watching videos pertaining to the state of the union and the cabal.

I didn't disagree with his political beliefs, but I knew he was taking on principalities and powers he could not spiritually tackle with so many cracks in his armor. Never swat a hornets' nest when you are completely weakened and defenseless.

He also began watching videos and researching endless facts about human trafficking, particularly child trafficking, the use of Adrenochrome in Hollywood, and other dark subjects.

I remember looking him in the eyes and telling him, "You are getting way off balance, Jeff, and you just need to go back to reading your Bible."

His demeanor was one of blackness, darkness, and a hollowness in his very core. He was still watching extremely inappropriate R-rated movies, in addition to the documentaries. I continued to find movie accounts he had opened.

His language became exceptionally offensive. I was glad we had pulled him out of the pulpit, but he had begun doing constant livestreams about Trump, our government, and things pertaining to the political season we were in, Adrenochrome and child trafficking.

He gained a lot of attention from the general public for this cause. Our nation was hungry for an answer!

He had thousands of followers. He even wrote a book about Donald Trump called "Trump - The Destiny of God's America". It was quite prophetic and I didn't know how he had managed to write such a book in his current state. Again, the gifts of God are without repentance.

I went on YouTube and watched some of his videos and I could tell that the man who was speaking was not Jeff, but he wasn't Jeffrey either.

He had hired a new partner coordinator. He had no intention of stepping back. He said all the right things to our staff, in response to the confrontation, but behind the scenes, he was preparing for another big launch.

In retrospect, the man had everything. He had acquired respect, recognition and fame. In the beginning, he had such a desire to see the lost saved. At this moment, I felt he was just building a bigger platform on which to stand.

Throughout his ministry, he had written numerous books, including Glory Rising, The Furious Sound of Glory, The Beginner's Guide to Miracles, Signs and Wonders, Enthroned, Revival of the Secret Place, Trump - The Destiny of God's America, and Exploring the Unseen Realm, which was his last book to be published.

He also created numerous worship and soaking CDs, including The Eye of God. He had a CD named Spontaneous, with all original songs he had composed. I even helped him write one of the songs. His gifts could not be denied, even in light of his current state.

When I look back at his accomplishments, I am awed and overwhelmed at what God had imparted to him, as far as wisdom, knowledge, spiritual understanding and anointing, and how he had used this to teach and minister to thousands of people. I remember saying out loud one day, "God, how could Jeff literally just spit on all You have given him?"

That question came from my heart because although I had witnessed it all, I still could not fully understand and grasp how this could have happened to my Jeff. How could this have befallen someone who was once so close to God, and who had ministered with such a God-given anointing?

I tried to tell his new partner coordinator that this was not the time to promote Jeff or the ministry. She didn't understand and I hesitated to tell her the whole truth at this point. In actuality, this was because I didn't want to hurt her, not because I wanted to protect Jeff.

She was a go-getter and very good at what she did. Jeff's political views and stand were a very hot topic. Jeff pushed using his political platform to build a larger partner base. He would tell me the basis for this was that he no longer had to travel to make a living. It was Jeff's desire to not have to travel as much, so he hoped having more partners would provide more provision.

"But Jeff, you are asking people to partner with you when you are nowhere near stable or even worthy of people's seeds of faith," I said it over and over.

Sometimes he would say under his breath, "I know, Jan." Other times, he ignored me and just changed the subject.

Our partner coordinator was starting to see mood irregularities and shifts. She finally asked me what was up. I was as honest as I could be. I tried to deliver it softly, and simply tell her that Jeff had some serious problems that so far, he had been unwilling or unable to fix.

She hung in there for a while, but I could tell she had lost a tremendous amount of faith in him. I felt sad for her, but glad she could see at least a portion of what we had all experienced.

She finally saw at least the tip of the iceberg came one day, when we were standing in his office. She wanted to confront him on some of his behavioral inconsistencies. He parked his behind on the corner of the desk, and acted like he was listening, but stared out the window into the parking lot.

"Jeff! Are you listening? This is serious! I feel that I cannot build with the Jeff I am seeing now!" she cried out to him.

There was no response. He simply stood up and left the room, murmuring something under his breath about having to go next door.

The church owned two adjoining properties, and he inconsiderately walked out of the room and headed over to our youth building next door.

I looked over at her, and said, "I've tried to tell you, but I didn't want to hurt you, just like I haven't wanted anyone else here to be hurt."

Shortly after that, she resigned and left our church. We remained on good terms.

Chapter Seventeen

THE NEXT LEVEL

Stranger In The House

After a blow-up one day, when Jeff was drinking heavily, I literally feared he had the ability to kill me, and he seemed to hate me enough in his fits of rage to do just that. This may have been an irrational fear, but years of stress and unpredictability had taken their toll on me.

Once again, the kids and I fled to a hotel as quickly as we could. We got away before he did too much damage. There was something very dark about him that I had never seen before.

His Covid test result had returned as positive. The hospital had called to inform me three weeks after his first visit to the ER. Somehow, he had survived having Covid, the flu, and double pneumonia, all at the same time, but his behavior was even more bizarre after his sickness.

One prominent internationally known minister we had walked with for many years contacted me and asked me, "What is wrong with Jeff?"

"Well, he actually just overcame Covid, the flu, and double pneumonia. What's up?"

He told me that Jeff had phoned him and, in his words, completely cussed him out. He would never have imagined Jeff would have done that. I would not have imagined it either. Even though Jeffrey would manifest to me, I could not begin to understand why he called a ministry friend out of the blue and spoke to him like that. Jeff loved this man.

While in the hotel, I put the kids to bed and spent the evening just petitioning the Lord for what to do. I was desperate.

When was enough truly enough? I'd had so many ups and downs, hope one minute, despair the next.

In deep prayer, I sensed the Lord impressed on me that a pastor at our church, named Arthur (not his real name), had the key to unlock the answer.

I isolated myself from the kids, and called him. He was the man who had most recently been traveling with Jeff.

I believe Jeff completely trusted this man. He knew of Jeff's drinking, and had witnessed his unusual behavior. It was truly in his heart to help Jeff.

I told him all I had experienced in a nutshell, and how things had been since Jeff had Covid, the flu, and pneumonia. He asked me to let him pray about it and said that he would get back to me the next day.

It was a long night.

The next morning, Arthur called me back and said the Lord told him to come to our house and baptize Jeff.

Baptize him?

"The Lord told me that he has a demon," he said.

So many times, I would cry out to God and say, "Lord, I truly feel as if I am living with a demon. It's not even Jeff or Jeffrey anymore."

Jeffrey was cruel and rude, but the man living in my house now was beyond cruel and rude.

He turned around in the kitchen one day and out of the blue, with no reason at all, looked me in the eyes. His eyes were black and dark. It was not Jeff. I wasn't sure who, or what he was. I had seen quite a few people before who had demonic infestations, and I'd seen the blackness in their eyes. But how can a Christian have a demon?

With a very intentional tone of voice, he said, "I hope you and the kids end up starving, with nothing, living in a trailer down by the river in your hometown where you belong, with all the other unwanted trashy people. Your own father didn't even want you, Jan. That's why he left you. Nobody wants you. You are a piece of crap."

You know, that would rattle most people. But nothing surprised me at this point. I didn't even wince. I didn't shed a single tear.

My response was, "No, I am a highly favored child of the living God. He loves me and I have a purpose in this life. You're not my husband. You will not be allowed to stay in this house!"

I walked out of the room. It had now been almost three months since Jeff became ill. I was quite sure I had not seen the real Jeff in that long.

I was addressing whatever had possessed Jeff. I knew this was serious. I don't think I was surprised when Arthur told me that he believed Jeff had a literal demon.

I knew from our deliverance ministry that Christians could, and do, get demons. When a person has alters, or parts that are not clean, and open doors as Jeff had, a demon can attach to those unclean parts. A demon cannot attach to our spirits. But it can attach to the unclean, fractured parts of our soul. Jeff was certainly sick enough, defenseless enough, and vulnerable enough, for a demon to attack him.

We had cast many demons out of people of all walks of life, ministers being no exception, so why not a man of Jeff's caliber? Could a general in the faith actually have a demon? We were about to find out if it was truly an actual demonic attachment or simply his alter Jeffrey, getting worse.

The following is from Mark Sandford's "Can Demons Physically Afflict a Christian?

[Quote]

But can a demon directly harm a righteous person physically? According to Scripture, the answer is yes, but once again, only with God's permission. Satan obtained permission to afflict Job physically, with boils. *"The Lord said to Satan, 'Very well, then, he is in your hands; but you must spare his life.'"* (Job 2:6).

I have heard Christians claim that when Jesus came, He prevented this kind of thing from ever happening again to a Christian, for Jesus defeated the demons.

"And having disarmed the powers and authorities, he made a public spectacle of them, triumphing over them by the cross." ~ Colossians 2:15

Satan cannot use any sin that we have brought to the cross in repentance. However, Job was not afflicted because of any personal sin. He was afflicted because God gave Satan permission, in spite of Job's righteousness. For that reason, I know of no commentary claiming that a predicament like Job's cannot occur today.

2 Corinthians 12:7 might confirm this. Paul said,

"To keep me from becoming conceited because of these surpassingly great revelations, there was given me a thorn in my flesh, a messenger of Satan, to torment me. Three times I pleaded with the Lord to take it away from me. But he said to me, 'My grace is sufficient for you, for My power is made perfect in weakness.'"

All commentators agree that the thorn had nothing to do with any sin in Paul. Rather, as the passage says, it was sent to keep him from sinning. The Greek word, "torment," kolaphizo, means to strike with clenched hands, to buffet with the fist.

Even though Paul offered Satan no sinful point of access, God allowed him to be buffeted with the fist. Does this mean demons physically harmed him, perhaps through discomfort or a physical ailment? (Some commentators suggest that Paul's "thorn" was poor eyesight see Galatians 4:15.) Or did Paul use the phrase, "messenger of Satan," metaphorically, of a spiritual or emotional buffeting? We don't know. No one knows exactly what Paul's thorn in the flesh was.

However, we do know the following:

* The thorn was in his flesh. The word, "flesh," can be used of the sin in us, but it is also used of the body. This makes it possible that the "buffeting" was physical.

* The Greek word for "buffet" means a physical beating. Although one might use any word metaphorically, this word's customary meaning was physical. Elsewhere in scripture, the word is used in this way (for instance, of the soldiers beating Christ (Matthew 26:67; Mark 14:65).

* The thorn was "from Satan;" Satan was afflicting a righteous man.

* The thorn was sent only by God's explicit permission, to accomplish God's purpose.

* Conclusion: In rare instances and only by God's permission and for His purposes, a demon may afflict a person physically who offers it no sinful point of access.

[End of Quote]

So if the Lord allows demons or Satan to afflict believers who have no sin in their lives, what about Christians who do have sin in their lives?

Jeff had opened many demonic doors, from his excessive drinking, to his watching inappropriate movies, infidelity, and spending so much time focusing on dark things. He had not brought his sins to the cross and laid them down. He had both wrestled with them and given in to them, continually. He definitely had many cracks in his armor, and his physical illness had left him very vulnerable.

Are we so blind to allow ourselves to think that the enemy would not look for ways to attack God's anointed? He tries even harder because if he can bring the elect down, he can disillusion and hurt many people.

Also, Jeff had an alter who was created before he became born again, and who was, most likely, not born again. How can a person be born again and Spirit-filled, and a part of them is not? I have seen it time after time, after time.

Again if a person is experiencing tremendous trauma and damage, a part of them will step up to rescue the core person, and if the core person is not saved or born again at that time, the alter will not be saved or born again either.

I have heard of a few instances where someone said without any kind of intervention, their parts had finally come to trust Jesus and that the core person was able to integrate the part into the whole.

We hadn't really seen this to be the case in our deliverance and freedom ministry at the church. It depends on the severity and level of the fracture of the person's soul.

I told Arthur on the phone that I was still at a hotel with the kids, and had to drive them to their home school tutorial.

I would wait for Arthur to tell me when it was safe for me to come home. Neither of us had any idea of whether Jeff would even let him in our house, but I knew that the real Jeff trusted Arthur. I just prayed that God would intervene. I didn't know what else to do.

I took my kids for breakfast and we checked out of the hotel and proceeded to drive to their one day per week tutorial.

I drove around for a while, waiting to hear from Arthur.

A few hours later, Arthur called me and simply said "Come on home. I'm still here."

I had a knot in my stomach and felt like I could literally vomit. I trusted Arthur, but had no idea what I was walking into. As I entered the house, Jeff was sitting in a chair in the den, and Arthur was next to him. They both had smiles on their faces. The emptiness and darkness that was previously in and on Jeff, was gone. He looked like my Jeff.

Jeff looked up at me and said, "Jan, I couldn't have believed anything like that lived in me." I simply let Jeff talk, and did not interrupt.

He added, "Arthur put me in the bathtub to baptize me. I'm surprised I even allowed him to, but as I went under the water, something dark and horrible came shrieking out of me!

"It was a demon, Jan. I'm free now." Tears were streaming down his face.

I could tell by his countenance that he was telling the truth. Arthur confirmed that this was what had happened.

Jeff hugged me and said, "It's over Jan. I can't remember anything that has happened in months. I remember going to the Emergency Room but can't remember anything after that, up to today. I cannot imagine what I have put you through. Thank you honey, for not leaving me."

I sighed a breath of relief. Was it over? Could it be? I had to stretch my faith, as I had done only a couple of other times in the past few years. I felt that we might have a chance, that the church might have a chance. The ministry might survive. Now we had to get Jeffrey integrated somehow.

After Arthur left, Jeff and I had a good talk, probably the best we'd had in a long time.

"Jan, I would have never thought I could have had a demon!" He took a deep cleansing breath. "But now, what will I do? I don't want Jeffrey in control. I don't want God to kill me."

Apparently, he was still afraid that he would die. He had contemplated suicide on several occasions because he just could not cope. He didn't want Jeffrey in control. He knew Jeffrey was destroying all the Lord had blessed him with.

He said he wanted to go to a rehab facility so that he would not drink again. He seemed serious this time, and I was open to anything that could help him.

A Huge Leap

I made numerous phone calls and was referred by someone I trusted to a facility in Texas. I was impressed with the counselors I spoke with on the phone. They stated there would be mostly one on one help, while he was there.

We scheduled an appointment for him to speak with them on the phone to be accepted.

They did approve him, and our insurance approved his stay. I felt we had been down a long road and now progress was being made, or so I hoped. I put him on a plane a few days later.

He called me two days after he checked in.

"This place is nothing that was promised. I have had absolutely no one-on-one sessions at all, and I was placed in group settings for eight hours a day."

I could tell that he was beyond irritated.

He said, "All I do here is listen to a bunch of rednecks complain about their lives and cuss and swear." He continued, "Jan, this place is not helping me, it's only making me worse."

I told him to be patient, that he had only been there for two days. He told me in no uncertain terms, that he was flying home, and would go to another rehab when he got here. We would work it out.

He booked his own flight home, and showed up at our door. He told me what he had to endure daily and I could see how this could potentially make him worse.

Finding a suitable rehab facility for an executive turned into a more difficult process than I imagined. Again, I was the one always doing the leg work, I was making phone calls, and I was the one trying to find help for him. He never put a minute into it. He just kept doing what he did.

He wanted a rehab center with more of a professional approach. Maybe businessmen? Surely there was such a place. I guess I could understand what he was feeling. He had nothing in common with anyone in that rehab facility, except the fact that they were all addicts.

Humility would have been great for him, but that was an area he struggled with. I did find a local rehab center that seemed promising and they put him on a wait list.

I was still very aware of Jeffrey's presence, but I thought Jeff was at least more out front now. He was still shocked that he literally had a demon, and this scared him. He was now asking for help to integrate his parts. He also stated that he was scared because when Jeffrey took over, he really took over.

Casting a demon out of a part does not integrate the part. Our deliverance ministry had cast many demons out of people. Getting the parts integrated still had to be dealt with.

Jeff was very open and honest about his acknowledgement of having alters and needing serious integration. Either he still didn't realize, or wasn't willing to talk about why he had such severe dissociation of his personality. Neither of us really knew at this point. I was still studying and trying to learn more about this condition.

I knew that if he were to receive complete healing, he would have to be integrated. If Jeffrey remained, more demons could attach, and Jeff could not stop it.

Jeffrey opened the demonic doors and Jeff often didn't even remember what Jeffrey did. Jeff was really a victim. I had to remind myself of this when things were bad.

It is difficult to understand how a substitute "you" could take control, but let me repeat that in our ministry, we have seen it hundreds and hundreds of times.

The way God made us to survive can sometimes destroy us if we don't stay balanced and in check with God's Word. The Bible is clear on how to prevent the enemy from attacking us. Often, we lack understanding of all of the enemy's ways. Few people understand parts, alters, and how this works.

This is the reason I am writing this book. I am not writing this to slam Jeff, expose him, or discredit the good works that he did. I want you to know that being D.I.D. or having dominant and controlling parts is more common than people realize. It is a spiritual affliction that any one of us could eventually succumb to, if left unchecked.

Intensive Treatment

I contacted a minister that I knew could integrate parts. He had ministered and taught at our church a couple of times. He worked with the worst of the worst, the most severe satanic ritualistic abuse victims, those who had come out of the deepest satanic backgrounds.

Who else was more qualified to integrate these parts and make sure there were no more demonic attachments?

Stephen Daniels (not his real name) was familiar with us, and when I told him the story, he agreed to have Jeff come to him for a few days to do intensive treatment. Jeff seemed eager to go. He had grown weary of the battle and the warfare. I purchased his airline ticket and with tremendous expectation, sent him to Arizona for the weekend.

Stephen did tell me not to express my disdain for Jeffrey. He said if it was obvious that I wanted Jeffrey gone, he would resist me even more, and potentially reciprocate with cruelty. He said, "I know it's hard for you to act like you love something that you perceive as evil and a threat, but if Jeffrey feels like you want to get rid of him, he will resist integration even more."

Perhaps this was why Jeffrey targeted Mercy and me. Parts often trust no one, not even God or Jesus.

It is common that victims struggle with seeing God as a God of love. They cannot understand how God could have allowed horrible things to happen to them.

A minister who understands the integration of parts, must bring the parts to trust Jesus, and lead them to submit to Him. He must also convince the parts that it is best for the core person that they all be integrated, and persuade them that they are no longer needed.

This can be a quick thing, depending on the level of trauma, or a long drawn-out process. One part may be easily integrated, while another may step up and take over repeatedly. Our deliverance ministers dealt with this continuously.

I didn't hear from either Jeff or Stephen for a couple of days but remained in prayer for my Jeff to come back whole.

I eventually got phone updates, and Stephen said that during a session, it had come out from Jeff's parts that Jeff was sexually molested by a male neighbor for years, probably from the time when Jeff was about seven, until he was maybe twelve.

Jeff had never mentioned anything even similar to this. To say that I was shocked, is an understatement.

So this was the beginning of his soul division? Why had he never mentioned this? Surely as long as we had been married, if this were true, he would have revealed this to me. I trusted Stephen knew what he was doing. Severe childhood trauma, especially sexual, is known to be a huge cause of dissociative identity disorder. This might explain everything.

When Jeff got home, he seemed more like himself, initially. He said Stephen had supposedly integrated Jeffrey, and that during a session, one of his parts, probably Jeffy Boy, came forward and told Stephen about the sexual abuse. Jeffy Boy had obviously been created to somehow shelter him from the horrific trauma of sexual abuse.

It was good to know why he had been so fractured, but Jeff, now realizing the trauma, was more needy and weak than ever, and I feared his parts would ultimately step up, stronger than they had ever been.

All the repressed memories of a neighbor horrifically abusing him suddenly came flooding back to Jeff.

I asked him why he never told me. He simply said, "I don't know. I think I was protected from remembering all my life, I guess?" He wasn't exactly sure.

We talked about it at great length. He was confused himself, that something so horrible had somehow eluded his memory. Part of the protective function of an alternate personality can be to block all memories of the event. Obviously this was the case with Jeff.

It was confirmed by Stephen in these sessions that Jeffy Boy was created when Jeff was about seven. This was the age when this sexual abuse began, or so Jeffy Boy had revealed. As previously stated, alters are typically created at the age of trauma and may act like someone of that age. This explained why, when he often played with our children, he acted like a child who could have been the age of seven, or so.

Though we had conversations about the abuse after it was revealed, he never spoke to me in detail about what had happened to him as a child. I could tell that this was extremely difficult for him.

He looked like a wounded puppy. I wanted to know more. I wanted to know the extent of the abuse, how this began, how it ended. But he refused to go into detail. He simply could not speak of the extent and nature of the abuse. He was never able to talk about it. He was very broken.

He did say memories were coming back and flooding his mind and that he simply couldn't handle it.

As you can imagine, sexual abuse is one of the most traumatic and damaging things experienced at any age, but especially to a child who should be innocent and simply enjoying school, toys, and normal childhood activities. When someone is severely traumatized, often it is more than the human psyche can handle, so a part, or alter is created as a coping mechanism.

Sometimes the memory of the trauma is completely blocked, sometimes the memory remains, but the alter prevents the harsh effects of the trauma from being realized by the core person. It helps them navigate the challenges of life.

An alter can come and go depending on the need for them. As Jeff had grown up and somehow couldn't remember the trauma, Jeffy Boy was no longer needed. But when Jeff began feeling he was harshly treated in his teen years, Jeffy Boy was not strong enough to help Jeff overcome that. He had been created only to buffet Jeff from the sexual trauma. Another stronger, more aggressive Jeff was needed now.

Stephen confirmed to me that Jeffrey came about when Jeff was around seventeen. This would explain why Jeffrey acted like a rogue, unsaved teenager.

Stephen confirmed that alters can literally be unsaved when the core person is Spirit-filled and born again. This was the case with other people that I had ministered to, who knew that they were D.I.D.

Let me just make this clear. The victims of dissociative identity disorder that I had worked with could describe their personalities. There was always one or more who served the Lord, and others who were living in blatant sin. As previously implied, this may be because parts blame God for not saving or rescuing the core person. They blame God for letting the trauma happen, and they react in rebellion.

The spiritual posture of an alter, or part, depends on the spiritual condition of the core person when the part was created. Jeff's part, Jeffrey, was created before Jeff was saved and born again, so Jeffrey particularly did not act like a saved person.

My Conclusion

In trying to reason this all out in my mind, it was my conclusion that repressed trauma may have caused Jeff to do some things as a teenager in order to help him cope.

I could relate because my father had left my mother when I was around nine years old for another woman. I began experimenting with recreational drugs and alcohol just to numb the pain. Perhaps this was what Jeff was doing. His rebellious behavior led to his father bearing down hard on Jeff in a manner that Jeff perceived was abusive.

My mom wasn't too happy with my rebellious attitude either. Remember, Jeff's father was the police chief in their town, and having a hippie, druggie son must have been significantly embarrassing to his father.

Teenage Jeff may have been too much to deal with. I'm speculating, as Jeff had never talked to me about this much. He just said his father was too hard on him, which was why he moved out of his parents' home and moved in with friends. He didn't even admit this to me until after he exited a HeartSync session one day.

As I said before, the level of trauma someone experiences is how the core person perceives it. Maybe, if Jeff hadn't been so damaged from sexual abuse inflicted upon him as a small child, the discipline of his parents wouldn't have made him feel so threatened that another part, Jeffrey, had to step up to save him.

Jeffrey was probably utterly impossible to control by his parents. If Jeffrey was as mean at the time of his inception as he had been in our marriage, I cannot imagine what his family must have thought. I'm sure they were doing their best to deal with a rebellious teenager and guide him as best they could. Parents are expected to discipline their children.

Jeff never told anyone he was sexually abused as a child. In my experience in dealing with people who have a history of sexual abuse, they are in total fear of either being blamed or not believed. Many never confess to anyone. Many who tell their reality, are not believed.

I actually know numerous people who were sexually abused or molested in their youth. Several are good friends of mine. One friend in particular told me that she did tell her mother that her step-father was abusing her, but her mother simply did not believe her.

Another friend told me she never felt confident enough to tell her mother that a family member had abused her, and had carried the secret her entire life.

Still another friend told me that when she told her mother that her father was molesting her, her mother blamed her and not her husband. My friend wasn't able to forgive her father until he was dying, and she continued to struggle most of her life to forgive her mother.

Imagine carrying the weight of something as severe as sexual abuse for your entire life, with no one to even disclose it to, and being afraid that you would be beaten or severely punished for disclosing it!

Jeff was obviously afraid of his father and couldn't bring himself to admit what had happened to him. This traumatized him even further. The combination of all these things caused his inner person to be unable to cope, thus Jeffrey's creation.

The automobile accident that I previously mentioned was when I was with my friend Mary and we had received warnings. I described feeling as if it were happening in slow motion, as the other car hit me. It felt surreal, as if a protective force took over so that I would not experience it in real time.

I think this is a good comparison to what a part does. It literally pushes the real person into the background somewhere, steps out front to take the trauma itself, and shields the real person from the memory of it.

The trauma of my wreck was small in comparison to Jeff being severely sexually abused as a small child.

The purpose is to save us, but an alter will sometimes make things much worse if it thinks a certain action or behavior will protect the real person.

When Jeff had a breakdown and collapsed in exhaustion on my floor years earlier, the dormant part named Jeffrey, stepped back up to save him. Perhaps Jeffrey had been dormant since Jeff was a teen. This would make sense, if Jeffrey didn't feel he was needed.

Another tremendous revelation I got was that since Jeffrey obviously perceived ministry as the cause of Jeff's recent breakdown, Jeffrey viewed ministry as traumatic and too stressful for Jeff, so he was willing to destroy the ministry to save Jeff. This is difficult to understand, but indeed reality. Jeffrey thought he was protecting Jeff, when he was really destroying everything the real Jeff valued and loved.

Stephen even told me that he had asked Jeffrey a question in a session one day. "Jeffrey, how do you minister?"

Jeffrey said, "I've watched Jeff for much of his life. I just learned to imitate him."

This explained how Jeffrey was able to step up on a stage, preach, and even quote scripture, but he lacked the anointing and sincerity that Jeff carried.

Jeffrey could imitate Jeff, but he couldn't prophecy from the Holy Spirit. This was why he could only get simple words of knowledge, like a name, address, phone number, etc. Jeffrey got his information from the wrong source, not the Holy Spirit.

The picture was becoming clearer and clearer. It all made sense. Or did it?

Chapter Eighteen

THE LAST NAIL

Wrestling For Identity

Stephen did tell me that without Jeffrey to carry him and cover for him, Jeff was very vulnerable. Stephen also warned me that Jeff was very weak at this point. Jeffrey had protected him for many years. In his current state of extreme vulnerability, even the slightest stress could push him over the edge. I lived this and witnessed it in the days and weeks after he returned home from Arizona.

Stephen did tell Jeff with me in earshot, "If you drink alcohol again, every demon in hell will have access to you, as that is one of the biggest cracks in your armor." Stephen was very adamant about this.

Jeff said he understood, but this added even more pressure to his very real struggle. He obviously thought alcohol had helped him cope. So how would he make it without Jeffrey, or alcohol?

At this point, Jeff just sat in a chair all day long. He didn't move, he didn't speak. He looked as if he would crack at any moment. He was irritable, angry, and volatile. I tried to talk to him, but he would just tell me to go away and leave him alone. I wanted to help, but even my love seemed to aggravate him.

The memories that came flooding back in his sessions with Stephen were more than he could process. Imagine suddenly remembering every last detail of such traumatic events.

Jeff said he needed to get away. He begged to go visit his parents. I agreed for him to go to visit his parents and siblings in Wisconsin, but phoned them in advance to tell them that Jeff was very much in need of a peaceful getaway.

I couldn't speak to them of the whole truth, but I did ask them to please remove all the alcohol from their homes.

His sister even talked to me about what a rebellious teenager he was, and how they couldn't manage him. None of them had any idea of Jeff's reality, and they had no idea how weak and vulnerable he was at this time.

They even blamed the adopting of our three children as the cause of his distress. They were grasping at straws, I guess, or perhaps this is what Jeffrey had told them.

After all, I did hear phone conversations between Jeff and his mom, where he blamed our children for his stress. I knew this was not the truth. He actually blamed me for even wanting more children, and said that was his breaking point and he never agreed to adopting all these children. That was typical of Jeffrey. Jeff loved his children.

He was gone for a few days. It was good for me and the kids to get a break. My kids had no idea what Jeff and I had just found discovered about his childhood. I felt this revelation was too deep for them to grasp.

I was hoping Jeff took a deep breath while he was away. I heard little from him when he was gone.

When he returned, he told me that he decided to drive around to familiar places from his childhood, which he had always done when he went home, even when I was with him.

This time was different, because now he had memories of abuse that he didn't have before. He said that as he drove around, he ended up seeing some of the places where the sexual violations took place.

This was too much for him. The visit only made things worse. He was particularly distraught and didn't know what to do to get relief. He was a wreck when he got home.

Although Stephen continued to have phone sessions with Jeff and was confident Jeffrey had been integrated, I didn't believe this was the case.

In fact, things at home became worse than ever, and Jeff was becoming increasingly verbally abusive, even when he was not drinking. The slightest thing would make him snap.

It was similar to what I suffered when Jeff had the demon. I was confused because Stephen was so secure in his success at integrating Jeffrey. This just brought more questions for me to try and get answers for.

I didn't see Jeff drinking at this point. He was trying to cope with not leaning on alcohol to numb himself, as well as dealing with extremely traumatic memories, and fearing his alternate personality, Jeffrey, may no longer be there to step up and save him.

Despite my now gaining understanding of the big picture, what Jeff inflicted on me had become intolerable. My children were afraid to even be around him. He wasn't physically beating us all up. There was no profound physical violence or abuse, but his behavior was erratic and extremely volatile. Again, I said repeatedly, "I feel as if I live in an insane asylum."

One day, Jeff seemed excited to take the kids into the woods behind us, to just build a fire and enjoy nature. I knew he was greatly relaxed by going into the woods, or even building a fire in our fire pit at the house, because it reminded him of his pleasant childhood days of camping. I was glad to see him pursuing something, anything. Otherwise he just sat in the chair.

I let the kids pack cans of Beanie Weenies and go into the woods behind our house, although I gave Jeff a stern warning to use caution. I didn't trust him, but I thought, "What harm can come from a walk into the woods?"

They were gone for hours! I began to be concerned. I prayed it just a pleasant "dad" experience. After all, I was not an outdoor person.

When he and the kids returned from the woods, my children had wide-eyed looks on their faces.

Later when Jeff retreated to his office as usual, the kids came to me and told me that on their walk in the woods, they had wandered up on a deer stand, which they said was about ten feet up in a tree. Their dad insisted they climb it and he was sitting between them. Jeff was in the middle, Truth on one side, and Given on the other.

They said that he had brought alcohol with him and that he was drinking on their walk. By the time he insisted they climb into the tree stand, he was already drunk. They were extremely traumatized by this.

Given said, "Mom, it was like he was trying to knock us out of the deer stand!"

They both told me he began sliding back and forth on the seat on the tree stand, as if he was trying to slide each of them off the side, and onto the ground. Keep in mind, this was at least ten feet up in the air.

To my knowledge, when someone places a tree stand, it has to be high enough up in the tree so the deer could not see it. I would venture to say it was much higher up than ten feet. I looked it up online and read that the ideal height for a tree stand is twenty feet or higher.

I was horrified! So he *was* drinking!

I determined that from that point on, he would never be allowed to be alone with the children.

There are many forms of abuse. He said very hurtful things to me that were completely out of left field. Can you imagine how this would make you feel, to hear the man who is supposed to love you as Christ loves the Church literally cursing you night and day? He called me foul names I had not heard since junior high school. You can imagine.

I called Stephen and said, "He's much worse. Either Jeffrey is worse, or there are more parts you didn't deal with."

"Oh, he is integrated. I know that. I walked him through that myself," he responded.

"Well, Stephen, I live with him. It's worse than ever. I just don't know what to do," I appealed to him.

It seemed to be more important for Stephen to believe he succeeded, than to realize that maybe this monster we were dealing with might be bigger and harder to defeat than he had thought. He insisted he had done his job.

Jeff continued to meet with him on Facetime, but Jeffrey was a habitual liar. Jeff had confessed to me many times that

Jeffrey had learned to lie, to protect him from his father. He admitted that he had, in his own words, a lying demon.

Lying is *very* demonic, in my mind. The Bible says the Lord hates lying. (Proverbs 6)

Every other deliverance minister he had worked with in the past was convinced that they had his parts integrated, as well. The Lord told me this was not true, as Jeffrey had convincingly lied to them all, including Stephen, who was an expert. Jeffrey was just pretending to integrate. He wasn't going anywhere. He thought he was the only thing that could save Jeff.

Although Jeff had stepped back from ministry overall since he went to Arizona, he still had a hard time resigning himself to the fact that he had to step out of the pulpit. Pulpit ministry had been a big part of who he was. He felt defeated and didn't know where he belonged. At times, he would confess this to me in moments when he trusted me enough to talk to me.

By this time it was late 2020. This man, whoever he was now, began doing more and more livestream ministry, in an effort to gain attention. This type of ministry had remained very popular and well accepted, post-Covid. Perhaps he just had to do ministry of some kind to feel validated.

As he immersed himself in Internet ministry, I noticed that his confidence had begun to slowly come back. He was finding his place of validation.

He still came to church, but it was really hard for him. He was embarrassed to just sit in a pew. In his mind, and in the eyes of many people, he was a highly recognized and gifted prophet. Had he not been the initiator and founder of the church?

As he wrestled within himself to find his identity and find a niche for himself that he could carve out, he took on a whole different personality, or persona, than Jeff or Jeffrey. It was as if the coin had flipped and he was an entirely different person altogether. He wasn't like the demon, but I had never seen such indifference. He was very secretive about what was obviously some unknown, new agenda.

Apparently, for some reason, Jeff opened a trust account in his name alone, eliminating me from it. I later found out he had been keeping all the gold coins and jewelry that people had thrown in offering plates for him over a period of many years.

Often people in other nations would give him jewelry in the offering. Perhaps they had no actual money. I saw him, a couple of times, with a big jug of gold and I asked if I could see it. He always just refused and ran off. This puzzled me.

He had taken the gold, sold it, and had his buddy, the men's leader, purchase him a large amount of foreign currency (Iraqi and Zimbabwe), which he believed would increase in value. He was creating a trust fund for this process, but didn't want me to have access to any of the money.

He had never been managerial and had always leaned on me for my administrative gift, so he became frustrated that he could not fill out the paperwork. He eventually asked me to help, but wouldn't tell me what I was filling out.

When he wasn't around, I called the trust company for information, and found out that he had asked that my name not be put on the trust. When confronted, he said the trust company recommended to him that I not be included. The trust company said it was Jeff who wanted me excluded.

Ironically, at the time, some people from my church were telling me that Jeff was instructing them not to tithe to the church, but to give money to him instead, so that they would receive the prophet's reward".

When they would ask him if they could give me a check, he would say, "No, she doesn't know yet. This is a surprise."

Later, I would find out that he had contacted friends and ministries all over the world, asking for large amounts of money, for one reason or another. It seemed he had collected thousands and thousands of dollars in his Cash App account.

Discovery of all these details hit hard. I was exhausted from it all, and was now trying to figure out what he was up to, this time. What was next?

I was notified that Jeff had been accepted into another rehab center in the town we live in. Apparently they had kept him on their waiting list from the time I had first called them. Was this God?

At this time, he had no eagerness to go although, when I told him this was his last chance, and that I couldn't take another round of alcoholic Jeff, he at least verbalized that he would go. A date was set for his check-in.

He told me he was not drinking at the time, but I knew that was not the truth, since he had been drinking on the outing with my kids. Later he admitted he had been drinking daily. In reality, I guess he felt that he might as well blow it out and drink as much as possible before entering rehab. He was also just having a very difficult time coping with life in general, post discovery of the severe trauma.

I'm not sure if he ever really stopped drinking after he returned from Arizona, but after he returned from meeting with Stephen and was warned never to drink again, I felt he at least tried for a short period of time. It was too much for him to deal with so many challenges, all at the same time.

He continued to lock himself in his office night and day and literally hid from me. I lived in constant suspicion and fear. I didn't even want my children around him, and they continued to lock their bedroom doors. He told me that he was staying in his office to relax and unwind. I knew that was not the case.

In January of 2021, we came home one day at one o' clock in the afternoon, after being out all day, to once again find him completely intoxicated, sitting in his chair in the kitchen.

"Really Jeff?"

I hurried the children to their rooms, waited till he was asleep and went into his office. I did not immediately confront him. His office was completely littered with alcohol containers. Most were empty, but there was a good stash of unopened beer cans behind the attic door and behind the curtains. Where had he gotten this alcohol?

I knew not to confront him when he was drunk but again, I had come to the end of my rope and the discovery of the alcohol containers made me furious!

He didn't even try to defend himself, as had become the norm. He had been sternly warned that if he drank alcohol again, he was inviting every demon in hell.

His response to this was to accuse me of being controlling. He began cursing and calling me horrible names, and told me to stay out of his business.

I insisted on an answer. "Where do you get this alcohol?"

Since the DUI convictions, he couldn't legally drive. He had not recovered his driver's license for his own safety and that of others. He begged for his own vehicle, but I refused to allow it. In order to drive our vehicle, it had to have a device installed that would require him to breathe in it at intervals. But I would also be subjected to this, as the machine could not tell who was driving. I refused.

"Jeff, I've told you before that if you can successfully go without alcohol for six months or complete a rehab program, I'd love for you to have your license back and a vehicle," I would always remind him.

He would routinely go to the gym with a friend from church. Jeff admitted he had asked the man to take him to the store. Jeff had no remorse and offered no apology.

"Doesn't he know what you are buying?" No response.

I had even recently spoken to this man and reminded him that Jeff had a serious alcohol problem, and asked him to please not take him anywhere that sold alcohol.

Jeff also admitted he had been having alcohol delivered to the house when I was not home. I didn't even know you could have alcohol delivered to your home! Yet another repercussion of the Covid shutdown, I assumed.

We had gone through the same repetitions for years now. Jeff would drink and get drunk, do something unacceptable, sober up, not realizing he had done anything wrong, and then apologize, insisting he would never repeat this behavior.

It had become a vicious cycle. His fruitless apologies were becoming old. I knew when he apologized, he was Jeff and he meant it, but those moments were just fleeting.

I went to the Lord again to petition for a release. I had asked the Lord so many times to either save him, or to release me from the marriage.

Day after day, week after week, month after month, and year after year, I interceded and called on the Lord to intervene. Now, I went to the altar once again.

"Lord, what am I to do? I've done everything in my power to hold onto hope. Please speak to me!"

This time, He responded, "You are released." This was in January, 2021. I had to reassure myself that this was a true word from the Lord, but I knew His voice.

I was actually stunned that God finally said I was released. I did not know exactly what this meant, or what to do next.

There was an established date confirmed for his admission to the alcohol rehab center, but I had no idea if he would follow through with it.

A few nights later, Jeff was obviously drunk, and he once again called me another horrible, disgusting name. This had become more normal than not. This time, a new level of boldness and righteous indignation rose up in me.

I raised my voice to him, and said, "You will never call me these names again! I am done!"

I *felt* done. My heart grieved, but I was done. Nobody should have to endure any type of abuse for any reason, especially for this long. Even though I knew the real Jeff would never treat me this way, it still hurt.

I know my self worth. God values me and my children far more than how Jeff, or Jeffrey, had treated us. As I previously quoted, "A husband is to love his wife as Christ loves the church." This is solidly biblical.

Many of you may have no idea how it feels to share a life with a man who is the complete opposite of who you married, a stark contradiction of who you knew him to be, and to come to realize that he is now a prisoner in his own body and soul.

It is heartbreaking and heart wrenching, but I knew I had done everything in my power to get him help, from taking him to therapists, counselors, pastors, deliverance and inner-healing ministers, setting him up with rehab, calling on trusted ministry generals to keep him accountable, and praying countless prayers.

Nothing I did seemed to last long, or have any long-term effect on him. I had no guilt or shame. I ran the race and did my best. I would never allow myself to become the perpetual victim of anyone, ever again.

I didn't pack up and leave immediately because it was complicated. I had to be obedient to the Lord and up until now, He had not released me.

Now that God had assured me that I was released from this marriage, what would I tell the church, and what would happen? Would it all simply end? I needed answers.

Jeff was supposed to enter the rehab facility in a week, so perhaps I was to hold on. I would wait.

A few days before his admission date, late one evening, the kids and I had gone to bed. Jeff went to his office and was heavily drinking. He apparently came downstairs at one o' clock in the morning. I wasn't even aware of it.

For some unknown reason, he wandered outside, leaving the back door open, and our beloved cat Gabriel got outside. This was discovered when I got up the next morning, finding the back door standing wide open and Jeff passed out.

I asked the kids if they had gotten up in the middle of the night, but they all denied it. Jeff admitted to going outside at one o' clock. I was surprised that he even remembered.

We were heartbroken that we couldn't find Gabe and although he had accidentally gotten out a time or two over the years, he always came back. Any time he accidentally got out, he would be on the front porch the next morning. But much to our dismay, this time he didn't. My children were devastated, on top of everything else they were already going through.

I was now on Facebook, and we posted on the neighborhood Facebook page. The neighbor at the end of our street had captured video of our cat following another cat, in their driveway. This was the last time we would see Gabe.

We had a couple of rabbit traps in the garage. Jeff felt bad that he had let our cat out. I saw a moment of compassion in him towards the children and me, however brief.

I made signs with pictures of Gabe and posted them online and in the neighborhood. We set a rabbit trap where one of the neighbors thought they had seen our Siamese cat. We baited it with raw salmon. We checked the trap regularly, and although we didn't catch Gabe but to our surprise, we did catch a frightened feral cat.

Jeff should have known better, but again, he was drinking and wasn't thinking straight. He brought that feral cat back to our house to show the kids, and tried to set it free in the garage. It somehow climbed up on the top of our parrots' large cage in the garage and Jeff climbed up to try and catch it.

I had stepped inside the house while this was going on, so I didn't see what happened. One of the kids opened the door to the house, and while the door was open the wild cat jumped off the bird cage and ran inside the house. It ran upstairs, and nobody knew what to do.

I somehow managed to remain calm, and was able to trap the cat in a kennel and release it outside.

Jeff showed me that the cat had bitten him on the hand while he was trying to catch it. I poured peroxide over it and bandaged it up, feeling that he got what he deserved.

I told Jeff that he had to leave the house permanently at this point. I was loving, but firm, and told him that the kids and I just didn't feel safe anymore.

We didn't know what he was doing as he stayed in his office all night with the doors locked. His threats towards me led me to fear what he might be capable of. Jeffrey admitted to me that he hated me.

Many nights I laid awake all night, knowing what he was capable of. I knew that these were not irrational fears. We had no idea what he might do from one day to the other. The children deserved to feel safe, and so did I.

He didn't even argue with me. He packed his bags and I drove him to a hotel and dropped him off.

He got out of the van without saying a word, and I cried all the way home. I just knew it could really be the end this time.

Apparently, he continued drinking in the hotel. I saw on our online banking where he walked to a local convenience store and purchased alcohol.

He even called me accidentally when his phone was apparently in his pocket and I heard him making the purchase. The clerk asked for his ID, and Jeff presented his passport.

I didn't personally hear from him for days. When he did contact me, he was lower than I had ever heard him. He had been thinking a lot and felt he was hopeless and could never meet up to anyone's expectations, especially those of the Lord.

He said he simply could not live like this any more. He told me that the Lord had again said that He would take his life, if he continued down this path.

This had plagued him for years, but not enough to bring him to a state of humility. Jeffrey kept Jeff from dealing with reality, or submitting to humility.

This time, I heard fear in Jeff's voice that I had not heard before. It was a "fear of the Lord" kind of humility.

"The fear of the Lord is the beginning of wisdom". (Proverbs 9:10) Would this be a turning point?

He had recounted to me many times about God telling him how He would take his life, beginning after his breakdown in the floor, years earlier.

I had never really sorted through that, but I could tell that Jeff had dropped to a new level of despair, this time. I knew the real Jeff was fighting for freedom, but he had internal enemies he didn't know how to control. He had given up.

I agreed to pick him up from the hotel and deliver him to the rehab center in the morning, if he would still go. I was very surprised when he agreed.

I left my younger children with Mercy, hopped in the van, and headed to the hotel to pick him up.

When Jeff got into our van, he told me he had been vomiting all night, felt hot, and that something was wrong. He then showed me his hand.

It was four times its normal size, very hot and red, and the bite marks from the cat were obvious. It was severely infected. As upset as I was at him, someone had to help him.

I called the rehab center and told them what was going on and they told me they couldn't care for someone with an open wound, and that I should seek medical help, as they didn't have medically trained staff. I was to let them know the findings of a medical doctor after Jeff had seen one.

I drove him to a local walk-in clinic, and after examining the wound, they told us it was far too serious for them to treat. We rushed to the nearest emergency room.

After an initial exam, x-rays and labs, he was taken to the operating room for emergency surgery to clean out the wound, which was, indeed, severely infected. The infection had even gotten into his bones.

I was angry and frustrated. The one chance Jeff had to maybe get free of his alcohol addiction was ruined by a drunken event that resulted in an contaminated cat bite!

He was in the hospital for four days, and I had to let him return home after his release so that I could provide wound care. The rehab center would not take him. I didn't know what else to do. After all, he was still my husband.

He never was a good patient, and this was no exception. I fed him and did his wound care. The wounds healed in time. During this time of healing and daily dressing changes on his hand, he sat in his chair all day, playing the victim. I realized it was challenging to do things with one hand.

I reminded him that if he had not been drunk, our cat wouldn't have gotten out, and he wouldn't have caught the feral cat while searching for Gabe, but of course, he didn't get it.

I was also dealing with heartbroken children who were grieving over their dad, and now over losing their pet. Gabe was really a good cat and a friend of the family.

I tried to get him to go to another rehab, or back with the same one that had accepted him, once he healed. He just didn't seem to care anymore, and it was as though he was pursuing something else. This was the new person I had been dealing with who wasn't Jeff or Jeffrey, and he was moving on with Plan B.

In hindsight, I see that Jeff gave up trying, and felt he was not capable of change. He was just too weak, too tired to try any more. He felt he had disappointed everyone. Sadly, he knew it, and he just gave up.

He said to me, "I can't do it, Jan. I keep failing God and the church, but especially you and the kids."

My heart was always willing to give him another chance, and another, but how many times can you do that, when wisdom says that continuing to give him chances isn't helping?

I went to my church leaders in January, 2021, and told them things had become intolerable and that I no longer felt safe under any circumstances. They called a meeting with Jeff and gave him a final ultimatum:

1. No ministry whatsoever, period, including livestreams, interviews, etc.

2. Get help, no matter what. Alcohol rehab, inner healing, whatever it takes.

3. No more abuse toward Jan and the kids.

He had an established period of time to prove that he was serious. After all, we had all been patient, we had all been forgiving but ultimately, if we failed to obey the word of God then, as He had said, we were as guilty as Jeff was.

We could no longer turn a blind eye.

His Final Decisions (Plan B)

Unfortunately, proof of my suspicion was soon revealed that something, or someone inside him, had already made the decision. One of my leaders overheard a conversation in the back of the sanctuary one Sunday morning.

"Let's go start our own church so they can't tell us what to do," he had said to a group of four, including the man who had been driving Jeff to the gym and other places.

As information began coming to me, Jeff had already been gathering money. It was clear that he had at least contemplated an escape, of sorts.

Instead of repenting, submitting, and fixing himself, it became obvious that he just planned to leave and start a new life, blaming me and the church for everything he had done. Friends, this is the demonic spirit of narcissism.

Although the ultimatum stated that he was to not engage in any ministry, he continued to do things via livestream and video. When I confronted him, he just ignored me and walked away. He no longer even tried to be a part of our lives. He just existed. He was very indifferent at this point, and wouldn't even bother to talk to me.

Out of the blue, he informed me that he had a ministry date in Oregon that was scheduled "a while back" and couldn't be canceled. He had booked a flight to depart April 6, 2021.

I warned him that he was to follow the plan that our leadership had laid out, and to stay out of the pulpit in order to be sure that the Lord's agenda for his healing was carried out.

He refused to cancel his plans to go to Oregon. The fact that I hadn't heard of this trip until now wasn't lost on me.

When he left the house at four o' clock in the morning, I looked at him, demanding his attention. I asked him to look into my eyes. That was when I could see the real Jeff, if he was anywhere to be found.

"Jeff, you know that this is the very opposite of what you were asked to do."

No response. Just cold, blank eyes.

He told me that his travel companion suddenly couldn't go. Later on, I was to find out that this was all part of the plan. There was never a travel partner.

"Jeff, if you drink on this trip, you will never return to this house. I promise you this. You were told by Stephen that if you ever touched alcohol again, every demon in hell would eat your lunch. You have not adhered to the warning of the Lord, and now, you are in grave danger."

He shrugged his shoulders nonchalantly, and simply walked out the door. I could feel the finality.

I felt pretty sure he was drinking as soon as he got on the plane, despite the hour of the morning. I knew it in my spirit.

Throughout the day, he wouldn't answer any of my calls. He spoke to me only once while he was gone for the weekend, very briefly. He basically just dismissed me and hung up. He sounded as if he had been drinking, even on this one phone call.

His ministry time in Oregon had been recorded and was live-streamed. Very soon, miscellaneous people were contacting me and asking me if I had seen the video. I hadn't, and I cringed at the thought. What did Jeff do this time? Several people commented, "He's acting like he is preaching drunk."

He made some very unusual comments on the subject of what he called patriotism. One of his comments was something to the effect that our church security team was "packing" and if you came to our church and messed with us, they would, (and I quote) "blow your head off".

He also made comments about the church, as a whole today, being effeminate, and even having a "homosexual spirit".

His Trump support had gained him a great deal of attention, both good and bad. In addition to Trump supporters, Trump haters had also been keeping up with all of his videos and interviews. Our church had begun getting threatening messages on our voicemail, as a result of his rogue preaching.

After he made his speech in Oregon, the intensity of these threats reached an alarming level. One voice message left on the church voicemail said they would "blow our church to bits".

We had a huge conference scheduled at our church with very popular ministers in May of 2021. At this point, we felt that it wasn't safe to host this event, as both of these ministers had also taken a stance for President Trump, but in a healthy way.

We canceled the event, for the protection of our church, the ministers, and everyone who would be in attendance.

Little did I know at this time that Jeff would never come home. In fact, even when it was time for him to return from his trip, he didn't contact me at all.

Jeff's grown daughter from his first marriage texted me the day after Jeff arrived back from his Oregon trip and said her dad had come to her house to rest. I knew he was just hiding from accountability. He wouldn't take my calls.

In fact, he blocked me from his phone and had no contact with me for over a month. He left me to deal with our children, who had no idea what to think. He left me to deal with a church body who had no idea why he wasn't present.

In a way, I finally began to feel somewhat safe. At least with him gone, I could sleep at night.

But I knew that just leaving things hanging and hiding, wouldn't solve anything. I feared what could be lurking. I feared that one night, any night, he might try to sneak back into our home, and hurt me. I had many nightmares about him, and I would often wake up in a sweat.

Although he had hurt me before, I had no tangible proof that this was his intent, now, and that he might act on it. These were just fears that manifested in my heart at that moment. I kept all my doors locked. This was difficult with children running in and out.

I made numerous attempts to contact him. I wasn't desperate for him to come home. I just wanted to know what he was thinking now. After all, many aspects of my life hung in the balance. Our income had come from Global Fire Ministries.

If it were to be no more, would I have to put my kids in public school and get another nursing job? What would happen to the church? So many questions, but no answers.

He ignored me and acted as if neither I, nor our children existed. I cannot tell you the enormity of emotions I felt at this time. I had to carry on, try to keep the church going, and encourage my children, as best I could.

"Where is Dad?" my two youngest would ask me.

"He is staying with your sister for a while", I would respond, but didn't know what to add to that. They told me that they also felt relieved to not have to fear what he would do next. Mercy was quite obviously just glad he was gone.

Trying my best to keep the church going was particularly challenging. I had many faithful people surrounding me, as I stood for the church, as the Lord had told me to stand.

As word got out that Jeff had not come home, ministers had begun contacting me, just to encourage me. I had so many visitations from the Lord and encounters during this time. God knew I needed them to be able to endure.

I received many, many words from generals in the Lord about how I was to simply stand and that the Lord would ultimately vindicate me and the church. This gave me strength. I was determined that Jeff's downfall would not be mine.

Still, the kids' father had disappeared. My husband had disappeared. Our senior leader had disappeared. I had no words.

I was inundated with questions from our congregation. "Where's Jeff? What's going on? Is he coming back?"

Not only were leaders all over the world contacting me with information, but now people in the church were becoming bold enough to tell me things that they knew he had done. The reports were steadily coming in, as word continued to spread that he had left me.

One ministry couple planned a crusade, highlighting Jeff's ministry time, in Brazil. I remembered this crusade very well.

They called me during this time to tell me that Jeff was "falling over drunk" the entire time he was there.

This husband and wife told me that he literally crawled up on the stage for the crusades, drunk out of his mind, and tried to preach. He was an embarrassment to himself, to his hosts, and those who had come. I remembered that Jeff claimed they had mistreated him somehow, and he didn't talk to them again after he returned from the trip.

It seems that I got a phone call every day or so with one shocking story after another, mostly about how Jeff was asking for money or ministering drunk somewhere. It was worse than I had even imagined. He had burned many bridges.

One of Jeff's grandsons texted my older daughter while he was apparently staying at his daughter's house and said, "Did you know your father is here in a drunken stupor every day?"

He was witnessing what was going on in the home. This obviously disturbed Jeff's grandkids as well.

Is this what Jeff called rest? He was still doing live-streams from somewhere in a country farm-like setting. People asked me where he was. I had no idea. He didn't even look like himself in these videos and I had a hard time trying to watch them.

After I tried many times to contact him, Jeff finally agreed to set up a phone conversation with me. This was about six weeks after he had abandoned our family, implying that we didn't even exist. There'd been no contact, no nothing. His agreeing to talk to me on the phone felt more like some sort of an official appointment, not a meeting of a married couple, who had shared life and love for twenty-seven years.

I took Given to a park to play, and I sat in the van to have this scheduled conversation. I wasn't sure what to expect.

I began by simply asking him, "Jeff, what is going on? What are you thinking?"

I sensed absolutely no humility, no remorse, no regret. He was stone cold.

Without hesitation, his immediate and aggressive response was, "Nobody will ever tell me what to do again, not a church, and not you! If I want to drink, I'll drink. If I want to watch rated R movies, I will do it. If I want to buy a truck, I'll buy a truck, and drive it! If I want to buy an RV, I'll buy an RV. If I want to go to the gym, I'll go to the gym. If I want to travel, I will travel. and if I want to buy a snake, I'll buy a snake! I will do whatever I want, when I want, and nobody, including you, will ever tell me what to do again."

Twenty-seven years to come to this?

He didn't even ask about my well-being or that of the kids, our house, our animals, nothing. He had no concern for our provision or whether we even had food to eat, or enough money to pay the mortgage.

I listened and realized he had planned his escape long ago and had made up his mind. This was why I felt he was even yet a different person than Jeff or Jeffrey.

I told myself to take a deep breath, and calmly responded.

"Jeff, you created your own prison by sneaking around drinking, and making the children and me feel unsafe. I didn't put you in prison. You did that to yourself.

"Do you think I wanted to have to act like your mother instead of your wife? If I'd just let you do whatever you wanted, you'd be dead right now, or would have killed someone else on the road, or Heaven forbid, hurt the kids and me far worse than you've already managed to.

"Look at the consequences of your actions. Doesn't that matter to you at all, in any way?"

There was absolutely no response, other than an abrupt goodbye, as he hung up.

I whispered to myself, "Wow, he's like Jeffrey on crack."

That was pretty much the end. Many of his demands were based on the fact he felt like a prisoner in his own home. Jeffrey had convinced him that all the attempts I made to help him and rescue him were simply attempts to control him.

That made Jeff feel like he couldn't meet any of my expectations or those of the church and the ministry, so it was easier to just bail. He had just resolved to quit trying, and then, in his mind, there would be no pressure.

I sat in my van for a bit longer and sadly relived our conversation. It was heartbreaking.

Chapter Nineteen

PRIDE WILL BE HIS DOWNFALL

Freefalling

True to the visitation from the Lord that I had in 2004, Jeff had fallen into pride. The Lord reminded me that He had said "pride will be his downfall".

He didn't say that it could be his downfall, or might be, but He firmly said "it will be" his downfall.

Jeff's demands to do whatever he wanted were rooted in pride, and Jeffrey just didn't care. I felt Jeff was gone forever, or at least being held a prisoner but, as I told him on the phone, he had created his own prison.

At the time of this writing, the movie Jesus Revolution was recently released. If you've not seen it, I suggest you do.

It is a very well done movie about the ministry of Lonnie Frisbee, Chuck Smith of Calvary Chapel, and Greg Laurie, a young man who was saved in the Jesus movement and went on to pastor Harvest Christian Fellowship in California.

I picked up on a lot of similarities in Lonnie that coincided with Jeff. I remembered Jeff's stories about meeting Lonnie and attending a huge event where Lonnie was ministering. He said Lonnie had called him out of the crowd and prophesied over him and laid hands on him.

He said, "Jan, that is the only time I felt literal lightning striking my body with a tremendous force." Jeff felt he received a special commission when Lonnie laid hands on him.

Lonnie had come from a dysfunctional home and was sexually abused by a neighbor, just as Jeff was.

Jeff was raised in a normal Catholic home, but he too was molested by a neighbor, for years. The struggles in Lonnie's life most likely came from early childhood wounding, as did Jeff's.

Lonnie seemed to feel that he couldn't go to his parents or others for help, so he ultimately turned to drugs to fill the void. It was the same with Jeff.

Lonnie was looking for love and acceptance in all the wrong places until he found Jesus. In some ways Lonnie's life story would almost mirror Jeff's. I remember, as I watched Jesus Revolution for the first time, I marveled at how many similarities there actually were!

Jeff talked about Lonnie with high esteem, and had several books about him. I'd never read them and had never heard the whole story until I watched this movie and I could see why Jeff was so drawn to Lonnie.

Notably, Lonnie had begun to show a side of his ego was getting the best of him, as his ministry with Chuck progressed. He began showcasing his gifts and giving glorious words of knowledge just like Jeff, and beginning to think it was all about him. Again, just like Jeff.

Being a true father and leader of his church, Chuck had asked Lonnie to check his ego. Lonnie had grace with Chuck, but he still chose to leave Calvary Chapel. Once he left, he struggled with many things, including truly finding his place of ministry again. The parallel with Jeff was uncanny.

People who are full of themselves do not easily submit to authority. Neither Jeff, nor Lonnie, were able to easily submit. They were both filled with pride.

Lonnie had been an incredible asset to the Vineyard movement, and Jeff had also done amazing things for the kingdom of God, but pride got the best of them.

Jeff had no one he was accountable to. Many offered, but it was his ultimate choice to be accountable to no one. Although I had asked him to be accountable to several ministers whom he trusted, he did so in word only, and continued to go down the path he had chosen. The door to pride was opened, and the devil walked right in.

I've said many times that words are cheap. Jeff's words that implied his accountability may have convinced some, but they weren't the words of an humble, truthful person. They were simply prideful lies.

Pride is the key to opening the doors for a narcissistic spirit to find a way to attack its victim. Remember, Jeff was completely humble and submissive to the Lord and to his family and marriage for many years, but he was not able to properly steward all the attention he began getting as our ministry grew. He had underlying issues of deep pain and trauma, that had been swept under the rug.

He had become a rock star in his eyes and that, coupled with unhealed wound, was a powerful target for the enemy. He was treated like royalty when he traveled and had begun thinking he deserved it. Humility had just flown out the window.

I often said I felt as if we had a target over our heads. At times, Jeff would shockingly announce from the pulpit, "The devil can't touch me!"

I would literally put my hands over my head and whisper, "Lord, don't let me be found in his wake."

"Jeff, you are challenging the enemy! Where is the wisdom in that?" I would chastise him for saying or even thinking that he was untouchable.

He would just laugh and say, "Well, it's true."

Pride always leads to a fall!

Proverbs 16:18-19 says, *"Pride goes before destruction and a haughty spirit before a fall. v. 19- Better it is to be of a humble spirit with the meek and poor than to divide the spoil with the proud."* (Amp)

Pride puffs up and brings division. Humility levels out and brings unity. Pride says, "Look what I have done!" Humility says, "Look what the Lord has done!" Pride says, "Look how messed up people are and how great I am." Humility says, "We are all a work in progress. Let's work together and we can achieve more!"

It's not that Jeff never wanted to do the right thing. Pride simply opened the door for the enemy to overtake him.

Once, in a somewhat humble moment when he had been sent to a hotel, Jeff called me to apologize. He even admitted to me that he knew he was a narcissist. If he could have found his way back to humility, there might have been hope.

After he left us, I would lie in bed and remember the times I saw desperation in his eyes. If I could not find Jeff, I could see him through his eyes. Jeff was still in there, somewhere.

I struggled to accept that Jeff had plotted his escape, and had actually carried it out. It was a hard pill to swallow.

He was not narcissistic when I met him. The psychiatric world will tell you that narcissism is a disease, or a personality trait. I find that it is a demonic spirit. I lived with the humble Jeff for many years, and there wasn't a narcissistic bone in his body.

When narcissism overtook him, it was because he allowed it, by not keeping pride in check. Bob Jones had warned him about girls, gold and glory. He had succumbed to all three.

Narcissism is found within the demonic family of Jezebel, Leviathan and Python.

Demons come in families, or orders, just as angels do. There is always a lead demonic spirit and following that one, are many other demons whose characteristics match that of the head.

Chapter Twenty

LEVIATHAN

Leviathan, Python, and Jezebel

"*I*n that day the Lord will deliver Israel from her enemies and also from the rebel powers of evil and darkness; His sharp, unrelenting, great and strong sword will visit and punish Leviathan, the swiftly fleeing serpent, Leviathan the twisting and winding serpent; and He will slay the monster that is in the sea."

~ Isaiah 27:1, Amplified

In Psalm 74, the Lord crushed the heads of the Leviathan, the spirit over the Egyptians, and fed them to the creatures in the wilderness.

The entire chapter of Job 41 is all about Leviathan. Verse 3 says, "Will he speak soft words to coax you?" In verse 34, Leviathan is called "king over all the children of pride." (Amp)

Pride is what allows the spirit of Leviathan to enter into people's lives.

By natural definition, the name Leviathan means a sea monster or something large and formidable. In a spiritual context, the serpent or dragon always symbolizes the devil. It is simply a powerful and terrible beast that humans cannot control, without the Spirit of God.

While it's true that all evil spirits are liars, the Leviathan spirit, rather than outright lying, specializes in twisting the truth in the mind of its victims without them even realizing it. It distorts intentions and conversations.

A person working under the influence of Leviathan is so prideful that they can't admit when they're wrong. They play the blame game, and everything is always someone else's fault. They can never admit that they are the ones in error. This destroys relationships and creates division.

This is the spirit of narcissism. A narcissist operating in a Leviathan spirit will always blame someone else for their sins, and sometimes will blame another for exactly what they have done or are doing. Their accusations can actually be a confession of their own sins.

One of the primary assignments of the Leviathan spirit is to break and destroy covenants. Leviathan hates covenants of any kind, especially the marriage covenant. Leviathan is most likely responsible for most, if not all divorces.

Beneath the head demon of Leviathan, you will always find pride and at least some level of narcissism.

The Spirit Of Jezebel

Many books have been written on the spirit of Jezebel. Because narcissism almost always works alongside Jezebel, I will touch on it here.

Many people who hear about someone operating in the Jezebel spirit conjure up ideas of a seductive woman dressed scantily, trying to lure a man into a sexual tryst.

In reality, most people who have the Jezebel spirit operate much less obviously than that, although most all will have a secret sexual side to them that is not healthy, but is selfish and manipulative. So, just what are the signs that a person might be operating in that spirit?

People who operate in the spirit of Jezebel will always have many similar characteristics across the board, whether they are a woman or a man.

The first thing that you will notice is that they exert themselves in an arrogant manner although in reality, they actually feel unsure of themselves.

Some have a history of very demanding and controlling parents, and some a history of childhood abuse.

They have an underlying fear and anxiety, which they try to cover up with control. They must be in control and get their way. They will manipulate you through statements to get you to side with them, believe them, or to make you feel indebted to them. Oftentimes, it will appear very obvious to you, while they think they are being discreet.

Other traits associated with someone operating in the Jezebel spirit are easily recognized.

There is fear and anxiety. There is insecurity. There is a lack of peace, and an unhealthy drivenness.

They have a compulsion to control and manipulate others constantly to be satisfied. They exhibit outbursts of anger to make sure you are afraid of what they can do.

They are masterful liars and deceivers. They are very prideful and arrogant. They feel that others should serve them and give them whatever they want and if you don't, they will become angry until you give in.

They practice sexual control through either manipulating you to not receive sex unless you do what they want, or they may want sex all the time, but in a perverse way. Those in a relationship may be unfaithful or be tempted to be. Some will become addicted to pornography, or have an extreme underlying disrespect, even hatred, for the opposite sex.

They remain unfulfilled, regardless of what you do to give in to their demanding ways.

They will try to shut you down if you are in ministry, and are often jealous of what the Lord does through you.

They try to gain friendship with people of influence and power, especially in the church and within ministries, so they can control people and ultimately cause confusion and obstruct true freedom in the Lord and deliverance from the enemy.

They will buy your friendship through gift giving so that you will feel obligated to them, allowing them to exercise their control over you.

If you are married to one of them, you will notice that their face will contort into a fierce look if you dare to resist their demands. That is how the demon of Jezebel manifests to intimidate you into getting what it wants.

They live a double life as they appear loving, kind and generous in public and before the church, while then behaving in very evil ways behind closed doors, undetected by those in church or ministries.

In a church setting, they will try to put their hands on you. They know they can control and manipulate you if they touch you in a way that will draw you into them and ultimately get them what they want. They will try to pray for you and put their hands on you, and they can subtly seduce you in that way.

They are wear fake smiles all the time but inside, they are always scheming to get their own way at the expense of others.

If you are not a person of influence or power in your church or ministry or at work, they will have no time for you, as you cannot help them accomplish what they want. They treat those of insignificance with disdain and will not spend time with them because they are of no benefit to them.

Every church and ministry can have people who operate in the spirit of Jezebel try to rise up from time to time. The more anointed the ministry is, especially if there are prophetic giftings, the more people with the Jezebel spirit will gravitate to them.

If this spirit is never addressed, it will continue to operate and cause confusion, stop true deliverance, and ultimately will cause a split in the church or ministry. Therefore, it must be addressed and not tolerated, as stated in Revelation 2:20-23:

"Nevertheless I have a few things against you, because you allow that woman Jezebel, who calls herself a prophetess, to teach and seduce My servants to commit sexual immorality and eat things sacrificed to idols. And I gave her time to repent of her sexual immorality, and she did not repent. Indeed I will cast her into a sickbed, and those who commit adultery with her into great tribulation, unless they repent of their deeds. I will kill her children with death, and all the churches shall know that I am He who searches the minds and hearts. And I will give to each one of you according to your works." (Amp)

I have seen many people who operate in the Jezebel spirit be delivered and set free. They can finally become who they are in Christ, as they can hear the voice of the Holy Spirit clearly, instead of being distorted by the enemy. It is possible, but they have to realize their need for deliverance.

Although Jeff was not a total Jezebel or Leviathan, I was seeing that many of these traits fit who he was becoming, and had become.

Python

Acts 16:16-18 says that while Paul and Silas were on their way to a place of prayer, they were met by a slave girl possessed with the spirit of divination.

This was known to be the spirit of Python.

The Python spirit was the serpent or dragon that guarded the Delphic oracle at Mt. Parnassus. Many readers of this story would assume that this slave girl was a positive witness, calling out in verse 17, *"These men are the servants of the most High God! They announce to you the way of salvation!"*

She was possessed by a spirit of divination, claiming to foretell future events, and to discover hidden knowledge what we would call a psychic. She was making a great deal of money for her owners by fortune telling.

Here are some traits of the spirit of Python:

Flattery

It loves to flatter. Those operating with a Python spirit, like the slave woman, attempt to flatter, to draw attention to themselves. The slave girl must have assumed that if she gained acceptance from falsely prophesying, she might also gain acceptance from the ones who would normally excuse her, those who followed the Holy Spirit of God.

Attention Seeking

This spirit demands attention. This is proven by the fact that the slave woman followed Paul around for many days. V.18 says Paul was "sorely annoyed and worn out". Can you imagine being followed around for days by someone who kept yelling and distracting from what you were really trying to do?

Beware of those who carry this spirit of prophecy, falsely trying to get into the limelight. They will even attach to legitimate ministers and prophets, just to be known.

It loves to be seen and heard. The slave woman kept putting herself at the center of attention.

Status Seeking

It wants to be important. Beware of those who use prophecy to gain status with pastors and leaders.

There is a monetary motive. This young girl was bringing in a great deal of money for her masters. Have you been around ministers who will even prophesy in return for money? The spirit of Python loves being financially blessed and convinces everyone that they somehow deserved this blessing by the favor of God, when in reality it was manipulation that bought the gifts.

You can see how narcissism goes hand in hand with all three of these demonic spirits. Each spirit has the trait of a narcissist, and a narcissist will have traits of all three spirits, even if not entirely. I believe the longer the spirit of narcissism goes without being checked, the stronger, more powerful, and more deceptive it becomes. It feeds on its success.

Jeff's prophetic gift, under the influence of Jeffrey, was often one of divination, where the information gained was not from the Holy Spirit, but instead from the second heaven. That is why people perceived Jeff was simply off.

Chapter Twenty-One

NARCISSISM

Narcissism Explained

Let's take a moment to talk about narcissism, itself. Narcissists are extremely insecure and damaged, even though they behave otherwise. They act grandiose, exaggerating their worth and abilities to others, although they feel very poorly about themselves on the inside.

They present themselves to be special in some way, and only other special or important people are worthy of their time and energy. If you can't benefit them in some way, they don't want anything to do with you. They are extremely entitled.

They fantasize about their success and boast to others about how elaborate their plans and futures are. They exaggerate how great their lives truly are.

They need constant admiration and praise. If they don't get it from those around them, i.e., friends, family, spouse, they will seek it elsewhere. Many narcissists get angry if their significant other doesn't give them the attention they want and think they deserve, and they even resent their significant other when they spend much needed attention on themselves. This unbalanced attention seeking can lead them to being vulnerable to an adulterous relationship.

The husband or wife of a narcissist is always unfulfilled, and can never meet the expectations made of them. If they confront the narcissist, they are blamed and are told, "You are selfish, controlling, cold, unloving", etc. They place the blame on their partner for exactly who they are. This is something that I experienced firsthand.

They exploit others. They take advantage of people and they think it is their right to do so. "I deserve it," they reason.

They are arrogant, self-serving, and patronizing of others.

They lack empathy for other people and have little to no compassion. They don't even understand the needs of others.

They are actually envious of others although they won't show it, and they believe others are envious of them. If they have a conflict with others, they always blame the other person and cannot even see their part in it.

The bottom line is that narcissists are delusional. They are not able to rationalize their bad behavior, and they feel justified that the other person deserved it. The narcissist feels they have every right to do what they did.

Just to recap, let me point out some of the narcissistic characteristics Jeff had portrayed that were very obvious to me, and to others who were around him a lot.

As he began to transform in a bad way, he began to criticize others, showing extreme disrespect, saying things like, "They will do what they are told to do."

Jeffery was at the helm and had no use for the church that we had built. He considered it a nuisance and a thorn in his side that took too much attention away from his ministry. This is exactly what he said to me.

He even required the name of the church be Global Fire Ministries World Miracle Center, instead of Global Fire Church. He began calling it a center for his ministry, and not a church.

This was an early wake-up call to me, although in faith I went along with it, not having total understanding. I always adamantly opposed this, as I felt the church was to be a family of believers who had tremendous love and mutual respect for each other with unselfish unity. I cringed when he called it a center.

He was very cliquish. He chose those who would elevate him and even accept his sin, and avoided others who were valuable to the church. He spent a great deal of time fellowshipping with those he felt he fit in with, but he basically ignored everyone else.

He would even admit publicly that he was not a pastor. From the pulpit, he occasionally said, "Don't tell me about your problems, I've got problems of my own. I'm not a pastor."

He was trying to be funny, but this was accurate. I always felt that I was the pastor, and he was the charismatic speaker. I could see that his behavior towards others was patronizing.

He began to expect being treated like a king, being driven around in limousines and getting tremendous attention and honor in his travels. The once very humble man, who bought his clothes at Sears and Roebuck, now demanded nothing less than the best of everything. If it weren't the best and most expensive item, he didn't want it.

I am a bargain shopper and enjoy the thrill of the hunt. Jeff would spend tremendous amounts of money to make himself look good. This was the complete opposite of the man I met and married. Again, humility was part of what drew me to him in the first place.

As previously mentioned, he was convincing people to sow into his ministry and asking them to deprive the church of their tithes and offerings. I cannot even conceive Jeff ever doing anything like this. He was always a very generous man in the beginning, and in his natural state, wanted to bless the church.

Neither of us ever took a salary from the church because we always wanted to give to and bless the church, not take from it. Our international ministry always provided for us.

Eye And Ear Gates

In retrospect, another concern was that Jeff's watching movies that contained violent content and murder, cursing, and nudity had opened many demonic doors.

This began slowly, as sin typically does. Jeff thought he was above the law in this respect, and claimed that all of that went over his head.

I've always been one who is extremely resistant to bad movies and media, so we had a lot of discussions about this. The only movies I watched were clean cartoons with the kids. I even avoided Disney for the most part.

He said his spirit was too strong to be affected by the content of movies and media. I told him repeatedly, "The more you open doors, the more doors will open."

If you open your eye and ear gates to perversity and sin, it will eventually live and grow in you. What you feed your spirit with is what will grow in your spirit.

Also, through the narcissistic deception of believing he couldn't be affected, the enemy lied to him more and more, and the content of what he watched had become worse and worse. This was total deception. Please hear me!

Although he thought he was hiding his movie watching history from me, I could easily go search the many accounts he opened. I was shocked that he would even want to watch these kinds of things! Why would any child of God, especially one who called himself a prophet and a minister of the gospel, want to watch total trash?

This had been going on for years, and nothing I had done to contain it had worked. He literally thought he was above it.

As is typical of a true narcissist, when I confronted him, he would turn it back around on me and call me controlling and manipulative. He couldn't just say, "That's sin, and it's wrong."

One level led to another level, and to another level. I can't say to what level he stooped to after he left us, but when he was still in our home, my children and I caught him watching inappropriate movies numerous times. I was horrified.

My innocent children would step into his office at night, hoping maybe to get just a little fatherly attention, and find him watching things that they knew were wrong. They didn't tell me about some things, until after he left us.

When confronted, he always adamantly denied it. He seemed particularly drawn to extremely violent movies full of guns, shooting and suspense.

When I met Jeff, he did not use curse words or swear. His use of foul language had started when Jeffrey stepped up after his breakdown, but had increased in frequency and intensity, as he watched so many movies with that content.

The "f-word" became something he commonly used to hurt me. Jeffrey knew how much I hated that word.

How many men and women have opened one door at a time, until they were completely trapped by addictions, unable to find a way out? It could happen to any of us.

Beware of thinking that you can peek into doors, or even tap on them. The devil is quick to grab you and pull you through that door. How many people in the church innocently knock on doors, thinking there is no danger, and later find themselves trapped behind that door?

I was upset that any level of perversion was allowed into the atmosphere of my home. What should have been a safe haven for my children, had become completely unpredictable and spiritually distorted.

Distorted is simply the word that comes to mind, because I can't think of a more accurate word to describe it.

I knew that Jeff had wanted to quit ministry since around 2013, or at least that was what he said to me. He was in distress overall and tried to express it, but was unable to follow the leading of the Holy Spirit.

In front of people, he was entirely the opposite, and would boast and brag about his infinite plans to expand the ministry. Although he had a desire to make a difference in the world, it seemed to me that later on, he went on crusades just to gain followers and attention, and sometimes to grow his partner base. It seemed to him that people would more easily partner with a ministry that was doing crusades.

I am not saying he didn't care at all about souls or people. When I first met him, he didn't seem to show a desire towards evangelism, particularly. His heart was about worship and music. He frequently verbalized his deep love for Jesus. There was an innocent and pure anointing on his life.

Narcissism didn't hit him suddenly, it came on step by step, precept upon precept.

I can't impress enough that the stand he took for President Trump brought him much attention, which he used to his advantage. That, plus human trafficking and other political hot topics became his main focus.

This was true especially after he was asked to step down from all ministry. I warned him over and over that he was getting out of balance. The darkness coming from his office and into our home had become tangible. This was not a spirit that I ever wanted in my home.

I remembered him watching a video called The Fall of the Cabal. That seemed to open up a door of curiosity that led him into a season of discovery when he realized how corrupt and perverse our government was. This was not harmless in itself, but any obsession is, and it became his obsession.

One video led to another and another. It seemed he had his face in front of the computer in his office almost constantly watching something. The more I warned him, the more movies, livestreams, interviews, and political programs he watched.

He was also doing many livestreams himself. Most were about the political arena. He seemed no longer interested in simply preaching the gospel.

As I began to search around in our history for what might have caused or created what I was now living with, I realized that I first started to notice the beginnings of a rockstar persona when he began taping his show The Glory Generation around 2006. It seemed manageable for a while, and he described it as growing into his ministry.

In my mind, he wanted the spotlight. I felt he thought he had something to prove to those who had discouraged him. This was particularly painful to him, as he had expressed to me. His former pastor who told him to just be quiet and sing and his perception of a father who did not believe in him were factors.

Because of his charisma, he had easily become a very visible figure. He was good looking and great behind a camera. He did many videos, tapings, shows, and recordings to propel himself. He was successful at doing just that.

He taped an entire series on Sid Roth's "It's Supernatural" and felt the release of this series would propel him into his destiny. This was around the year 2020. It was never released.

"Pulpit ministry is a lesser ministry anyway, Jan," he would say to me. Jeffrey said the same about worship. As much as Jeff suffered by being pulled out of the pulpit, he still tried to rationalize it, acting as if it were his idea, since he had more time to do "Internet stuff".

He would be heard telling people that this was the reason he no longer ministered and preached at our church, instead of telling the truth that he was asked to step back numerous times and even eventually asked to step down due to his own struggles.

I recall a very revealing moment. I call these "arrow" moments, when the Holy Spirit grabs you and shows you something that goes deep into you.

Even though he would occasionally sing into the microphone during one of his performances, as I call it, of charismatic exuberance, he had literally quit playing the guitar and leading worship as he once did. He would sing out, but it wasn't the humble spirit I once knew in him.

In no way did his onstage singing carry the pure anointing that Jeff's earlier music had carried. He no longer wrote songs, and no longer seemed to care about music at all.

I asked him why and he simply said, "It's beneath me."

How could worship be beneath us? Worship should be the most important thing we do. If we don't worship, if we don't cry out, the rocks will!

He was once such a beautiful worshiper, and had written amazing songs that had gone around the world. He even had songs that he had written recorded on Promise Keepers CDs in the 90s. He was so dedicated to his music then, but now it was beneath him? He always had such a Davidic psalmist anointing.

It dawned on me that Jeffrey was created before Jeff learned to play the guitar and sing! Jeffrey was not interested in music or worship. Jeffrey was not a skilled musician, so when he was out front, he avoided worshiping all together. I was deeply saddened by this. He would sing, but not worship. It was really just a performance.

Jeff, or Jeffrey, had also become a habitual liar.

At the sake of repeating, this is important enough to stress: Jeff, himself, admitted that he learned to lie when he was being challenged by his father, in his youth. He said if he didn't lie, he would be punished beyond what he could handle. He even admitted he lied frequently to his first wife when he was being confronted.

As I looked back throughout our marriage, he had always turned to lying when confronted with anything. He never chose to just say, "I was wrong. I made a mistake. Please forgive me." Not, at least, until the reality of things he did were completely obvious and couldn't be denied, such as his horrendous binges.

It would often take him days after a binge or a major offense to admit he was wrong. He confessed he truly struggled to be able to tell the truth, for fear he would be crucified for his mistakes. I had not yet known his lies, like I was about to experience them.

Chapter Twenty-Two

THE WORST IS YET TO COME

Grasping At Anything And Everything

So here I was, abandoned and forsaken. The worst was truly yet to come, I feared. I didn't want to try and restore the marriage if it were to be as it was when he left. I could no longer tolerate the drinking, the abuse, or the lies.

God had released me. I had begged the Lord for years to release me, but I knew it had to be God's way, and in His timing. In light of it all, I had to be obedient to the word of the Lord.

Many times I had felt forsaken. My children and I had lived with such trauma and drama for so long now. I use the word trauma a lot, because trauma best describes our experience. All I could do was continue to believe that somehow the grace of God had us.

When it became apparent that nothing involving Jeff was changing, and he was not seeking help, the Lord issued a warning to him one last time.

He was given a final warning in January of 2021, which led to April 2021, when he went to Oregon and defied us all, letting it be clearly understood that he would not adhere to a healing and restoration process.

The board and leadership of our church, and of Global Fire Ministries, informed me they had no choice but to fire him, and remove him from both. It was never my idea. I intentionally removed myself from the voting process because I was too close to the issue. It wasn't that I didn't agree, but for ethical reasons, I chose to stay out of the legalities of it.

A letter was drafted and presented, involving our entire board, as well as our attorney. The letter was sent to Jeff via text and email, as we had no idea where he was living at this time and had no address to mail such a letter to him.

He had blocked me from his phone so I couldn't even contact him in case of an emergency. He had allowed me that one conversation, and had made it clear he was rebelling from what he perceived as control.

I was still totally shocked that he seemed to have no concern about the welfare of me or our children. I had once believed he loved us all so much. How could he just be happy to move on and forsake us?

I will never forget his response when he realized he could legally be removed from the ministries he and I founded. He obviously claimed some sort of ownership and felt it was his church and his ministry. He took credit for both.

He didn't seem to understand that Global Fire Ministries and Global Fire Church were ruled by a board of directors that he himself had appointed, along with myself. He didn't appear to care that he and I were partners in the founding of the church and the ministry.

He had been warned many times in the past few years, and he was reminded of the legalities and consequences. He had choices to make, but because of his arrogance in thinking everything was all about him, he remained in deception. He had already made many reckless choices, and one choice turned out to be especially unwise.

He had failed not only to properly father, nurture and protect what he had helped birth, but now had selfish motives that ruled every aspect of his life. I can't say for sure who it was making his decisions for him now; whether it was hopeless Jeff, or arrogant Jeffrey.

I think perhaps somebody gave him really bad advice, and he didn't consult legal counsel throughout his removal. He was also seeing through the eyes of Jeffrey. We don't know what he was told or what he was thinking but apparently, he felt he had rights to half of all the assets of the church and the ministry.

This may be true with personal assets in a divorce, but not when it involves a church or a corporation.

We knew other ministers who had been fired from their ministries after falling into sin, and subsequently lost all assets, properties and rights, as an example.

Jeff and I had talked about this at length and he had made the comment that it wasn't fair to fire the founding member of a ministry and have everything taken from that leader for any reason, whatsoever.

"This will never happen to me," he said. Never say never.

I told him that this is why a board of directors is installed in the first place. It protects the church or ministry itself, and prevents a leader from becoming a dictator.

"How many ministers have you seen just go completely off the wall?" I asked him several times. Actually, we had known quite a few of those.

He obviously didn't do his legal research and listened to the few surrounding him, who were as deceived as he was.

They had become the cheerleaders that he surrounded himself with, which is typical narcissistic behavior. He drew those to himself who applauded him and accepted his behavior, regardless of what he did.

He had tried to convince people that it was he who had been wronged. He told people that he was fired for no reason and that we had stolen all that he had worked so hard to build.

Although he had his posse who couldn't see stark reality, there were those who could tell how the enemy was at work. They were the ones who came to me and told me what Jeff was saying, and what I was being told shocked me. It broke my heart to know that he would rather see all his good works die, rather than simply submit to healing.

In his deception, a couple of weeks after he left and was fired, he made a decision to go to a bank in the small town where he was staying with his daughter. He apparently inquired about all the balances in the church and ministry accounts.

I was always the admin person for our personal lives and ministry. I had always managed the finances, and he admitted that this was simply not something he was capable of doing. He stated that he was not administrative.

I tried to keep him abreast of all things financial, but he would say, "Jan, you've been an excellent manager over everything including money, so I trust you."

Our church had an official administrator, who handled church finances. After firing Jeff, one of our priorities was to remove his name and his ownership from anything related to church or ministry.

We were in the process of changing bank accounts and removing him, but it was not an instant process. At the bank he visited, it seems he found his name still on three accounts.

We discovered that he asked the teller how to remove money from these accounts. This small town branch had no idea that we were in process of removing him from all accounts, and the teller unwittingly gave him three over the counter checks, which he wrote and signed, removing a total of $15,000 from them, almost exactly half of the sum total of what was in the accounts that still bore his name.

Notably, the Lord had urged me several days before to move all assets, because Jeff would try to access them, deciding that the money was his. Again, I didn't completely understand, but I had to be obedient. I had obtained an attorney by now, simply because I did not feel safe regarding anything that had to do with Jeff.

My attorney had also pressed me to move any assets of any accounts his name was on, as matters would ultimately be worked out legally in court. I'm sure all attorneys have seen just about every nightmare known to man. Dividing assets had to be part of the process along the way.

Honestly, many things that I had seen Jeff do in recent days shocked me. Telling faithful church members to stop tithing to the church and give only to him really shocked me. The real Jeff would never have taken from the church.

I wasn't surprised that he would take ministry money, feeling it was his, but to steal from our church? I thought he would have enough consideration and respect for monies that our faithful people had sown in their tithes and offerings to maintain the church's needs, and would realize that none of the church and ministry money was personally his, but I was wrong.

Losing this much money from our church account was a terrible financial blow. We were not a large church with huge assets, especially since Jeff had brought about division.

People had been steadily leaving, in light of Jeff's rebellion. Tithes and offerings had been given for our building expenses, employees' salaries, and other needs, but we rarely had much if any left over, after bills were paid. We were hurt, shocked and very concerned.

We consulted corporate and ministry attorneys, as well as our accountants, and we were told that we had to report this theft to the police. If we failed to report it, any of us could even be held liable for the missing money. You can't have this much money disappear from a church or 501c3 organization's bank account, and not expect to have to account for it.

Subsequently, after reporting the loss to the police, we got a call from a detective. They asked for an appointment to meet with us. The detective and a police officer came to our church in order to investigate.

Several board members, leaders, and I met with them. We told the detectives that we weren't seeking to press charges, and that this wasn't why we had reported the theft. We were simply following the instructions of our attorneys and notifying law enforcement of the missing funds because our lawyers had been clear that this was something that we must do.

It was always our intent to protect ourselves, the church, and the ministry, and in this case, it was the same. We would leave the consequences to the Lord.

The detective investigated over a period of weeks, and she decided to press charges, as she felt he intentionally stole from the church out of spite. The district attorney agreed. We had no choice but to leave it in their hands.

Rumors got back to me that Jeff was telling everyone he came in contact with that I had stolen the church from him, and that I had stolen all his money and left him penniless.

The truth was that in the end, he abandoned me and our family, and never offered me one penny of support for our children or our needs, but had literally taken my only source of income by destroying what we had built with the ministry.

Our salaries were always taken from the ministry, which was funded by love offerings, honorariums, crusades, book and product sales, etc., but not from the church. I no longer had a source of income. My church was not able to pay me in such a difficult and challenging time. We had lost quite a few people.

God was my husband and my provider and He has never failed me. I had to walk it out, one day at a time. I found myself completely dependent upon the provision of the Lord.

Jeff continued to try and cover for himself. He even told many people that not only was I the one who was stealing from the church, but that I had been for ten years. He said I was under investigation and audit. How could he make up such an audacious lie? Everyone who had any discernment at all knew that nothing was further from the truth. I honestly couldn't believe the extent of his lies and his own deception, and I wondered if he truly believed the lies he told.

The next shocker was that Jeff located literally less than ten miles from our church and started another church which he called Global Fire Family Worship Center. He felt the name Global Fire was even his and since we robbed him of the church, he had a right to the name.

Here we were, still a married couple, and he started another church, while ours was still alive and well. We were adjusting, but very much alive and well. The Lord was with us.

Jeff took no responsibility for any of his actions. One former church member followed him and was helping him plant this church. A few other very deceived people stood with him as well. Somehow they were convinced that all his lies were truths.

Some people put Jeff on a huge pedestal and couldn't believe he could do any wrong. Isn't that typical with the man of God syndrome?

He was on a mission to convince everyone that I was at fault, instead of him.

This was when I could see narcissism in him the most. He was literally blaming me for exactly everything he had done.

I think some of his followers knew of his sins and they just didn't care. As previously stated, he drew those around him who would accept anything he did.

I had gone to this former friend of his who stood with him now, more than once, and shared with him what Jeff was doing behind the backs of church members and ministry followers. I asked for his help, intervention, and prayer. I asked him to make Jeff accountable.

Did he ever even confront Jeff? I wondered if he gave Jeff an "atta boy" instead of offering any correction. And now, he was Jeff's sidekick.

To give the benefit of the doubt, lying spirits are very convincing. I cannot condemn all those who fell for his lies. They just didn't know the whole story. How many times I wanted to just do a magazine article, video, or TV interview, something, to just tell everyone the real truth.

Jeff actually had what I will call recruiters contacting people who were still at our church, the church Jeff and I founded together in 2009, to try to get them to leave and come to his new church.

I tried to reach him by phone. He did finally answer a few of my texts. He must have unblocked me.

When I confronted him on his recruiters and told him I simply couldn't believe he was attempting to start another church and destroy the one we had founded together, he commented that he had not appointed people to contact my church members, but he knew it was going on.

I told him that he had gotten what he wanted. Nobody could control him, as he desired, but he now looked like a crazy person, starting a new church and we were not even divorced. As expected, there was no comment from him.

"Leave Global Fire Church and come over here with us," these recruiters would say when they called, or left messages on a church member's voicemail.

You can't imagine the chaos that was created, both in the natural and the spirit realm.

Needless to say, my church began the process of changing our name. Initially I wanted to call it the Path. We prayed into this a lot and had many meetings about it.

"Why should we give up the fire in our name? It's not Jeff's Fire! It's the Fire of God!"

We all agreed. Our children's pastor told us that often the children who came to our church loved it so much they would tell their parents, "I want to go back to the fire church."

So, this was the name we agreed upon. We simply dropped the word global. Nobody would steal our fire!

I always wanted the church to be a community church, not a global center. The word global was chosen by Jeff and I because of our international ministry. I decided to keep the name Global Fire Ministries for now, for the ministry, but not the church, loosely based on a dream a prophet friend of mine had.

He said he saw Global Fire Ministries in his dream and that the ministry still had many mandates which were huge and this had not changed since Jeff was no longer a part.

Global Fire Ministries was God's ministry, not Jeff Jansen's. He said, "Jan, don't give up Global Fire Ministries. It is not finished."

My church was trying to heal from feeling that Jeff had deceived us all. (I call it "my" church to differentiate from what he was trying to start now, and the church I was still standing with and was now leading in his absence.)

A few of the people who left when Jeff was fired have since come back to apologize. I can only say, "I understand."

Things like this should never happen and I realized people were disillusioned. Most told me that they sensed he was off for quite a while. Many more who had left before all this even happened, contacted me to say they left because they knew Jeff was off. Nobody seemed to know how to define off. Again, "off" was a word that I heard a lot.

On one hand, I had never felt more betrayed, but on the other, I never felt so supported.

It seemed people I didn't even know were coming out of the woodwork to encourage me. I'm so thankful for those who stood with me and embraced the truth and the hope.

Others felt they had to choose a side. Then there were those who wouldn't take sides. They insisted it was a marital dispute. Only my staff, close friends, and those I had confided in, understood the fine details of all that was going on. This was definitely not a simple matter of a marital dispute.

I was reminded of the old James Taylor and JD Souther song that said, "Some of them his friends, some of them her friends, some of them understand."

There were those who simply got tired of the recruiting and of being harassed, and eventually filtered out of my church. My worst fears were happening.

All those years I cried and petitioned the Lord that I never wanted my church family to be hurt or disillusioned, but Jeff was making sure they were. Although our numbers declined some, God hand selected the faithful discerning the ones who would stand with me.

I say this a lot, but words cannot express my feelings and emotions at this point. The Lord made it very clear I was to stand, despite it all. So, I did.

Jeff's behavior was narcissism at its finest. His lies only increased and magnified. Nothing hurt me worse than hearing that the man that I had loved with all my heart, was now trying to destroy the church and ministry that he and I had built together in faith. He was trying to destroy me. I had done nothing but try to help him. I had devoted well over twenty-five years to him, our family, our church and our ministry!

The Lord told both of us in 2009, "Build Me a house in which My glory can dwell", and now he was literally trying to shut it down, in an attempt to make himself look like the victim, instead of the perpetrator.

My faithful ones told the recruiters to leave us alone, so eventually they stopped calling.

Later, a few told me they went to Jeff's church just to see what he was doing, out of pure curiosity, because this was so inconceivable.

They could clearly see that Jeff was not okay, and they immediately left. The faithful knew it was the Lord who had built our house, not a man or a woman, and they publicly and privately continued to support me, and my church. I still thank God for them every day.

Jeff and I had many ministry associations and ministry friends. God had networked us with many credible and anointed men and women of God. There were a few highly respected ministers that I considered my own personal friends. One day, I reached out to one of them by phone. I wondered what her thoughts were on all that was happening.

She said, "You don't have to tell me anything, Jan. The Lord has already shown me everything. Be sure you stay quiet and let the Lord do the exposing. Step out of the way and keep your mouth shut." I never forgot those words.

My heart was crushed, but the Spirit of the Lord Himself had girded me with strength for this kairos moment in ways I cannot explain in the natural. To begin with, I had many, many generals in the faith contact me and tell me that the Lord had prepared me for all of this, and they confirmed what the Lord told me. I was to stand, no matter what. If I had one prophetic word, I had a hundred.

"Stand Jan. Do not falter. God has prepared you for this." Those words were strength to me! I can't express how, as word got around of Jeff's actions, one minister after another reached out to me to offer their love and support.

I believed God, and let Him lead me and guide me. It didn't make sense in my human mind and emotions.

"How am I going to do this, Lord?"

I often said to myself, and to my friends and confidants, "My soul mate, my one true love, was lying about me to everyone he came in contact with. He doesn't even care that he has abandoned a faithful wife, and three beautiful innocent children, who I thought were once his pride and joy."

Trying to be mother, father, counselor and friend to my children and leading a church out of the ruins seemed... well, I have no words.

It had to be sort of an Esther moment for me. I had to believe that God truly had prepared me for this. If He had not, I would have possibly not made it.

As I am writing this, the Lord spoke Psalm 127:1 to me, *"Unless the Lord builds the house, they labor in vain who build it."*

(Amp)

I was determined to plant my feet firmly, and let the Lord build this house He had ordained to be a place for His glory to dwell. I claimed that over my personal household as well.

I will always trust God to do things His way. During the unfolding of all that transpired, I had no agenda of my own and I never did. It is a simple fact that I was the victim of the totality of Jeff's actions, and not the perpetrator.

Jeff was soon arrested on theft charges. Both by law and ethically, he had no right to any of the money that he took, especially church money.

As I said before, Jeff and I deliberately chose to not ever draw a salary from our church. We were fully taken care of by the funds generated by our international ministry and didn't want to be paid from the church.

Jeff fully supported this until he changed.

He had begun to say things like, "The church does nothing for us. They literally give us nothing."

He often said that he wanted to close the church because he it was a burden to him. This was absolutely inconceivable to me. My church was my family.

In hindsight, I see that I should have taken some of his comments more seriously. I wanted to think maybe he was just speaking through a filter of fatigue.

He vacillated back and forth. One day he would be ready to just quit all ministry, and the next day, he was going to shut down the church and focus on building his ministry empire.

Another day, he seemed to need the church to house his ministry center.

He had lost his love for the church, the Bride of Christ. Did he ever really love our church as a true shepherd loves his sheep? Or, was this just the difference in Jeff and Jeffrey?

Chapter Twenty-Three

ADJUSTING

Coasting To A Stop

The next year or so was a roller-coaster ride I wanted to get off. My first priority was my children, of course. Becoming the sole everything in my home was consuming. I prayed to continue home schooling my children. I was concerned that at some point I would be forced to get a job and put them in public school. This alone was a nightmare to me.

I graduated my older daughter Mercy from high school during this time and I threw a grand Sweet Sixteen birthday party for her. For her to graduate from high school at the age of sixteen was quite an accomplishment in itself and speaks highly of her determination. I was very proud of her. She graduated with a 4.0 grade point average!

There were happy times, but there was always an overtone of grief and the unknown. Their father was somewhere, living a life that didn't mirror reality.

Someone told me he had moved out of his daughter's home and had purchased a $250,000 RV and that he was living on property that belonged to one of his friends. Having an RV was something he had always wanted. He enjoyed just going to look at them on sales lots.

I think this was part of the freedom that perhaps Jeffrey desired. It was a freedom he thought he deserved, but it wasn't Jeff's reality. He was living the life that Jeffrey felt was paradise.

I know Jeff felt differently. Jeff loved his family and his home. Occasionally people would send me videos that appeared to be filmed in a large RV.

As we prepared for a high school graduation ceremony for my daughter's home school tutorial that she had attended her entire life, she said, "Mom, I always thought both of my parents would come to my high school graduation, but I honestly don't think I can take Dad walking in."

We prayed God would have His way. We chose to not invite Jeff, for fear he would create some kind of drama and make it all about him. Thank God he didn't come uninvited.

My children had begun confiding different things to me that they had seen Jeff do, and even types of abuse he inflicted on them, as they now felt safe to release these burdens that they had been carrying for a long time. I was thankful they trusted me enough to confide in me.

Mercy even asked me to please have Jeff's belongings removed from our home. She was quite insistent upon it.

He had already removed many of his important belongings from the house. All of his guitars were gone, as well as many other things he considered important to him. It was clear he had planned his escape for a long time and had been sneaking things out, from time to time.

I hired a moving company and had everything pertaining to him moved to a storage unit. This brought peace to my children, particularly to Mercy. Maybe I didn't realize the level of damage that had been done to them because I had so many plates spinning. I trusted God to just cover them in His love.

I could somewhat relate to "father" trauma. My father was not the best influence on me either, as he had left my home and abandoned me at age nine.

My parents' divorce was somewhat of a scandal as he was a deacon in the church and was having an affair. He married the woman he had an affair with, and although he said he didn't want children, he adopted hers. I did pursue a relationship with him throughout my lifetime, and accepted things as they were. I grew to love his wife and her children. My mother remarried and moved on as well.

My dad did come back to the Lord before his death and make things right with me. Perhaps somehow Jeff would see the light at some point and make things right with me and our children? All I could do now was pray and do damage control.

One Day At A Time

I walked through the next year or so one day at a time. I remembered the old Christy Lane song, "One day at a time, sweet Jesus, that's all I'm asking from You. Just give me the strength to do every day, what I have to do. Yesterday's gone, sweet Jesus, and tomorrow may never be mine. Lord, help me today, show me the way, one day at a time."

I continued to hear rumors of Jeff telling others that I was just out to get him and he continued blaming me for all he had done, playing the innocent victim role. Any discerning person could read into his behavior.

Why didn't the people now telling me the ways that they had noticed Jeff coming off the rails, come forward at the time? Why didn't the church members who admitted they were giving him money behind my back tell me then? Why were they all coming forward now?

I don't blame them for putting him on a pedestal, but that is never healthy. If a man or woman of God is asking you to give them money privately, and withhold from your church, there is an ungodly hidden agenda at play.

I had shed so many tears because of sense of being let down by those I thought were my friends. A few intentionally betrayed me because they had similar spirits to the kinds Jeff was operating in. Many didn't understand and didn't want anything to do with any of it.

Regardless, for the few months that he was still trying to conduct a church, my worst fears had come true. I had often expressed my fear of my beloved church family being hurt, and I couldn't deny that on some level, this was happening.

Jeff spent months trying to destroy our church and pull people out. I don't think his church ever grew beyond the few that left with him and backed him up. He bragged online that his church had grown so much he had to get a larger facility.

People who had visited there told me this was simply not true. He must have failed to make expenses in the building he rented. Although he told people he needed a facility that would hold up to a thousand people, in reality he rented a small room inside a facility that could hold a thousand people if all rooms were filled. The room he rented was really small in comparison.

He eventually changed the name of his "church" (I can't keep calling it a church with a clear conscience, which is why I apply quotation marks) to Father's House 360. I guess he was finally convinced he had no rights to the name of Global Fire Ministries or Global Fire Church.

While he continued to try to build a new work, I always felt that it left a black mark on us at Global Fire. Rumors went around like spreading wildfire. More and more people were coming to me just wanting to know the truth.

He eventually closed his "church" without pomp and circumstance. There were no announcements, they just stopped meeting. It only lasted a few months.

He still had a website for a while, stating he was founder of Father's House 360. I wondered if he had any concept of reality at this point.

He continued to point to Trump in many of the videos he still released, as his patriot stance had gained him a lot more followers and a lot of attention. Thousands of people still followed him on Facebook.

Magazines, including Newsweek, in the secular market, and Charisma in the Christian arena, had done articles on him at this point, and none of them were positive.

His reputation had been tarnished. It was all preventable, if he had only listened to our warnings.

All you had to do was Google "Jeff Jansen" and you could clearly see the controversy. There were talk videos where Jeff was the main topic. The discussions were about him leaving his wife and family, and being released from his church and ministry, as well as his very public stand for Trump. Very few gave him the benefit of the doubt. Of course, a lot of the secular market tried to attach his failure to his stand for Trump.

The accusations being made about him were becoming more blatant. Many churches and pastors continued to text me, email me, or call me. A surprising number of them, on top of the ones who had already contacted me, told me that he had been drinking or was drunk when he came to their churches.

Pastors told me he had contacted them and told them I had left him and was divorcing him for no reason at all, so that I could achieve power over the church. Somehow, he coerced them into giving him great amounts of money. Some of his friends had given him thousands of dollars not realizing what was going on in our lives. They all expressed deep sorrow for me and my children.

They all encouraged me with, "Hang in there, Jan. God's got this!" They repented to me for sowing into such a broken man. Of course I didn't blame them.

Everyone still loved him, but they were insulted that he would take advantage of them and jeopardize their churches and ministries by ministering impurely while he was with them and taking advantage of them.

I was shocked at all the information that came to me without my seeking it. Some of the comments I heard from other churches and ministers were:

"We could clearly see he was off, or not right." (There was that word "off" again.)

"We didn't know what was wrong with him, but he acted as if he had been drinking."

"He seemed very different from the Jeff we had known earlier on in his ministry."

I can honestly say that it hurts me to tell you these things and it hurts me to know these things.

I did ask a few people why they didn't come forward at the time of the offense. The consensus was that they wanted to believe the best and didn't want to hurt me, or his reputation. They also didn't want to admit they had been taken advantage of.

It was apparent that he had led a double life on a much deeper level than even I knew, while presenting himself as a pure and clean vessel of God outwardly.

I wasn't contacting anyone to gather information about Jeff. I knew what I knew about what was going on, and what had been going on for a long time, but suddenly I realized, I didn't know the half of it.

The minister told me to keep my mouth shut because God would do the exposing, and it was happening.

I seemed to be swirling in a sea of negativity and I was in shock with all I was hearing from so many places and people from all over the world.

Being a glass half full, rather than glass half empty person, I recognized that all of the trusted ministers who reached out to me during this time gave me confirming and encouraging words. Not one was against me. The positive was beginning to far outweigh the negative. This was a huge foundation to stand on.

I cannot say this enough: I am very thankful for those who believed the truth and were discerning, and I offer many thanks to those who stood with me throughout this ordeal.

I knew the Lord stood with me and with my church. I continued to stand with Him and press into what He told me to do. We continued to host conferences, and ministers who had once come and ministered when Jeff was here, graciously agreed to come. They all made it known they were standing with me.

They publicly spoke out in support of me and the church from the pulpit. My confidence was beginning to build and I clearly realized nothing had been a surprise to God. I've had many powerful prophetic words from guest ministers who spoke over me and our church. We have held onto these words in complete faith that they will come to pass.

Women came forward telling me of encounters they had with Jeff, none blatantly sexual, but definitely not ministerial.

Now that he was gone, I felt led to contact Emma, the lady from Australia, to ask her what really happened.

My main question, and reason I needed closure, was if they'd actually had a physical affair or was it only emotional, or ministerial, as he had told me repeatedly.

I messaged her on Facebook and simply asked her, "Was your affair with Jeff physical?"

She responded without hesitation and said, "I am so sorry, I lied to you. Yes, it was physical. I was hurt very badly by him. He targeted me, as I was a new Christian. He spiritually abused me, and I went to the ACC (Australian Council of Churches) and complained of the damage he had done to me. They suggested I sue him, but I didn't want to relive the drama."

Of course, I confronted her on the messages I found where she said she couldn't meet with him in 2017 unless her pastor was present, but she still agreed to meet with him. Her response was that she was still emotionally and even physically challenged from his abuse.

She cut me off short and said she could not answer any more of my questions. Then she blocked me from Facebook, saying she was too damaged to talk about it further. At least I had confirmation that this was a full-blown affair.

It also became known that he had been talking to a woman I will call Alicia (not her real name). I knew that he had been talking to her for a long time, but he would never explain who she was. He always claimed he was mentoring all these women I caught him talking to.

Alicia also lived in another country. I didn't even know if they had ever met face to face. I went to her Facebook profile, and she looked as if she were twenty-years old, but even she admitted her profile photos were filters.

Interestingly, Jeff managed to leave his iPad behind and I was able to log onto it and see messages for a month or so.

I clearly saw he was in a relationship with this woman, and had been for at least a year or more. Mercy had somehow come across Jeff's passwords and the password to his iPad was simply the name, Alicia.

I could also see conversations he was having with other people as well, which was very enlightening.

I could see the lies that he was telling people on Facebook Messenger and email. Somehow he figured out I could see his messages, and blocked my access.

In the end, it is a fact that while he was married to me, he was involved in a relationship with Alicia and that he told her he had been divorced from me for a long time. She even called herself his fiancé.

The truth is, I did file for divorce in May of 2021, after it was apparent that he wasn't coming back and that he made no attempt at repentance or reconciliation. I knew I had every biblical reason for divorce, and had known this for years, which was why I begged the Lord for so long to release me.

I felt that my safety and the safety of my children was in jeopardy. I felt I needed protection, physically, emotionally, financially, and legally, which led me to consult an attorney.

I loved Jeff and I would have always been willing to talk about a restoration process, if only he were humble and willing. I sought out great counsel on the decision to file for divorce from ministers, counselors, and pastors that I trusted. It was not a flippant decision.

I again tried to reach out to Jeff a time or two toward the end, to see what he was truly thinking. There were one or two occasions where he would contact me unexpectedly and tell me he missed the children and wanted to see them, but he wasn't willing to humble himself to make that happen. This had to be court ordered.

I tried to have conversations with him to see if there was anything left to save of our relationship and former life together. I got nothing from him to indicate that there was.

Pretty early into any conversation we had, he would begin accusing me, and blaming me for all he had done, and he refused to listen to reason. If I disagreed with him, he would quickly hang up then block me from his phone.

I concluded that even if I had an emergency with the children, he was not stable enough for us to rely on. I couldn't reach him anyway, because he had my number blocked.

By now he had changed all of his contact info except his phone number, so I just left it in God's hands and felt there was nothing else I could do.

Soon after he left, his mug shot was sent to me by someone I didn't even know, who had found it online. He had apparently received his third DUI. It was circulated all over social media, as was the mug shot from his theft arrest.

It broke my heart to realize that a man, who was given so much from God had fallen and become a source of contempt and embarrassment in the Christian community.

Through it all, Jeff continued to make videos and livestreams and publish them, so the general public had no idea of the real truth. He acted as if it was business as usual.

He looked like he had aged so much, and just looked unwell to me, and to others who spoke to me about it. He didn't even look like the same person I had once known. He looked sunken and sallow, and the color of his skin was even different. He had grown quite a beard as well.

He rambled and didn't even make sense at times on his videos. I couldn't keep watching them.

All of his videos were now being shot in his RV. He was living the life that Jeffrey felt was paradise. I often wondered if my Jeff was ever allowed to be out front, at all any more.

After much delay, it was actually months before we finally had our first court date for divorce, child support, and alimony.

Jeff showed up with his entourage, those who had supported him in his bad decisions and who had played the recruiter roles. They all looked at me with hatred in their eyes, and wore offense like a garment.

I had asked my daughter Mercy, my associate pastor Kim, and Jerry Bryant, the pastor who married us, to accompany me. Jerry wasn't choosing sides, but he did know the truth.

As information was brought out in the brief hearing, it became very obvious that Jeff had misled his own attorney, and even the judge, with the information he brought to court. This was another confirmation that Jeffrey believed his own deception.

The court documents his attorney brought clearly stated he had been drawing his salary from Global Fire Church and that he was an employee of the church. This was patently untrue.

There were several other pieces of false information. His attorney didn't know any better, so he simply put what Jeff had told him on the documents, without doing his own investigation.

The judge found that both Jeff's attorney and mine were unprepared for the hearing. It seemed they hadn't communicated with each other at all. The judge called me to the stand.

"Mrs. Jansen, is any of this information presented by Mr. Jansen's attorney factual?" he asked.

"No sir, it's not. Neither of us ever drew a salary from the church at all. The rest of the information is not accurate either."

Surprisingly, the judge announced that apparently neither attorney had properly prepared for this hearing, so he dismissed the hearing in order for discovery to take place before we could come back to court.

The judge did have to order some kind of temporary visitation agreement regarding our children. This was something I had grieved heavily over, and one of the reasons I stayed with Jeff for so long. I was afraid for him to have visitation with my children without supervision. He had proven he could not control his drinking, so I feared what he might do if he had my children, unsupervised.

What if he drove drunk with them in the car? What if his actions were as dangerous as had been demonstrated in the past? I had known him to drive drunk many times and he now had three DUIs to confirm he had no restraint. He had even driven his Harley Davidson through our residential neighborhood drunk at great speeds with no helmet on. It is a mystery as to how he was never caught, early on.

I was horrified at the thought of him having my children without my being there to protect them. I prayed and prayed and asked the Lord to please not allow him visitation at all, or at least not without supervision.

The Lord heard my prayers. The judge ordered supervised visitation with me, and another appointed person, who was to be agreed on by both of us, and would be present during the visits. We agreed on the former Vineyard minister who had married us, and who still loved us both, Jerry.

This pastor had reached out to Jeff many times to minister to him. He'd said Jeff was unresponsive and blamed others for everything he did, particularly me.

Jerry still agreed to sacrifice every other Saturday because he loved us both so much. He still wanted to believe Jeff could be restored. This was a great sacrifice, in my eyes.

The first time we were to meet, it was at the chapel next to our main church building, which was our youth building.

Mercy absolutely refused to see him. My two youngest children were inside our main building, but were hesitant to see him. They were just fearful of the unknown.

I simply wanted to talk calmly to Jeff before bringing the children over. All they felt toward him at this point was fear and uncertainty, understandably so.

He had abandoned us with no explanation or apology. How do you explain this to a child who so desperately needs love and stability from both parents? I had no explanation.

I met him at our youth chapel and simply said, "I need to tell you how our kids feel."

Without allowing me to explain or even hear my concerns, he jumped up and without hesitation said, "Oh no! If they aren't here, I'm out of here."

I told him they were in the main building, but I simply needed to talk to him first to explain how they feel. My daughter, Truth, had written him a letter to express to him her feelings. I told him that, and offered it to him but he sternly said, "I don't want to read that!" He bolted out of the building.

Jerry was there to supervise of course, and witnessed the whole thing. He followed Jeff out to his vehicle and tried to reason with him.

Jeff refused to listen and just drove away. Jerry had offered him the letter again, but he refused to take it. I was baffled.

He had a second chance for visitation two weeks later, which was court ordered.

In an absolute state of anxiety that Saturday morning, I drove to the main church building with my older daughter and my son. My older daughter wanted nothing to do with him and at this point, due to the severe PTSD she had been dealing with, I was not going to force her.

Truth had spent the night with a friend and refused to come to the visitation. Her friends had become more important to her, by now.

Mercy had the job of cleaning our church. When we arrived, she quickly darted out of the van and unlocked the door of the main building of our church to go in to clean. She ignored Jeff, as she had so often done, recently. She had no intention of even speaking with him. She only came with me to clean the church, and that was it.

Jeff was supposed to stay at our chapel, by court order, but seeing us pull in, he came rushing over to the main building, opened the door to our van without warning, and grabbed my son by the arm. I was terrified!

Given was deeply afraid at being yanked out of the safety of our van. A man he once called Dad, but who had put him through years of uncertainty then had just abandoned him, now grabbed hold of him and pulled him away from the only stability he had ever known, his mother.

Jerry saw what was going on, then got into his own car and drove from the chapel over to the main building. Jeff walked away with Given, unsupervised, and headed towards the chapel.

"Jerry, what should I do?" I pleaded. Jerry headed towards the chapel on foot.

Jeff walked around with Given for a couple of minutes, whispering in his ear. When Jeff saw Jerry coming towards him, he let Given go, and walked up to the main door of our church and demanded to see Mercy. Given ran to me. Jerry walked over to Given and me.

I told Jeff as kindly as I knew how, that Mercy had no desire to see him and that she was locked in. He began demanding that she come out and confront him.

I warned him that he was being recorded on our doorbell cam, and that my staff could see him in real time. He said he didn't care and would break into the church, if he had to. He was raising his voice and flailing his arms, as we had so often seen him to before.

Realizing anything was possible at this point, I opened the door with my key, locked it behind me as I entered, and went to talk to Mercy, while Pastor Jerry had Given. I told Mercy that her Dad was very threatening, and that he said he would break into the church if she didn't come out. Although I knew he could not literally break into the church, I told her she needed to confront him herself, or he wouldn't relent.

My heart was pounding out of my chest. She finally, very reluctantly agreed to come out. I could see the fear on her face.

As she hesitantly walked out the door, he immediately marched up to her and began to verbally challenge her.

He hurled accusations against Mercy and me, claiming that I had turned her against him. He accused her of lying to people about him and yelled, "I'll make you take a lie detector test!"

I couldn't believe that Jeff was given two opportunities to see his children, and he blew both opportunities because he simply couldn't control himself!

Mercy ran back into the building and later told me she was so upset that she became sick and literally threw up.

Jerry came to Jeff and said, "This was supposed to be a visit between you and your children. This wasn't meant to be an opportunity for you to attack your daughter and wife in front of your young son."

Jeff didn't hesitate to push his chest up to this sweet man, who had pastored us and mentored us so much early in our marriage and yell, "Hey old man! You're taking up for her!"

I was actually afraid for Jerry and realized that Jeff, or Jeffrey, could truly hurt him.

It was Jeff's disadvantage that this was all recorded on our doorbell cam. Jerry wasn't going to accept being threatened as if it were two men in a brawl. Somehow, Jerry was able to talk Jeff off the ledge.

Jeff dragged Given next door to the chapel, and walked around with him for about an hour or so. Our dear pastor and friend stayed close, and followed them around. I was humbled that Jerry didn't just leave.

I went inside the chapel to sit down and just pray. My heart was in my throat at this point. Unexpectedly, Jeff stepped inside for a brief minute. I saw a glimpse of the real Jeff, but just a very brief one.

He surprised me by saying, "Jan, I don't want to fight with you. I want this to be good for both of us. Please tell me that you still love me."

I knew it was the real Jeff, in a momentary state of his being able to step out front, despite the obvious Jeffrey behavior he had just demonstrated.

I didn't know what to say. I stuttered, "What? There's a lot to this. You just threatened our daughter and me, for no reason."

I was calm and noncombative, but resolute.

He walked away without saying another word. I felt like I had just encountered both the real Jeff and the absolutely impossible Jeffrey in a matter of seconds.

I took the confrontational video from our door cam to my attorney, and visitation was temporarily suspended.

Because Jeff had pending court appearances with the third DUI and the theft charge, he could not be questioned in a divorce court because he had the right to remain silent. Our divorce was basically halted.

The DUI was eventually heard in court after he had postponed this hearing three or four times. He was sentenced, but somehow got the charges lowered to a second offense.

Amazingly he was sentenced to just a couple of days in jail. I couldn't believe it! His third offense DUI occurred in my hometown of McMinnville, which was about an hour from where we lived.

I was told that the one jail there was full, so minor offenders were being let off with mild consequences.

Word got back to me that he was telling everyone that he was never really arrested for anything, but that I had made it all up and that I even created fake mug shots myself, on my computer. Did anyone believe him? This was the second time he circulated these lies, the first time being when he was arrested for theft and that particular mug shot was circulating.

The reason Jeff's church didn't survive was because it was not built on the plans and the desires of the God of Heaven and Earth. It was built on Jeff's desires to make a point and destroy me, and to make himself look innocent. If he could destroy me and the church, he could continue to blame me and tell everyone that I was the guilty sinful one, and not him.

I was still reeling from the betrayal I had experienced from him and from the few who followed him who I once considered to be faithful members of our church.

Some who'd separated themselves from both of us stating that they didn't want to take sides later came to me and repented for doubting, saying that they just didn't want to be in the middle of things. Others repented for leaving the church and came back to be a part of what the Lord was doing at the Fire Church. Still others have made peace with me since.

I still wonder how those who clearly knew Jeff's lifestyle could stand with him and just turn a blind eye to sin. I still think about what other lies he may have told. I shouldn't care, but it's hard not to, if I'm being honest.

During this time, the Lord said to me, "Those who you see standing with you are those I have caused to stand. Some of them may surprise you, but trust Me. Embrace them. Those who obviously do not draw to you, dismiss them. They are not meant to be in your life, at least not right now."

Those words were more valuable than I can tell you. I developed new relationships and had old relationships restored. New people have continually come into my life and church since that time. God is so good.

It would be an entire book, in and of itself, to tell you all the information that people brought to me in this season of betrayal and adjustment.

I was amazed at how many great men and women of God sent me Facebook friend requests at this time. It just showed me that I had an alliance with many of God's great ones, and that they were with me. I do not have words for my thankfulness.

In later reflection, I had begun to realize that Jeff traveled without me and our family just so he could drink, because so many pastors were contacting me continuously to tell me of their experiences. I didn't know why so many people bothered to contact me after he left, but in a way, it brought me more confirmation and more closure. One minister friend even told me that Jeff had confessed he prevented me from traveling with him so that he could, in his words, "do whatever he wanted".

I admit, I was forced to wonder if this information had gotten to me sooner would it have changed anything? But Jeff's downward spiral was already well underway. At the end of the day, even if I'd had more information, it would have been just that... more information. I don't see how I could have tried any harder to rescue him.

It was all so inconceivable. In the aftermath, all I could say was, "This is a book, or maybe even a movie."

I was now living completely by faith. God showed up for me so many times, in so many unexpected ways. I never doubted Him. I just thanked him for my miracles before they were seen. I thanked him for the unseen to manifest into the natural. He has never failed me, to this day.

It is easy to become bitter and angry with God when you are tested to this level. But I know, that I know that God saw it all from beginning to end, from His vantage point of being outside of time and He walked through every bit of it with me.

Instead of being angry that I wasted twenty-eight years on Jeff, I have learned to praise the Lord for all that I was so honored to encounter. I would often ask the Lord why He allowed twenty-eight years of my life to be wasted. Or at least, that was how I saw it.

I had many fears that if Jeff wouldn't submit to a healing process, that I would end up in the place where I now stood. These are the many petitions I laid out before the Lord, the deep concerns that I had.

One concern was that I would have to get a full-time job as a nurse, stop home schooling and have to put my kids in the public school system. I didn't want that for them. God knew I would end up being a single parent. I had asked the Lord for one child, and He had given me three.

In prayer, I asked him once, "Lord, why did You give me three children, knowing I would be left alone with them? Why did I waste twenty-eight years of my life?"

His answer was simple. "They are safe in your hands. They need you, and you need them. They will overcome all they have experienced from this. I've got this."

He added, "None of those years were wasted. You had to be with Jeff to get to where you are going. You would never have had the experiences and opportunities you have had, especially regarding My glory. It had to be this way. You would also not have your children, if it weren't for this marriage."

His words have been words of Life that have kept me hanging on. He has been faithful to speak and lead me on.

One of my intercessors had a vision, once. She saw me lying in my bed, and saw Jesus enter the room. He walked over to me and laid a sword over the top of my body, the handle over my chest with the blade pointing towards my feet. Jesus whispered over me, "This is the sword I have used to fight for you. Now, you will experience My glory!"

I have received countless other words to confirm how God was in everything, and He has covered and protected me, my children, and my church. He truly had prepared me "for such a time as this".

Don't misunderstand me. God never brings tragedy and despair. But for some reason, sometimes He allows it. He will always use that which was meant for harm, for our good and for the good of the kingdom and His glory.

My other great fear was that the church would not survive. The Lord has brought many generals of the faith to me to decree and declare that the church was God's church, not Jeff's church, and that the purposes for which it was established still stand.

The Lord spoke to me about the deep wells that had been dug here. He showed me that the enemy had tried to fill those wells with trash and garbage, but that we were redigging the wells, and they were being filled with the glory of God.

An angel appeared to me during one Sunday service and stood in the middle aisle at the altar. He held a huge rod in his hand. He took the rod and rammed it into the ground. At this moment, I shook violently in my natural body. In the Spirit, I asked the angel, "Who are you and what do you bring?" The angel said, "I have come to bring the restoration of all things."

This has been a theme of our church since. We humbly carry the fire, in Him!

Jeff's obsession after he left us, was to have everything he always felt he deserved, but had been denied. He had no realization that God had something different in mind. His main responsibility was to the Lord God, then to his family, then his church. But he had his priorities twisted, due to deception. He left me, and got everything he felt that the church and I had denied him, not realizing he had created his own restrictions. He had satisfied his flesh in every way.

He got his driver's license back. He bought his SUV. He had his RV. He had snakes. (I hated snakes and would never allow one in the house). When he left, he wasted no time purchasing two snakes, I suppose just to spite me.

He went to the gym regularly. He took testosterone and hormone shots, that he purchased at the co-op, meant for animals, to increase his muscle size. I knew this because I found them in his belongings before he left.

I wondered if these medications contributed to causing his behavior to be even more volatile.

He got all of his weapons back from our associate pastor. The pastor had no more rights to keep them, nor did I, as Jeff was no longer at the church and no longer lived in our home.

True to the words he said in the back of our sanctuary that Sunday, Jeff tried to start a church where no one would be able to tell him what to do.

As I told him on the phone in that one conversation he allowed a month and a half after he left, "Well, you have everything you thought you wanted and were deprived of. Let me know if that makes you happy."

God doesn't give us everything we want just because we think we deserve it. He's a good, good Father and gives us what He decides we can handle responsibly. He only gives us our heart's desire when and if those desires are pure and are in agreement with God's word.

Jeff was not responsible with what he had been given, so there had been restrictions applied. If he could't leave the house unsupervised, without buying alcohol and becoming abusive to his family, there should be restrictions. If he had talked about suicide, he had to assume that perhaps he shouldn't be entitled to have an arsenal of weapons and perhaps those should be taken from him for his own protection. If his travels brought destruction to him, perhaps he should not travel.

Jeff was warned over a period of ten years that if he perverted the anointing of God, God would take his life. Although he said this scared him, it didn't scare him enough for him to humble himself and change. Like Jacob, he wrestled with God many times.

As the Lord had spoken to me, "Jeff never humbled himself long enough to go through the process of healing." As deeply as he was wounded, healing would have been a process, and not instantaneous for him.

I had no hopes of reconciliation in our marriage. Too much damage had been done. I was no longer willing to tolerate abuse, and he had made no real effort to even acknowledge that he cared about me or my children. He had not made even one effort to support us, contact us beyond a couple of texts early on, or even check on us.

Jeff and I had a mutual friend who committed suicide in 2021 and, to my surprise, Jeff came knocking on my back door soon after that. I often ordered groceries or other items, so I assumed this was that.

Face To Face Encounter

I opened the door, not knowing it was him, and without even saying hello, he said, "Jamie killed herself."

With much grief in my heart, I told him I had already heard. Of course, the younger kids ran to the door to see who I was talking to.

Given pushed his way through the door and said "Daddy? Are you back home now?"

Jeff answered him with a quick, "No."

Truth stuck her head out and said, "Hi, Dad!" She waited to see what he would do.

He said, "Hi, Truth", but made no effort to talk to either of the kids, showed no emotion whatsoever, then just returned to his SUV and drove away.

My kids stood there with a blank look on their faces. Although I didn't want them around him, my heart hurt for them. I had experienced rejection from my father. I understood the depth of that pain.

All I could say was, "I'm sorry." I couldn't even explain why he didn't missed his children and our family.

We are all responsible for our walk, our journey. Jeff had more guidance and counsel than anyone I have ever known. Many people loved him. Many people looked up to him. Many people believed he could be amazing. But ultimately, he himself didn't feel he could be amazing, so he succumbed to his own insecurities that came from severe childhood abuse.

In the end, he had no money. His church had failed. He had no outlets of ministry. I heard he had a couple of invitations only at the end, from people who had no idea what he had done.

His attorney contacted my attorney and said Jeff was engaged to Alicia, and wanted to move to the country she lived in immediately.

They had gone public with their engagement and although Jeff and I had never divorced, he was pushing for the divorce to finalize now so he could supposedly marry this woman.

I felt impressed by the Spirit of God, he was trying to flee the country before his court date for theft, because he truly feared he would get jail time.

Again, neither I, nor my church, ever pressed charges. It was out of our control by this time. We couldn't have dropped the charges, because he was tried by a judge, then the charges were bound over to a grand jury.

The grand jury believed there was enough evidence to prove him guilty, and the district attorney had scheduled a trial.

Jeff had managed to postpone his hearing four times for various reasons, all to buy him more time I suppose, until he could get out of the country. Maybe he reasoned that it might be dismissed, but the court finally said there would be no more cancellations and his court date was scheduled in August 2022.

Although his taking the money was so wrong, I had sympathy for the real man who I knew would never do this.

Jeff did contact me by text a time or two, in complete desperation, and begged me to drop the charges. I reiterated that I had not pressed the charges, so I could not drop them.

He got very angry and said that if I really wanted to drop the charges, I could. I told him I was sorry, but it was completely out of my hands. He must have indeed been a very anxious man.

Never once did I rejoice in his calamity. On the contrary, I was deeply sorrowful.

An intercessor, who I mentioned before, who frequently had encounters and words for me and the church, contacted me and told me that, in the Spirit, she saw Jeff, pacing the floors and wringing his hands. She said he was desperate and afraid.

He had been asked to take his RV and leave the yard of the friend and former church member who had supported him, for reasons unknown to me.

I suspected his drinking was more noticeable and couldn't be tolerated. He was losing his RV because he could not pay for it and had no provision. He was afraid he might go to jail. His decisions were catching up with him.

If you wonder how I knew these things, details always had a way of getting back to me.

He put his RV up for sale and, after losing it, he moved in with an old friend, the one who had lost his wife to suicide in 2021. She was the mutual friend Jeff came to the house to tell me about. I think the two of them living together was not an arrangement made in Heaven. They were both troubled, and together, it seemed volatile. That is just my opinion. Apparently, they had lived together briefly when Jeff and his first wife were getting a divorce.

The Download

In June of 2022, I was in my bathroom getting ready for bed, and suddenly a download from the Lord fell on me. As I said earlier, many times the Lord would speak to me in what seemed to be an audible voice, sometimes He would just whisper into my spirit, but at times, my "knower" would just know what He was saying.

Now and then, He would just drop a download on me, into my Spirit, and I would get a sudden awareness of His divine inspiration, in a moment. This was one of those downloads.

I suddenly just knew that Jeff would die soon. I can't tell you how I knew this, except by the Holy Spirit. If the Lord God wants you to know something, He will communicate it to you, one way or the other.

Even though Jeff had told me the Lord would take his life if he perverted the anointing, he had also told me in moments of seriousness, that he would die young, and I would live to be very old. I never really gave it much thought at the time.

The sudden reality that God was telling me this, and not Jeff this time, hit me like a lead balloon, and I just fell to the floor in grief and tears. It wasn't so much that I still felt I was in love with him. I think love can fade, when faced with abuse and rejection, but I loved the man I had met and married, and I grieved for that man who had seemingly been kept a prisoner of his broken parts.

I wept for about forty-five minutes and cried out to the Lord for the man I had once intimately known. I petitioned the Lord to save his soul, based on who the real man of God was, the general that God had invited him to be. I cried out for the potential that was seemingly wasted. I cried from the depths of my being.

Chapter Twenty-Four

THE PRECIPICE

A Long Way Down

What I saw at this point was a precipice. A precipice is a very steep rock face or cliff, especially a tall one. I even shared about the precipice at church. I felt I had certainly been digging my heels in, climbing a mountain to overcome all the obstacles that I'd been forced to encounter.

My children and I were settling into a routine the best that we could, to get a grip on our new normal.

I had the greatest church family I have ever known. It was truly an answer to much prayer. The Fire Church was not a center. It was a family. We were growing, and not just surviving, we were thriving. As I looked around me, I saw nothing but humble, servant-hearted people.

God truly was restoring all things. God was now leading the church and doing things His way.

As for me and my staff and leaders, we just yielded to His desires. The glory of God manifested in our services. The tangible Presence came in like a tsunami at times. There were times I felt so blessed that I said I could pinch myself.

After Jeff's church closed, and there were no more recruiters trying to bring division and destruction, a sense of peace had fallen over us.

Someone put it that we had climbed the heights and won the race. God was pleased. We could breathe now. I could breathe now. My children could breathe now.

This was my precipice. I felt I was looking out from this high place, seeing that the future was bright and hopeful.

Although my spiritual father, Bob Jones, had died years before, his widow Bonnie and I had remained friends. She was one who had stood with me faithfully.

She and Prophet James Goll agreed to come and be part of a conference at the church, which we'd felt led to call The Restoration of All Things.

It was a powerful event, where we felt the Lord did many acts of restoration in the Spirit as well as the natural. While here, Bonnie confided to me that Bob had always known Jeff would not end well.

Bob had said to her, "Jeff was not accountable and was disrespectful to authority".

She said Bob knew Jeff would not see another move of God's great glory, and that he said, "I believe Jan will see it".

I learned so much from Bob. Bob tried to warn Jeff more times than I can tell you. Jeff always thought Bob was just being comical, but I knew Bob was serious. I wish Jeff had listened, and yielded to his fatherly authority.

I also believe Jeff had reached a precipice. I feel he had come to a place where he saw very little hope. Perhaps he was realizing that he had ruined everything. Someone once confirmed to me that he had just given up.

After he left, he showed up in many of my dreams. In the dreams, he was always in the background, just watching. It was as if he realized what he had thrown away. I prayed to the Lord that Jeff would stop appearing in my dream life. I felt I was almost being pursued by Jeff. One night I was even awakened to Jeff's audible voice calling my name. I sat straight up in bed with chills running down my spine.

I prayed, "Lord, if he ever truly repents, I ask that he come and repent to me and my children, so we will know he is serious."

After I had the encounter in the bathroom, feeling his death was imminent, I tried not to think about it. I had suffered too much reality already.

During this time I had several people tell me that they had dreams or visions that Jeff had died. Some saw him as the victim of an automobile accident. Others saw a different fate.

I have to admit, every time my doorbell rang from that point, I cautiously peered out of the glass at the top of my doors, almost expecting to see a police officer standing there to bring bad news.

I wanted to pray for the Lord to spare Jeff, but in my heart of hearts, I felt the decision had been made. That was a sobering thought, so I tried to dismiss it and focus on the priorities at hand. I just prayed his soul would be saved.

After that bathroom encounter, I got a couple of phone calls out of the blue from people Jeff and I had once walked with, who wanted me to know they had spoken to Jeff recently. This would have been in Spring and Summer, 2022.

One was from a former member of our church. Another man had an unexpected encounter with him in a Nashville restaurant. It seemed that Jeff was, in some way, feeling at least some level of acknowledgement and maybe even remorse for what he had done.

One of the men said Jeff confessed to everything. He said that Jeff told him, "It was all me, Jan did nothing wrong." This man and Jeff had a long conversation. The man prayed with Jeff.

Jeff was still unwilling to come forward publicly, repent, and ask for restoration. I did feel relief that Jeff at least had moments where he recognized reality and was confessing some of his sins to at least somebody. At least, he had moments when he was not living in complete denial. God is a good God and He was convicting him.

The man who ran into him in the restaurant had no prior knowledge of Jeff's actions. He spoke briefly with Jeff, then invited him to come to a prayer meeting. He said Jeff did show up, and that he and several men prayed for him.

Jeff spoke few words while there, but he did say, "I've made a lot of mistakes and ruined everything," although he didn't go into specifics.

Around this time, Jeff's fiancé contacted my daughter, Mercy, through Instagram. Mercy showed me what was said and asked, "What do I do?"

Alicia said a lot of horrible things about me, and invited my daughter to come and live with her and Jeff after they were married. Mercy told her Jeff was still married to me. It was obvious that Jeff had deceived her, and that she believed his lies.

"Your Mom is lying! She and Jeff have been divorced for years," she proclaimed to my daughter.

She told Mercy that Jeff told her that he and I were no longer married, and had been divorced for a long time, and that he was free to marry her.

She said that I was a Jezebel and had taken everything from Jeff. She also said some things that were just inappropriate to say, especially to someone my daughter's age.

Mercy handed me her phone and I felt I could not ignore it, this time. I commented to Alicia that I was Jeff's wife, and that she should stop messaging my young daughter. She immediately began lashing out at me.

Before I said anything else, I paused and prayed about how to handle this. Very obviously, Jeff had lied to her like he had lied to everyone else. I remembered how he had told me things about his ex-wife when I met him. I tried to show her compassion, based on her deception.

I told her that I was so sorry Jeff had lied to her, and that we were definitely still married, despite what Jeff had told her. I told her nothing she had been told was the truth, and that I truly felt sorry for her.

I responded to her with as much love as I could muster, considering the circumstances, as I felt it was the best thing to do. She only knew what she had been told. I also told her she needed to examine the fact that she had been having an affair with a married man for quite some time, even if it were only through cyberspace. I told her that he had not left me until April of 2021. I told her I had evidence of them being involved way before that.

She did not respond well and simply got nasty with me, so I had to block her.

I could see Jeff, or Jeffrey, was beginning to deal with his sins and his choices on one hand, but was still carrying on with this woman and filling her with lies.

I also felt he was using her as an escape method out of the country to skip out of his court date.

Our attorneys were trying to push the divorce through. We ran into one obstacle after the other. I even said, "It is as if God doesn't want us divorced."

My attorney said he had never seen anything like this before! The judge refused to sign the papers three times, on minor technicalities.

I just wanted closure. I honestly didn't care if he got married and moved to another country. I just needed peace.

My children were getting ready for the 2022-2023 school year to start. We had to change home school tutorials for several reasons. Change was imminent in our lives. It was difficult for them. We had all experienced an overdose of change.

We were preparing for the orientation at a new home school tutorial. My children had been at the same tutorial for years, so this was a big change to them. There was some degree of anxiety. We had to leave the tutorial we had been at for years for reasons beyond our control.

My children had attended a tutorial since they started school. It's like school to them where home school students go to have teachers, or tutors, make assignments and teach them. It takes a great load off the home schooling parent. The tutorial was one reason I had been able to continue home schooling.

On August 9, 2022, I took my two youngest to their new tutorial for orientation. It was a very hot day, topping out at about 95°F. It's very hot and humid in Tennessee in August. The dog days of summer can be miserable.

Orientation began at six o' clock, p.m. We gathered in the sanctuary of the church that the tutorial meets in.

As the orientation began, I could see my phone ringing, even though I had it on buzz. I saw it light up in my purse.

I picked it up to see who it was, to see if I could message them that I would have to return the call later.

It was one of our daughters-in-law who was married to one of Jeff's twins. I had not heard from them since Jeff left me, so I got a really bad feeling, and felt nauseated. Adrenaline immediately began to flow through me. I knew I had to answer, so I told my kids I'd be right back and went out in the foyer to take the call.

Without beating around the bush, she said, "Jan, Jeff has been found dead".

You can never be ready for those words. Even though you may have had some foreknowledge, you are still in denial.

I was beginning to shake all over.

"What? What happened?"

I could tell that she was really choked up and emotional.

"He was found in the hot tub where he has been living. A worker on the grounds found him. We don't know the details yet." She said that they would keep me informed.

I hung up the phone with a huge lump in my throat, forcing myself to realize that this was really happening. I couldn't keep from weeping. I almost threw up several times. The ladies in the foyer could tell I was very badly shaken.

"Can we help you? What's going on?" they asked kindly.

"I was just told that my husband was found dead. I have to get my kids and go."

They helped me collect my children and exit. They asked if I needed someone to go with me or drive me. Although I was trembling, I said no and that I would be okay.

There was one family who were my church members and were also there for the orientation. They saw me leaving, and asked what was going on. I told them Jeff was dead. They were in shock with me. They also offered to drive me home and I thanked them but told them I would be fine.

I called my daughter Mercy as soon as I closed the door to the van, and told her that her dad was found dead. She had very little to say. I told her we would talk more when I got home.

Truth and Given knew something was very wrong and wanted to know what happened. I told them their father had been found dead. They were stone-faced, and I knew they simply did not know what to say or how to respond.

After all, Jeff had abandoned us a year and a half prior, and we had essentially no contact with him since. I knew they just needed to process. This had to be extremely difficult and shocking to them, but they didn't know what to say. After all, they were only children.

One of the realizations I had in these quiet moments in the van on the way home, was that I had not completely forgiven him while he was alive. It was tough, when he had told so many people lies about me and my church, and had literally tried to destroy the reputation of both, to vindicate himself.

Somewhere from the innermost core of my being, I spoke out loud, "I can forgive him now." A wave of reality flooded me. I repeated, "Lord, I forgive him."

When I got home, I gave my children all of the few details I had at this point.

I said, "Children, I forgive him now. He can't hurt us anymore. I urge you to forgive too, even if you don't feel it yet. Just choose to forgive."

They were still speechless. I asked if they wanted to talk. They just shook their heads. Nothing.

Our daughter-in-law eventually got back in touch with me. Jeff was indeed found dead in a hot tub on his friend's property. His friend had left in the morning to run errands, but the friend had an employee working on his property. He had found Jeff dead in the hot tub.

Jeff was found at approximately four o' clock, p.m. He was floating face-down in the hot tub.

His body was taken to the medical examiner, where a forensic exam was performed. Blood was drawn, including drug levels, blood alcohol level, and toxicology.

It would take weeks to get the results back. His cause of death was a mystery at this point.

The priority at this time was planning the funeral.

We all know about the rumor mill. As word got out about his death, people began to speculate as to the cause. Some thought he overdosed on some kind of drug. Others thought he had a heart attack. Those who knew he had a drinking problem, suspected alcohol could be a factor.

His so-called fiancé was posting on Facebook that a snake had bitten him, and that I sent it to him. She called me a witch and said witchcraft had killed him.

She was extremely angry and venting all over Facebook and social media. She stated in no uncertain terms that I had killed him. Imagine how this made me feel.

I contacted a minister who had walked closely with both Jeff and I, and resided in Alicia's home country, and asked him if he knew this woman. He said that indeed, he did. He told me not to worry about anything she said because she was a person of little reputation in the ministerial world. He told me a lot more as well, but I will leave all that unsaid here.

"Ignore her, Jan," he urged.

Jeff's daughter-in-law had apparently been nominated as the spokesman for his four children. They messaged me and asked me if I wanted to plan the funeral.

I told them, "I know that he wanted to be cremated. We discussed this many times. He didn't want a big funeral. He wanted to be celebrated in life, not in death."

Jeff said to me many times, "If I pass away before you, please don't glorify me in my death. I want to be cremated, and you and my kids can have my ashes."

His adult children did not agree, so I bowed out of the funeral planning. Since I'd been pursuing a divorce, I felt that his children should plan their father's funeral. I did tell them that I truly hoped they would honor their father's wishes, and not put on a big show.

They did ask my daughter, Mercy, to be involved with the decision making. She went one time to a meeting with them and felt she had no voice, so she didn't go back.

She said, "They're going to do this their way."

I wasn't exactly sure what that meant. I was simply trusting that they'd do a good job.

They wanted a big funeral. I told them again that Jeff did not want that, but I had no choice except to let them do it their way. I wanted them to be satisfied. I knew they had not had a great relationship with their father in their adulthood. I trusted that planning his funeral would somehow bring them peace.

They did all the planning, and my children and I simply showed up.

The Funeral

One of his sons was the youth pastor at a church that Jeff and I had actually taken our kids to early in our marriage. Back then, it was called Smyrna Assembly of God. It was no longer called an Assembly of God, but was now called Springhouse. The funeral was held there.

The family had a hospitality room set up and we decided that the right thing to do was to step in there before the funeral. It was probably one of the most uncomfortable moments of my life. There was so much sadness in the room, but of course, why wouldn't there be?

Jeff's parents were very kind and warm, and my heart went out to them. No parent should ever have to bury a child.

After a few minutes of feeling that we were somehow outsiders, we left the hospitality room and entered the sanctuary. Jeff's sisters refused to speak to me at all, although his brother was quite cordial. I didn't understand.

The family was allowed to view the body first.

It was surreal to see the man who was once my soulmate, lying lifeless in a casket. The funeral home had done a good job, but he looked bloated, and not like the Jeff I had once loved.

I have to be honest. I think I was somewhat dazed.

As my children viewed their father's body in the casket, there were a few tears, but little emotion. We were all numb, still tremendously disillusioned by so many things.

After the family viewing, guests began coming in. I stood on one side of the room, his grown kids remained on the other. My younger children didn't know what to do.

I was overwhelmed at the number of former church members who came to show their respects. I felt so sad, but so loved at the same time.

One of his children had put together a slideshow from photos on Jeff's phone, which was playing on the screens above. His phone was found at the house he had been staying at, along with some of his other belongings. They'd had the difficult task of removing all of their father's things that were found at the scene, including his SUV.

The funeral was very difficult; there's no other way to describe it. A few who stood with him during his rebellion sat together on one side of the room. They didn't even speak to me, acknowledge me, or my children, and I was okay with that.

To this day, I pray for mercy for them. They were all just tremendously deceived. Grace, grace, I shout to the mountain!

Being betrayed by those you once walked with and called church family is one of the most difficult things I had to deal with throughout the past year and a half after Jeff left. I knew I had done nothing wrong. I was very hurt at Jeff for lying to so many people and pointing the finger at me. (I had to remind myself that Jeff loved me. It was Jeffrey who was vindictive.)

Emotions flooded through me during the funeral, and my mind raced. I kept telling myself, "We will get through this. We will get through this."

My children's names were only mentioned once, when the obituary was read, as Jeff's surviving children, but I was not mentioned at all.

My daughter, Mercy, suddenly ran out of the funeral service, broken-hearted. She'd had many wonderful years with Jeff before he snapped. It broke her heart that we were not even mentioned at his funeral.

There were pictures of me and the kids on the slide show. Otherwise, I was considered as Jeff's ex-wife, even though I was actually his widow.

My partnership with Jeff in establishing and serving in the ministry and the church, and all that evolved in our twenty-eight years of marriage, was completely ignored.

My heart wanted to break. I wanted to lay on the floor and cry. But I held my head high. The Lord had stood with me, and told me to stand with Him. It didn't matter what anyone knew, or didn't know. God was my vindicator. He was Justice. He was my Father, Friend, Savior, and Rescuer.

Throughout the funeral Jeff was glorified for being a hero, a man who was loving, compassionate, and generous. I had to choke back everything I was feeling at the time. Jeff was being hailed as the greatest man who ever lived. It was more difficult than words can express, for me and my children.

Yes, he had many years of fruitful ministry and his life was not in vain. I didn't want it to be. I wanted the good things to be celebrated, but so many people knew of his downfall, I felt there should have at least been some mention of this, instead of just acting like it never happened.

There were many chapters in his story. I acknowledge that his older children were grieving and needed to do what they felt would honor their father. A funeral is a time for celebrating the life of a person, and the legacy they are leaving behind.

I'm a big girl, but I have to admit, it truly did hurt me that my name wasn't even mentioned once and I was given no credit for being half of the ministry years we'd had together. I literally went through hell for many of those years and I wasn't even mentioned. It was as if I weren't even a part of Jeff. But God knew all of it. God knew, and that was enough.

I knew it would take a while for the kids and me to heal from the fact that even Jeff's funeral had managed to bring yet another layer of pain to us.

Many of our church members had come to pay their respects to me, because they didn't know his grown children. I did feel very honored and loved by them.

They knew Jeff and I were a couple and were once in love. They knew we were always a team. They knew we had both built the church as a couple, and that for many years we had both worked hard to do what the Lord wanted to do with it.

They knew that I had served the ministry well, and stood by Jeff's side to assist him in fulfilling the mandate that he felt was from the Lord. I believe God sent them to me, that day.

I was surprised that only a few prominent ministers came to the funeral, considering how many great men and women of God Jeff and I had walked with over the years. I thought at least those who were local would have come.

Perhaps Jeff had burned more bridges than I was even aware of. Perhaps it was just too painful for those who knew him. Joshua Mills drove for three hours to be there, which touched my heart.

Of course our early Vineyard pastor, Jerry, was there and sat right behind me. I could feel his strength and prayers all during the service.

I tried to somehow connect with Jeff's family, but most of them now shunned me. Had they believed his lies?

But why wouldn't they? Wouldn't you want to believe your family member? Wouldn't you want to believe your father, your son, or your brother?

His family members were well aware of his struggles with alcohol, but at this point, very few knew that Jeff had dissociative identity disorder. Only those very close to him who walked with him regularly, knew this. I was sure his immediate family and grown children had no idea.

People who are D.I.D. can hide it well. You almost have to be around someone continuously to figure it out. You would just think "so-and-so" is in rare form today! Or "so-and-so" is in a really bad mood or must just be having a bad day. Many people noticed something was unstable about him, but they had no understanding or explanation for his personality shifts.

I did ask the one person that I knew who had severe D.I.D., how she hid the fact that she had at least seven or more personalities (according to her).

She said that each of her personalities fit somewhere in her life. She had one alter who enjoyed work, so that part came out when she needed to function at her job.

She had one alter who was sexually promiscuous. This part was created when she was being sexually molested as a child. It is not uncommon for someone who has experienced sexual abuse to be promiscuous. She said that alter stepped out in front when sexual temptation presented itself.

The other parts, because of wounding, were unable to perform sexually, and would run from the possibility.

One reason I am writing this book is to inform you that if you have unhealed wounds, issues not dealt with, addictions, deep inner struggle, please don't try to lead a ministry or minister to others until you deal with all the cracks in your armor. The devil looks for ways to bring ministers down and discredit their ministry, and even God.

At the time of this writing, many prominent ministries who are highly respected are being exposed.

I hear from the spouses of pastors all the time. Their spouse has succumbed to pride and left them, cheated on them, molested someone in the youth group, etc. This is an epidemic! If this book saves just a few ministers from succumbing to the same fate that Jeff succumbed to, then it was worth it.

One of my biggest hesitations in writing and releasing this book has been that Jeff's grown kids and his close family might be upset that I have told the whole truth.

These are truths that, up to this time, none of his family members know, that I am aware of. They knew something was wrong with Jeff towards the end and even made comments to me about it.

His family, including his grown children, simply weren't with him on a daily basis and only saw the Jeff they saw, when they were around him.

None of them had any knowledge of the severe sexual abuse he had suffered that was the root cause of much of his troubles.

I was the closest person to him. I know the whole truth. Others who spent a lot of time with him and tried to help him, know the truth. I made no efforts to advertise the truth. Some knew of the magnitude of his condition, but most did not.

Two of his sons did later tell me that they believe me, and that they had seen signs of the realities I experienced. That is very comforting to me. I love Jeff's kids. After all, I co-parented them for many years.

I had contacted all of Jeff's sons right after he left me and told them that he had left me and the kids. I spoke to them about his alcoholism, infidelity, and ultimate downfall. I tried to limit the information I gave them, but I needed them to know what was going on.

Knowing Jeff had spread horrendous lies about me was probably the most difficult thing I had to walk through, overall. I cared what his children thought and believed about me. The boys admitted that they had seen evidence of their dad's alcohol problem. They knew he had left, because he was staying with his daughter (their sister) for a while.

As I said, all of this is hard for me to even talk about, but if I can prevent further tragedy by telling the truth, then perhaps Jeff's legacy, and his ministry is still alive. I want his legacy to mean something.

Perhaps, even in his death, his blood cries out from the ground, as his story is being told.

Chapter Twenty-Five

TURNING THE PAGE

Saying Goodbye

I want to give the guest speaker at the funeral honor. He was the brother of the pastor Jeff moved in with, when he was a teenager. They started the church in Wisconsin together, which grew to 3,000 members. He later told me that he only came because he wanted to take the time to honor his dear friend.

Jeff's children were not aware of who Jeff had walked with during our long time together, so they invited people to speak who had not even seen him in many years.

This man, Bob, took the time to mention from the pulpit during the funeral service, that Jeff did have other children, and that he had a wife. God bless him for that! He at least offered an acknowledgement of us. I knew that he hurt for us.

We got through the funeral that day, somehow. I simply can't express just how difficult this day was for Mercy, Truth, Given and myself.

Mercy did not come back into the sanctuary until after the end of the service. I thank our children's pastor, Sharon, for going out to comfort her. I couldn't just walk out. Too many eyes were on me, and it would have just raised questions.

When the funeral directors called for the immediate family to exit the sanctuary, many looked over at me, wondering what I would do. Were we immediate family? I looked at my kids, then keeping my chin up, we stepped right into the procession. We knew who we were.

Afterthoughts

I am not sure if any other ministers ever heard the Lord warn them that He would literally take their lives if He had to.

The warning He gave Jeff should have been regarded as the very serious and yet very humbling one it was. God knew that Jeff would ultimately succumb to pride, and fail. But in His goodness, He gave Jeff numerous warnings and chances to turn around, to change his ways.

He offered this particular one, cautioning him of the consequences of perverting God's anointing so that when Jeff stood before him in judgment, He could say, "Jeff, I loved you enough to warn you."

The Lord God is a patient, compassionate God, who is extremely long-suffering, but He is also Holy. He cannot go against Who He really is, and He will not.

God, being a God who cannot lie, (Numbers 23:19, 1 Samuel 15:29, Hebrews 6:18, Psalm 89:35) had to fulfill that which had been spoken, if His warning went unheeded.

Jeff, in his spirit man, knew his life was in danger. He knew he would not live to be an old man. We talked about it many times. Jeff had choices to make, and I believe he could have prevented losing his life at such an early age.

We all know the story of King Hezekiah in 2 Kings. He was sick unto death, and the prophet Isaiah came to him and told him it was his time to die, and he should get his house in order, Hezekiah pleaded that his life would be prolonged, and the Lord said, "I will add to you fifteen years."

God granted his request, but in those fifteen years, he had a son, Manasseh, who became king and *did great evil in the sight of the Lord.*" (2 Kings 21)

Perhaps, for Hezekiah's legacy, it would have been better for him to perish and not have the additional fifteen years. God, in his great love, will often give us what we petition Him for.

My mind always went back to, "What if God had given Jeff an additional length of time to get it right?" Would he have gotten it right or would he have made an even bigger mess?

God, alone, knows the answer to that, and His wisdom is beyond our human understanding.

Some part of me felt that God took Jeff in order to spare him. His hearing for the theft charge was scheduled for the week after his death.

He could have easily gotten many years of jail time. I knew Jeff couldn't handle being in prison.

Perhaps God was saving him from a worse fate. I know Jeff was almost frantic not knowing what his immediate, or even long-term future would be. I could often see him, in the Spirit, in tears and filled with apprehension.

Father God also knew this was not cookie cutter, as much of the church as a whole, was used to. There were severe issues at play here, including serious unhealed wounds, which lead to severe fractures in his soul. He had given Jeff ten years to turn it around, since He spoke his first warning to Jeff.

One of my greatest prayers during the two years after Jeff left, was "God! You are the God of Justice! Only You, in your deep love, know how to execute justice so that Jeff can no longer misrepresent You and hurt himself and others."

Jeff had hurt himself, as much as he had hurt me.

God is the God of Justice, and He has to execute Justice, because Righteousness and Justice are the foundations of His throne. (Psalm 89:14 Amp)

My heart kept reminding me of the humble, Jesus-loving man I had met and married. He had taught me so much. He had served the Lord and the kingdom well for many years.

His ministry truly touched thousands, and brought thousands to salvation. God even used him in his imperfection. None of us are perfect. None of us are disqualified because we are a work in progress.

The key is that God told me, "Jeff would never humble himself long enough to go through the process of healing." That is something worth repeating.

Healing is not always instantaneous. It is often a process.

We need to strive to be whole. We need to strive to be healed. We need to strive to receive the pruning of the Lord, for that is what leads us to fruitfulness.

Jeff did not yield to pruning. Pride caused him to resist it. Pride caused him to blame everyone but himself, for his failures.

As for me, my church, and my beautiful children, the day after the funeral, my son Given cried for a long time. It took him until that next day to be able to feel and grieve.

My girls are still working through everything on their own level, in their own time. With the Lord's help, we are all in His hand and doing well.

Mercy gets her degree in health sciences at the age of nineteen this year, 2024. She is on the deans' list.

Truth is an accomplished actress and drama has been a great source of healing for her.

Given has looked at me a couple of times and said with much thought, "I wish I had a dad."

This breaks my heart, but I still see so much healing and growth in all three of my children.

We all enjoy looking through my photos at the "good ole" days. We try to find good memories.

I am so blown away at God's goodness. I am amazed at how He spoke through all of this, and how faithful He is. I am humbled to my knees at how He has always been with me in all that I have been through.

Many of you may not understand how I stayed so strong in the midst of a horrific storm. Many asked me, "How did you not crack up?"

Philippians 4:13 *"I can do all things through Christ, who strengthens me."* (Amp)

This is not just a suggestion. These are words to live by! I am thinking of another scripture the Lord reminded me of.

"A little leaven (slight inclination to error, or a few false teachers) leavens the whole batch." (It perverts the concept of faith, and misleads the church).

~ Galatians 5:9 Amp

The devil's assault against my husband was presented little by little, so Jeff couldn't see it for what it was. It started with just a few compromises.

He knew he was traveling too much and was warned by people who loved him. That was the straw that broke the camel's back and resulted in a breakdown. His alcohol use had also left a huge crack in his armor.

Jeff thought he was above the law, so to speak. He thought his anointing was so strong that the devil could not touch him. This is total deception, based on pride! We are all subject to attack.

If you think you can jump into ministry with sin in your life and unhealed wounds, you are a target.

Just a few open doors can make you vulnerable, especially if you are in high level ministry. The warfare involved in taking on crusades, deliverances and moving in a very public ministry, is overwhelming. New levels, new devils. Take this seriously!

Jeff, in his weakness, opened many doors. A mental and physical breakdown left him unable to cope. For whatever reason, he opened the door to Hell on Earth. Hell was looking for that open door. Don't think for one minute that it couldn't happen to you.

Jeff literally believed the glory and power that came in his meetings was proof that God was covering him, no matter what. He became deceived, believing that no matter what he did, even embracing sin, he would just be covered by the glory. This is simply not true. Ephesians 6:10-18 is truth. It is necessary. Nobody is exempt.

In hindsight, I also feel that the real Jeff, the Jeff I married, was making provision for the kids and me, in his own way. It may sound like the opposite of what I was seeing at the time, and the opposite of what you've been reading in this book, but in retrospect, I can see the real Jeff knew what was coming. He made sure we had a comfortable home. He even said to me, "Jan, this will be your house, you and the kids."

I feel his self-esteem was so low due to the abuse that he felt he had suffered, and simply due to his exhaustion, he honestly felt we would be better off without him. He made this comment to me more than once.

He felt he had failed us, and rather than just stepping up and doing the right thing, he gave in to his weaknesses, somehow thinking this would be better for us.

I don't have the right words to explain this, but I knew the man fell in love with. He was not arrogant or proud. I knew the real man was mighty in the Lord, but also mighty in humility. This was the man I came to know and love. Humility was one of the most attractive qualities of Jeff when I fell in love with him.

Let me say again, I knew him. I knew the man I married. The man I had been with for the last few years was not the same man that I married.

The Bible says many times that a man "knew" his wife.

The word for "knew" is yada. In many of these scriptures the word yada connotes a sexual meaning. This is seen particularly in Genesis 4:1 when Adam "knew" his wife and the immediate result was Eve's conception of Cain.

The real, fuller meaning of yada is "to comprehend something, to understand something, to learn something."

In Exodus 6:7, God says, *"Then I will take you for My people, and I will be your God; and you shall know that I am the Lord your God, who redeemed you and brought you out from under the burdens of the Egyptians."* (Amp)

To know someone, is to understand them in a way that no one else does, in an intimate and unifying way.

Another definition of the word yada is to "reveal". Sex in marriage is, in effect, totally revealing. When we truly know the Lord, we know that He reveals His secrets to us. (Amos 3:7, Proverbs 25:2, 1 Corinthians 2:10, Luke 8:17, Daniel 2:28, Colossians 1:26, Deuteronomy 29:29).

It is quite apparent that if we know God, He reveals things to us in an intimate way.

So although Jeff put me through a gamut of confusion, change, struggle, abuse, emotion, hopelessness, and ultimate attack, I knew the real Jeff. I knew that the real Jeff truly loved me beyond measure.

In the wake of Jeff's death, I continued to have, and still have, afterthoughts, as this section is entitled.

I've had periods of sensing that Jeff was not yet in a heavenly place. It has felt to me that he was in a holding place, which is the best way I can describe it.

I felt it was a waiting place of sorts, for the purpose of allowing him to realize all the deception he had caused, and all the damage that he had done, until such a time that he could be taken into his eternal home.

I only confess these moments of uncertainty, these afterthoughts, in an effort to be transparent. It is not a declaration, and I am not presenting it as a doctrine of any kind.

One can't deny that Jeff had done some unbelievable and intentional things, and had hurt and deceived many people, things that are even perceived to be evil in our Christian circles. I believe the alters that had overtaken him, had prohibited the real Jeff from realizing much of what he had done wrong.

Of course, I also know that part of my unrest about Jeff's place in eternity could stem from the simple fact that I long to be able to somehow reconcile the humble Jeff that I fell in love with, and the unfaithful, arrogant, and reckless Jeff that I had to protect myself and my children from.

Yes, he eventually abandoned me and our children, but he was still very much alive and regardless of what he continued to involve himself in, and the shocking behavior he exhibited, I at least could understand about his parts and alters, and make some sense of what was going on. It was clear, here in this realm.

But then, he left this realm suddenly, quietly, and all alone. What was the last thing he uttered, that day? Somewhere between that first swallow of alcohol and that last one, before his body succumbed and surrendered his spirit, did he talk to the God he had served before, that he had worshiped? Did God talk to him? Did he ask for forgiveness? Was he rescued?

Finally, after the long battle that had been waged inside him, his body was rid of the turmoil, and silent. But what of Jeff, himself? What of Jeffrey and Jeffy Boy?

Afterthoughts. Questions. I had them, and still do.

While Jeff was here, on Earth, things were at least able to be observed, but eternity's realm and how God chooses to deal with us, once we stand before Him, is hidden from us, to some degree, and that may very well be the mercy of God. I admit, I questioned what I was feeling. This would not be a common theological belief in my Christian circles. I prayed and said, "Lord this doesn't make sense. Please correct me if I am wrong."

In light of all that, I'll just share what happened next, after I prayed that prayer. Unexpectedly, my daughter Mercy had a prolific dream. In her dream she, Truth, Given, and I were looking at Jeff's body in the casket at his funeral. Suddenly, we were taken to a place where we could see him in the spirit realm, not in the natural realm, although he was dead. His spirit man appeared alive to us, and he spoke to us.

"Do you forgive me?" he asked us. "I will not be allowed to go to my permanent home until you forgive me completely."

Mercy said that we answered him by saying something along the lines of, "You are dead. You lost your life. We choose to forgive you."

In her dream, we verbalized it, but in reality, I'm not sure we all totally felt we had yet forgiven him, at this time.

She said he humbly thanked us and said that once we could completely forgive him, at some point, he would be taken to his eternal home, and that he was being held where he was, until that time.

If you think you are confused, imagine how I felt! These questions I had and this impression I got were being overlaid by my daughter's coming to me with her dream.

My daughter said she had truly seen in her dream that God, the Father, wanted the true Jeff to understand what had happened to him, and why.

As you read this, remember that I am not presenting this as a doctrine, nor do I teach this concept of souls being held between Earth and Heaven for an interim period. I'm aware that, for the believer, to be absent from the body is to be present with the Lord. I'm simply sharing with you, the reader, of the afterthoughts immediately following Jeff's death, and that sometimes revisit me. When they come, I don't shy away from them. I ponder them, and I talk to God about them.

I have been allowed to see my mother and father, and my grandmother in Heaven.

After my mother passed away, I had a vision of her, way up high, in what looked like an upper luxury skybox at a football stadium. It looked like she was behind the large glass panel and she could see the world below from it. She was waving at me, and smiling. She looked like she did in her youth, glowingly beautiful. I knew the Lord was showing me she was in Heaven.

Similarly, I had a dream of my grandmother after she died. She walked up to me in a heavenly form with a beautiful pink dress on. Pink was her favorite color.

Jeff had seen my father in Heaven when Jeff was severely ill, and seeing into the heavenly realm.

Although it would greatly comfort me to be able to claim that I have seen Jeff in Heaven, I can only say that, as to my questions about Jeff's transition, once his spirit left his body, I must put my trust in a God who knows every fiber of our being and understands far more about us than we ever could. He, alone, knew Jeff before he was even formed in his mother's womb, and He, alone, knew the very instant that it would be time for Jeff to leave this world.

His ways are perfect, and whether or not He ever gives me that image of reassurance, where Jeff is concerned, He is not willing for me to continue to camp out in fields of uncertainty. I may still have questions, but I'm at peace with having them, because, at the end of the day, whether God chooses to answer them or not, He remains constant and unwavering. I am to pursue peace, and so I press on.

Chapter Twenty-Six

THE REVEAL

All Said And Done

The results of Jeff's autopsy and toxicology took forever to be released. I called and called the Coroner's office, but I was repeatedly advised that the results were pending.

After about seven weeks, I insisted that there must be available results by now. We all needed finality. When I was finally able to get the coroner's office to send me the results, it was exactly as I expected.

Apparently he had climbed into his friend's hot tub on a very hot afternoon on August 9, 2022. It's hard to think of a despondent Jeff who began drinking hard alcohol during the day, all alone, and then climbed into a hot tub at a time when the summer temperatures had risen upwards of 95°F. I can only speculate that he was in such distress, that he just couldn't cope with his natural man being in a state of severe anxiety.

A former church member later told me he had called Jeff that day and spoke to him for a while. He thought it was around noon. He told me Jeff was planning to go visit a friend and play guitar. Nothing seemed out of the ordinary. He did say Jeff confessed to him all the sins he had committed, even adultery. Something must have changed his plans for him to have begun drinking and die in the hot tub, a short time later.

Jeff didn't want to die. Yes, at times he would say that he did, but he really didn't. How many of us have been depressed or discouraged and said things we didn't mean? He was frightened, and felt out of control.

The man he was staying with did express to Jeff's grown children that Jeff's drinking had become enough of an issue, that he was considering asking him to leave.

Toxicology showed that his blood alcohol level was 0.293. Alcohol poisoning in Tennessee is 0.30.

The results of the autopsy said that either he died of alcohol poisoning and just went under the water after he died, or that he was so intoxicated, he passed out and drowned. The official cause of death is listed as accidental drowning.

As broken as I was over this news, I was not surprised. He had struggled with a drinking problem for years. He was in deep anxiety over the state his life had become. He had lost everything that meant anything, and I'm sure the real Jeff didn't even understand how this happened to him. He just knew that something he could not control had taken him over. Jeffrey had finally had his way.

My heart ached for his family and grown children. I knew they had hoped that his cause of death would be listed as a heart attack or something physical.

His alcohol counselor said alcoholism is a disease. I walked through every step with him, and although alcoholism may be a disease, there was much more at play here.

He had been able to postpone his trial for theft numerous times, but had run out of excuses, so he was to stand trial the week following his death. I found this out a few days after he died when the detective phoned me. I believe Jeff was in great distress over this. This is worth repeating, as I believe it played a big part in why he may have been drinking so heavily that day.

He was also broke. He had no source of income. I'm sure pride made him unwilling to get a normal, everyday job after he had traveled the world over, ministering for almost twenty years.

He had ruined his reputation as a minister, and was unable to provide for himself in the manner in which he was accustomed. He was obviously planning a relaunch, if possible. I drew this conclusion based on something that was said at his funeral by a man who was working with him on releasing a new book.

I mentioned earlier that an intercessor friend of mine had a vision of him walking the floor, ringing his hands in worry. I believe this is accurate.

I can't imagine what Jeff must have thought, as he saw his spirit man leaving his physical body. Did he ask, "God, why?" Did he know why? Was he surprised? Or was this what he really wanted, to escape all the deep struggles and pain he was experiencing? Did he just want to go home?

I may not know until I get to Heaven, myself.

Let me reiterate what I do believe, in my heart of hearts. I know that the real Jeff Jansen was a good man who was in love with Jesus. He knew the true heart of worship, in Spirit and in Truth. He knew faith, and he knew the boundless love of God his Father. He knew his Jesus.

Outside of what I knew, I discovered that he was just too broken inside to walk out the call he felt was upon him. He created an empire that he simply could not handle.

Sometimes we wonder why God allows such things, when He could obviously stop them. Why does God allow bad things to happen to people? I know God is good, all the time, so I have to believe He always knows what is best, even though it may not compute with our natural, human mind.

8 "For My thoughts are not your thoughts, nor are your ways My ways, declares the Lord.

9 For as the heavens are higher than the earth, so are My ways higher than your ways and My thoughts higher than your thoughts.

10 For as the rain and snow come down from Heaven, and do not return there without watering the earth, making it bear and sprout, and providing seed to the sower and bread to the eater,

11 So will My word be which goes out of My mouth; It will not return to Me void (useless, without result), without accomplishing what I desire, and without succeeding in the matter for which I sent it.

12 For you will go out (from exile) with joy and be led forth (by the Lord Himself) with peace; the mountains and the hills will break forth into shouts of joy before you, and all the trees of the field will clap their hands.

13 Instead of the thorn bush the cypress tree will grow, and instead of the nettle the myrtle tree will grow; and it will be a memorial to the Lord, for an everlasting sign (of His mercy) which shall not be cut off."

~ Isaiah 55:8-13

Jeff made a tragic mistake in thinking he had risen to levels that prevented him from being touched by the enemy. I am happy to memorialize all the things he achieved in greatness for the Kingdom. I am also quick to speak a stern cautionary word of truth.

Chapter Twenty-Seven

IN SUMMARY

Things To Remember

I pray this book makes it into the hands of those who really need to hear this story. In summary, I pray you will walk away from reading this book with the following revelation and also a warning:

Address Wounds & Healing Needs

Don't judge, criticize or condemn Jeff for the mistakes he made. Remember, Jeff's struggle was an attempt to medicate a much deeper need. If it weren't for God's tremendous grace, we could all succumb to the same or similar fate.

Ephesians 2:8-9 *"For it is by grace (God's remarkable compassion and favor drawing you to Christ) you have been saved (actually delivered from judgment and given eternal life) through faith. And this (salvation) is not of yourselves (not through your own effort), but it is the (undeserved, gracious) gift of God, not as a result of (your) works (not your attempts to keep the Law), so that no one will (be able to) boast or take credit in any way (for his salvation)".* (Amp)

Beware Of Demonic Doors

The Bible is very clear about sin. Listen to your conscience. I am talking about what you put in your eye and ear gates particularly here, because this was one of the doors the enemy opened and used to deceive Jeff.

There is never a justifiable reason to watch filthy movies and put garbage in our eye and ear gates. There is no acceptable moderation to this either. It is black and white, with no gray.

Don't stand on the fence of impurity. If it doesn't match the Word of God, it is not acceptable. Once a door is open, the enemy camps out there. A demonic door is easy to open, but so very hard to close.

I have found that there is always some sort of tempting reward placed before us to lure us through these doors. There is always a deception. The deception is often that we are above being affected.

I have actually heard many Christians say that watching rated-R movies has no negative effect on them at all. They reason that we are over-reacting, and that exposing ourselves to the world ultimately teaches us warfare.

Brothers and sisters, there are many ways to learn warfare besides watching tormenting, demonic movies and media.

Remember the man we ministered to at the church who watched zombie movies? A demon manifested through him and actually admitted that the man had opened the door to the demonic realm from watching these movies. Satan inserts demonic content in the media intentionally.

In regard to watching movies, media, etc., one seemingly innocent open door can lead to a far worse open door. Watching rated-R movies, and even some rated PG-13, can eventually open the door to watching pornography.

Our own thoughts can also open a door. Protect your thought life. Keep it pure. You will eventually become what you consume, whether good or bad.

I remember taking a church group to see the new Noah movie that debuted in 2014. We expected the movie to be Biblically based, but about fifteen minutes into it, we knew that it was not. We walked out. Other church groups did the same.

Do not compromise. Compromise is an agreement with the enemy. This includes dark documentaries, deceptive secular news, or anything that will grow, once inside you. Jeff watched a lot of documentaries about very dark things in the end. There must be balance.

Although it is never okay to watch a perverted movie full of nudity, cursing, and horrific violence, it might be okay to watch an informative documentary, but if that is all you consume, it can take over your thought life. If all you ever study is child trafficking or other dark subjects, then it can become all you think or focus on.

"Finally, believers, whatever is true, whatever is honorable and worthy of respect, whatever is right and confirmed by God's word, whatever is pure and wholesome, whatever is lovely and brings peace, whatever is admirable and of good repute; if there is any excellence, if there is anything worthy of praise, think continually on these things (center your mind on them, and implant them in your heart)." ~ Philippians 4:8 (Amp)

Jeff started out saying all men enjoy a good movie with "man stuff" in it. One thing led to another, to another.

Balance

Be balanced. Remember my encounter where Jesus spoke to me about how important balance is? This should pertain to every area of our lives.

We must even balance how much time we spend sitting in our office studying or reading, if we are ignoring our families and children. If we are spending more time on any other activity, even an enjoyable hobby or watching senseless TV, than we are spending with our family or the Lord, then we need to examine ourselves.

Even if you are doing great exploits for the Kingdom of God and traveling all over the world ministering to people but are neglecting your family, you are out of balance.

Hezekiah failed to raise his son in the ways of the Lord. He was probably prioritizing too many other things, and assumed that his children were just fine.

Reading the Word, studying, watching educational videos, and doing live-streams to help others is always beneficial, but if that is all you do, twenty-four seven, and you are neglecting your spouse, your children, and your church, just to do your own thing, you are out of balance.

Jeff spent countless hours isolated in his office saying he was doing things that would ultimately help others, while his family, his spiritual health, and his church were ignored.

I have seen many great men and women of God dabble into questionable theology, including New Age, simply out of curiosity, but when they began to camp out there, they got out of balance. Delusion and deception overcame them. While they claimed to be sinking into spiritual education or higher learning, they were simply focusing on everything but foundational Biblical beliefs. They eventually lost their ministry or fell into total sin.

Accountability

Be accountable. In the words of Kim McLester, an associate pastor at my church, "Don't just surround yourself with people who need you. Although it's great to be able to minister to others, you also need to be accountable to someone who will minister to you. Otherwise, you will end up drained and empty, with no one to help fill you back up."

We all need someone to stand with, grow with, and be able to be transparent to. Your pastors should be some of these people. If you do not feel trusting of and comfortable with your pastors, then you are not in the right church.

I urged Jeff to be accountable to many great men of God over a period of time. He was too ashamed to admit his weaknesses and submit. Don't be ashamed that you are human. None of us are perfect. Transparency is absolutely required for overcoming.

Stress

Keep your stress level down to what you can handle. Remember, Jeff's repressed parts were not needed until he pushed himself beyond the limits of what he could handle. He traveled too much, wore himself out, and ignored the warning signs of burn out. Many wise generals warned him.

If you are starting to feel stressed, step back, at least long enough to assess what is going on.

Are you just tired? Can you rest for a season and feel like all is well? Or do you feel you need an extended time to just seek the rest and peace of the Lord? Learn to listen to the warnings of the Holy Spirit.

Jeff was warned by many, many leaders that had been there and done that, that he was overdoing it. He was driven, and didn't listen. The end result was that he literally collapsed on the floor in total exhaustion and the enemy saw this as a perfect time to begin his assault.

Girls, Glory, and Gold

Girls This was Bob's number one warning to Jeff. We all know one of the biggest baits the enemy sets up for men is the opposite sex, and vice-versa. A woman is not exempt from this either. Attraction of the opposite sex is a natural design of God, in a pure sense, but anything Heaven calls pure, the enemy will try to mock, copy, or pervert.

Jeff did not adhere to the number one rule of ministry. Do not find yourself succumbing to enjoying the attention of the opposite sex. If you entertain this, you have opened a door. A married person should particularly keep the marriage undefiled.

We need to never be in a situation where the enemy could use a member of the opposite sex to try to lure or seduce. We must never even minister to the opposite sex alone. That's just solid wisdom.

Jeffrey obviously was not the mature, humble Jeff. Jeffrey was not pure, so he could easily be swayed by sexual temptation. Because of this, he had at least two affairs that I know of.

Do you know how many times someone reaches out to tell me that their husband, pastor, youth pastor, etc. has given in to the temptation of sexual sin? It is as old as time! Keep your thoughts and intentions pure.

Gold   Never seek money as your focus and main goal! God will provide. He is faithful to His word. If He appoints you to ministry, He will provide. He has not failed me yet.

I have seen many ministers make major mistakes based on the need for provision.

Several times, I saw ministers who had a signs and wonders ministry that was pure and legitimate, but they put too much faith in the sign and wonder, rather than in the provision and call of the Lord. When the sign and wonder no longer appeared, they began to manufacture it falsely.

I knew one minister who got some pretty amazing signs and wonders, and particularly gold dust. She apparently got the sign of the stigmata that Jesus experienced.

When this dried up and the Lord cut it off for whatever reason, maybe it was just a season, or maybe there was more to the story, this minister began to bring the gold dust to the meetings with her. I began to see her show up with it in her palms and she would keep her hands closed while holding the microphone until she claimed God had brought it.

She would also have people bring offering envelopes up and throw them on a cover cloth, and she would pray over them. She would read the information written on the offering envelopes, then give words of knowledge, based on the facts that she had read, and memorized. I witnessed this with my own eyes in more than one meeting.

Another minister, who claimed to get supernatural gemstones at his local church, began stepping out to minister in other places all over the world. At one point, the gemstones were no longer appearing.

So, he brought gemstones from his own church, and would somehow toss them out, so that people thought Heaven had just produced them.

We drove to another state to witness oil flowing out of a bible into a plastic tub. This was similar to what we had seen in Puerto Rico. The oil just kept flowing and replenishing itself. The humble ministers gave away thousands of vials of it and many people traveled there to see it.

One day, it just stopped flowing. I was told one of the ministers apparently began purchasing the oil at the local co-op when it stopped flowing supernaturally. The man at the co-op exposed him. This revelation destroyed the ministry. I will say that I am only sharing what I was told and cannot verify. I do, however, know that this ministry ceased to exist at this time.

I have seen signs and wonders that seem to be seasonal. For whatever reason, they come, and they go. We thank God when they are here, but we do not worship them, or claim they are the entirety of God.

If they leave, we continue to hold firm to the tasks the Lord has put before us. We hold onto Biblical truth.

Most of these acts from the ministers faking things were from fear that nobody would want them to minister if the signs and wonders dried up, and that the signs and wonders were all that the people wanted.

If you minister by the Spirit of God, the signs and wonders are secondary, no matter what. We seek the Lord Himself, and whatever He wants to do. We don't put our priorities on money and provision, or signs and wonders.

Jeff was very pure in this area until close to the end, and in his deception, he began to think that the monies of the church and ministry belonged to him, and him alone.

He knew he couldn't handle the pressures of the ministry he had built, but kept pushing himself, not only in pride, but also because he feared we would not be provided for.

Glory I can tell you that it is very easy to realize how the Lord is using you, and you begin to feel like somebody special. It is easy to say, "Wow, look what I just did!" A humble person says, "Wow, look what the Lord just did!"

The devil seeks out pride because then he can bring arrogance, destroy humility, and promote self.

Jeff fell victim to this, and he didn't even know what hit him. He basically had a low self-esteem, and rockstar syndrome was not his friend.

He began to say, "Look at me! Look at the way I am worshiped, doted on, and recognized!" I watched this happen over time. I would always shake my head and say "No, Lord. This is not You."

At first, my warnings were heard by him, but eventually I could not reason with a demonic spirit. Pride is a demonic spirit. Pride leads to arrogance, it leads to egotism, and to narcissism.

Check yourself on pride.

1. One of the signs that you are operating in pride is that you refuse to admit it.

3. You do not accept constructive criticism.

4. You always seek attention drawn to yourself.

5. You have come to care too much what you look like or what people think about you.

6. You feel like you are above everyone else.

7. You are no longer teachable.

8. You think you know so much you are unable to take the correction and advice of those you should be accountable to.

9. You don't like anyone shining brighter than you. You don't even like those you have mentored to rise above you, and you are critical of those who seem to do better than you.

10. You think you are too important to perform simple acts of servanthood.

Many times, Jeff would skirt out early at a church event, so he didn't have to participate in mundane activities, such as moving chairs, vacuuming, or washing dishes. He would even pull me out, saying this was beneath us. How can you overcome this kind of mentality? Forget the pronouns "me, myself and I" and ask the Lord to keep you humble.

Do you know how many scriptures there are on humility in the Bible? There are at least eighty-three!

Step number one in identifying pride is to read the Word in regard to humility.

God wouldn't have had it mentioned so many times in the Bible if it were not one of the main keys to our victory!

If you have learned nothing else from this book, hear this: Never, ever, ever just give up! I think Jeff finally just gave up, when in reality, his victory was so obtainable.

Never forget, "Humble yourself long enough to go through the process of healing!"

It's not as simple as that, but as we have heard many times, we are like layers of an onion. One layer at a time needs to be peeled away as we get revelation of what is needed for us to be a finished work. We are never really a completely finished work. Humility says we are always a work in progress.

The Lord has shown me that He is greater than anything the enemy or the world can throw at us. We just need to believe that. Simply believe!

"It is for this that we labor and strive (often called to account), because we have fixed our (confident) hope on the living God, who is the Savior of all people, especially of those who believe (in Him as the Son of God and accept Him as Savior and Lord)." ~ 1 Timothy 4:10

True to the dream my prophet friend had, the Lord spoke to me recently and said, "All the mandates I gave Global Fire Ministries did not die with Jeff. They are still My mandates and need to be fulfilled."

One of the mandates Global Fire Ministries was given was the writing of books. Jeff was an accomplished author, but how would this continue with him gone? This is fulfilled in the writing of this book, and another book I am writing about my supernatural adoptions called Windows.

Another mandate the Lord highlighted to me was His call for crusades. I said, "Lord, I am not someone who desires to minister in crusades in third world countries!"

His response: "You can send, if you cannot go".

I just sent a team of ten missionaries to Kenya at the time of this writing. Pastor Jerry was one of them. Seven were from my church. I organized a missionary trip to Kakamega, Kenya, where there is a ministry and school that my church has supported and sponsored for many years. My team ministered to the local people, to the children, and did two nights of open air crusades. Many, many were saved and healed, and there were hundreds were in attendance.

The team also preached at a conference for all of the churches in the region. The pastors there said that great seed was sown in their region.

The lead pastor in Kenya sent me this message after the team returned: "I met with several pastors. They testify that this was the most successful meeting ever to be in Kakamega. The presence of God was felt intensely in Kakamega, and forces of darkness have been shaken and defeated."

This team was led by Pastor Jerry, and another minister who is a seasoned missionary. Another friend of Jerry's joined the team and she had been in ministry for over fifty years. But the rest of the team were my church members, many who had never been out of the country and none of them had ever been on a mission trip or done a crusade.

Never say you cannot do something. If God calls you to do it, He will bless it and empower you to represent Him well.

I also organized an orphanage last year called Blessed Arms Home of Mercy. Many of the students of the school my church supports in Kenya had no home, or their living circumstances were unsafe. There are over thirty precious children who reside there now who call me "Mom". This is also a fulfillment of all the prophetic words spoken over me that called me "mother of many".

I remain senior pastor, and "mother" of the Fire Church! The Lord has done beautiful, amazing things in my church and we know the best is yet to be!

Watching the Lord continue to use Global Fire Ministries and the Fire Church is truly the fulfillment of the restoration of all things. To God be the glory!

I have done more than my share of laboring and striving, but the victory belongs only to the Lord! I pray victory for all of you in your journey and pray you have been touched by the truth of this book.

In retrospect, Jeff achieved much in his years of ministry. He believed and trusted the Lord on a high level. His faith was not limited.

Because of this, he saw tremendous miracles, signs, and wonders in the glory realm of God. He had a child-like faith that we should all take note of. He believed in the power of the spoken Word and it manifested in amazing ways in his ministry. Healings, deliverances, and even manifestations in weather and the elements were commonplace. He believed what he released into the atmosphere would happen and it did.

He had a kingdom mindset that many cannot conceive. He had a high level of understanding of the ways of the Lord and applied this to his ministry.

The Lord spoke to him on a very elevated level. He had a supernatural ability to understand the higher things of God. I believe this was an impartation from Bob Jones in many ways. My Jeff knew the Lord on a very personal level, and His God spoke to him very personally.

We saw tremendous signs, wonders, and miracles in our ministry and held conferences at our church where hundreds and even thousands were imparted to, in a powerful way.

He imparted so much to those in our Kingdom Life Institute school. He was a father to many.

He conveyed a level of faith in so many people that I can't even explain it. He just had such a supernatural understanding of who the One True God was. He tried to put it into words in his ministry, our school, our church and our international ministry.

God saw a pure heart in Jeff. Although the Lord knew how fractured Jeff was, He also knew his heart.

The Lord knew Jeff had a great call to be a kingdom representative. God honored this, even though He knew his flaws. Isn't that just the great God we serve? He is a God of patience, grace, and mercy.

Alex and Jordan Parkinson were both students at Kingdom Life Institute. They met at our school, fell in love, and eventually married.

They subsequently founded The Zion Company. This is Alex's statement:

"In 2011, I moved by faith to Murfreesboro, Tennessee to attend Kingdom Life Institute under Jeff Jansen. I am forever grateful for those pivotal years in my life, and I often become emotional thinking of my time around Jeff's ministry. He imparted more to me than I may ever realize.

I write this actually overseas as I've stepped into my own ministry calling as an evangelist. It was his deep love for the glory of God and raw faith that went with him all around the nations that seeded those values in my life. Jeff always preached about the glory generation (Isaiah 60:1-3), a message that came alive to me.

In my own way I'd like to say I'm carrying the baton for that message to become a reality in the church as a memorial and a tribute to Jeff. He is missed, loved and I'm forever thankful for how the Lord used him in my life."

Kim McLester was a three year student in Kingdom Life Institute. This is a message from Kim, who is my associate pastor and is also the leader of my deliverance ministry:

"My time at KLI was full of impartation and stretching of my understanding about the higher and deeper things of God. I had several light bulb moments and impartation, whether it was due to hands being laid or just the sheer presence in the room. The skills, impartation, and information I learned during that time helped to grow me into who God has called me to be today. God led me there and I will eternally be grateful for what I gained while attending KLI".

If I were to call for testimonies of what Jeff imparted to the world in his short life, they would fill a huge book!

I pray my story has blessed you and validated the ministry of the true Jeff Jansen. I pray that it has imparted to you a sobering message that would push you to strive for the true mission of the Lord in this season, and serves as a strong reminder of what could be.

Jan Jansen

GATEWAY

For more information:
gatewaypublishinghouse.com